Teachers' Know-How

The Journal of Philosophy of Education Book Series

The Journal of Philosophy of Education Book Series publishes titles that represent a wide variety of philosophical traditions. They vary from examination of fundamental philosophical issues in their connection with education, to detailed critical engagement with current educational practice or policy from a philosophical point of view. Books in this series promote rigorous thinking on educational matters and identify and criticise the ideological forces shaping education.

Titles in the series include:

Teachers' Know-How

A Philosophical Investigation

Christopher Winch

Registered Offices
John Wiley & Sons, Inc., 111 River Street, Hoboken, NJ 07030, USA
John Wiley & Sons Ltd, The Atrium, Southern Gate, Chichester, West Sussex, PO19 8SQ, UK

Editorial Office
9600 Garsington Road, Oxford, OX4 2DQ, UK

For details of our global editorial offices, customer services, and more information about Wiley products visit us at www.wiley.com.

Wiley also publishes its books in a variety of electronic formats and by print-on-demand. Some content that appears in standard print versions of this book may not be available in other formats.

Library of Congress Cataloging-in-Publication Data applied for.

9781119355687 (Paperback)

Cover image: © Hero Images/Gettyimages

Set in 11.5/12pt Times by Aptara Inc., New Delhi, India
Printed and bound in Malaysia by Vivar Printing Sdn Bhd

10 9 8 7 6 5 4 3 2 1

Contents

Preface

What is good teaching? What is the know-how that teachers need? Around the world, and as never before, governments are vexed by questions about the quality of teaching and the preparation of teachers. Economic competitiveness is dependent upon having an educated workforce, and this in turn depends upon high-performing schools. Yet recurrently there is uncertainty as to how exactly such schools are to be created and how the right teachers are to be produced.

Now, as never before, however, we do have global measures for that performance, and hence conclusions can be drawn about the kind of teacher training and education that works best. *First, the appeal of the teaching profession is of critical importance.* In the countries with the best examination performance, teachers enjoy relatively high social status and competitive remuneration. This status is reflected in the comparative autonomy they have in the classroom: where teachers are not regarded as mere technicians or servants of the system, greater respect for them is generated, within and beyond the school. *Second, it is clear that teacher education matters.* The best courses provide extensive practical experience in schools, research-based teacher methods and emphasis on specific expertise in the subject to be taught, as well as the ability to work with a wide variety of child-development issues. *Third, it is clear that ongoing professional development matters too.* Apart from leading to improvements in practice, this enables teachers to develop as people in their profession, reinforcing their confidence and commitment to that practice. Time allocated for working together is an important contribution to this, as is the shared study of method and technique with support from fellow teachers.

This at least is the prevailing wisdom, as expressed in OECD recommendations based on PISA studies and other policy recommendations. Governments are disposed to pay careful attention to the comparisons that PISA has provided, not surprisingly given the economic pressures that can be brought to bear on those that do not take such findings seriously. But many have also found it convenient to push responsibility for reform down towards the schools themselves, rather than investing in the teaching profession and specifically in teacher education in the ways outlined here. Sometimes there has been a tendency to debunk educational expertise and to champion simplistic notions of the skills the teacher needs. In these circumstances, political debate about teacher education becomes ideological in new ways, mired in confusion about what it is that teachers need to know, about the qualities they must bring to their professional roles and about the ongoing development in expertise needed to sustain them in this. And even in circumstances where governments *have* acted on these three main recommendations, the tendency has been for teaching to be turned into something formulaic. The variety of the circumstances and the challenges that teachers face, and the complex and again varying demands of their relationship with the subject matter they are passing on, are rarely appreciated in the way that is needed. Comparisons can be immensely valuable, especially where they serve for something more than simply shoring up an orthodoxy. But too often the appeal of a systematic approach that the orthodoxy offers obscures the benefits such research might otherwise provide. So how might things be moved forward and a better understanding of teaching achieved?

As is evident from the beginnings of philosophy, the role of the teacher is crucial to human flourishing and to the development of a good society, and understanding of this has been important to the development of philosophy itself. Over the course of the centuries, some of the greatest philosophers have returned to questions about what it is to teach and to do this well. In contemporary philosophy of education, the challenge of teaching has been addressed in fresh ways in the present series, as indicated by Nigel Tubbs' *Philosophy of the Teacher* (2005) and Christopher Higgins' *The Good Life of Teaching: An Ethics of Professional Practice* (2011), as well as the recent collection of essays, *Philosophical Perspectives on Teacher Education*, edited by Ruth Heilbronn and Lorraine Foreman-Peck (2015).

The present addition to the series, *Teachers' Know-How: A Philosophical Investigation*, extends work on the topic to address more specifically epistemological questions: these are matters of critical importance, yet they are often neglected or treated in only a cursory manner. Winch broaches questions about the quality of education in a way that answers to the concerns not only of teachers but also of policymakers, the public and parents. Crucial to his exploration of teacher ability is a careful examination of the relationship between teaching and learning. His focus is on the know-how that is involved in teaching, understood in the broadest sense. And his preference for the unfussy and practically attuned expression 'know-how', as opposed to 'competence', 'expertise' and other more fashionable terms, avoids the tendency towards jargon that often characterises theorising about these matters: it suggests an embracing of the knowledge and various practical abilities that teachers require, with a strong sense of the ways in which such knowledge is integrated and realised in those abilities. What kind of knowledge is it that teachers need if their practice is to be effective? And how far does the acquisition of such knowledge contribute to the characterising of, even the constitution of, teaching as a profession?

Inevitably such questions need to be addressed with an eye focussed realistically on the practical demands of particular institutions and on the educational systems within which they operate, and Winch's attention is turned in particular towards the relatively formal setting of public school-centred education. But this specification of context in fact contributes to the book's ability to say things that can be seen to extend more widely through practices of teaching and learning: fundamental questions about teaching, learning and assessment are, after all, not confined to those contexts but of relevance more universally. What the book provides is a grammatical exploration of these concepts, as a means to become clear about what the know-how of a good teacher consists.

A salient feature of the account is the attention it gives to the important work Lee Shulman has undertaken into the pedagogical demands and possibilities that arise in relation to specific subject knowledge. Indeed, enquiry of this kind is important in the generation of coherent curricular and teaching strategies, and its value is obscured where teaching and learning are understood in generic terms or in generalised thinking skills. The book makes an invaluable contribution in taking this discussion forward.

It is possible to find a number of models for conceptualising teaching. Winch takes particularly seriously the ideas of teaching as a craft, but he eschews any simplistic assumption that the know-how that this implies is necessarily devoid of theoretical knowledge. He shows how it is necessary to become clearer about the relationships between craft knowledge and more systematic technical knowledge. What becomes clear, in addition, is that a proper examination of these matters cannot leave the concept of the 'professional teacher' undisturbed. Addressing such matters takes the reader further into the relationship between teaching and content knowledge. The discussion leads not only through the 'Taylorised' views that have exerted such influence, including contemporary reincarnations of these, but also into such central philosophical literature as is provided by Gilbert Ryle's *The Concept of Mind*.

Winch has undertaken important research into the thinking of Georg Kerschensteiner (1854–1932), with its insights into the social role of work and the bearing this has on vocational education. Such a conception invites us to think in terms of not solely specific skills and expertise but also forms of know-how that involve aspects of a person's character and sense of who they are. Here these ideas are extended in inspiring ways, addressing the question of what it is to pursue a career in teaching in terms of what Winch calls its 'civic' role.

Winch leads the reader towards a view of initial teacher education that nicely balances the practical and academic. With the recognition that the expectation of complete precision in respect of matters of teaching and learning is likely to be the basis of fantasy, his approach is healthily pragmatic: achieving the 'greatest precision possible' in the light of the demands of the content being taught will be, in his phrase, no mean achievement. On a rather more sombre note, he recognises that that achievement may well be compromised in a socio-economic environment that places too much faith in 'market forces', constructing learners as consumers with consumers' expectations and teachers as technical operatives whose function is to 'deliver', while indulging in excessive faith in high-stakes testing and imposing punitive measures on those who do not 'perform' (in what are, in effect, often bogus forms of competition). This degenerate model is to be contrasted with a 'service' conception of teaching, but here once again Winch avoids simplistic solutions, with a sensitivity to the demands of large-scale educational provision that pitches realism against formulaic answers.

In this way the book holds onto a pragmatic and robust account of the nature of knowledge and the specific know-how that is at the heart of teaching. Winch takes the reader through obvious and less obvious (though in fact essential) steps along the way, and he does this with exemplary clarity. This is a book that marries careful analysis and commitment. It will assist policymakers and practitioners, as well as interested members of the wider public, in coming to a better understanding of what it is that teachers need to know.

Paul Standish
Series Editor

1
Introduction: Education and Teaching

WHY THIS BOOK?

This is a philosophical essay on the knowledge and know-how of teachers.[1] There are a number of reasons for undertaking such an exercise now, particularly if one wishes, as I do, to reach beyond the immediate philosophy of the education community to address some of the most pressing current worries about the quality of education that are alive in the minds of policymakers, the public and parents, as well as teachers. Since I published *Quality and Education* in (1996a), the focus of public concern about education has undergone something of a shift from a preoccupation with the effectiveness of schools and the possibilities for their improvement (Mortimore *et al.* 1988; Tizard *et al.* 1988) to a growing concern with the quality of teachers and teaching (e.g. Hattie 2009). Although the research on improvement and effectiveness drove much education policy in the last 20 years or so, the results have generally been judged not to have fully lived up to their original promise. 'School effects' although significant, are small and the importance of background factors like school intake characteristics (Butler and Webber 2007) and relative social inequalities (Wilkinson 2005; Wilkinson and Pickett 2010), not to mention the stability of 'value-added' data (Gorard 2010), continue to exercise a powerful effect on the outcomes of education at the national level.

---

[1] For the sake of brevity, I will use the term 'knowledge' in future to cover know-how as well as propositional and acquaintance knowledge.

Teachers' Know-How: A Philosophical Investigation, First Edition. Christopher Winch.
© 2017 Christopher Winch. Editorial Organisation © Philosophy of Education Society of Great Britain.
Published 2017 by John Wiley & Sons, Ltd.

However, it is interesting to note that, despite the apparent importance of background social factors in determining school effectiveness (Gorard 2006), there is evidence that *within-school effects* are of greater significance than *between-school* ones (OECD 2013, p. 46). In other words, whatever the background effects, the role of teachers and the ways in which they teach are very important for the progress of pupils and students (see also Tizard *et al.* 1988), and there are wide differences in individual teacher effectiveness within individual schools. Although the political nature and the culture of a society are critical in contributing to educational achievement, we cannot ignore the possibility that improvements will, to a large degree, be dependent on improving the quality of teachers and teaching. This remains true even when one acknowledges the very important interaction effects that exist between a society and the kind of education system that it is prepared to support. Failure to understand this has led to a rash of policy borrowing in the developed countries which, because it is not based on careful analysis of the background to success in the countries from which the policy is borrowed, has led to limited improvement (cf. Harbourne in Baker *et al.* 2013).

The focus of policymaking has thus tended to shift towards scrutiny of teacher effectiveness and, inevitably within the 'Anglo-Saxon' (shorthand for the UK, US, Australian, Canadian and NZ polities), has led to the reinforcement of performance management systems relying on a mix of command and control and market mechanisms, approaches which, despite their favour with liberally minded politicians and policymakers, have had at best limited success. Not least amongst the problems has been that of the provision of overwhelming incentives to gaming behaviour in an attempt to mitigate the negative consequences of high-stakes accountability systems. I do not believe that there is a general 'agent–principal' problem in the public services, but it is very easy to create one with the wrong sort of accountability mechanisms. To use the language of le Grand (2003), if educators like all public servants lie somewhere on the spectrum between altruistic 'knights' and egoistic 'knaves', the wrong accountability system will not turn knaves into knights but make knaves of knights, hardly a desirable outcome for anyone who is not a fanatical believer in Public Choice Theory (cf. Stretton and Orchard 1994). 'Knights' in le Grand's classification are relatively altruistic employees; 'knaves' lie at the egoistic end of the spectrum. There are, of course, intermediate positions between these two.[2]

---

[2] See also Lynch and Walsh (2003) for a similar classification.

Much the same problem threatens with the new focus on teachers, not because teachers and teaching are unimportant (they undoubtedly are important), but because insufficient attention has been given to the nature of teaching as an occupation, what the nature of teacher expertise consists in, how teachers should be recruited and prepared for their roles, how their careers should develop and what the governance and broader civic role of teachers should be. There has been in particular a disturbing tendency to adopt a regressive model of teaching as a kind of craft, best acquired through a traditional form of apprenticeship, which prepares the teacher to work within a particular school or group of schools, rather than within the education system as a whole. This development is associated with a tendency to fragment schools into small, quasi-private bodies working within a market. This in turn is itself partly the outcome of the misapplication of research into the effectiveness of schools, which misunderstands the relationship between the school and the society in which it exists (see Grant 2009). This craft model will be subjected to critical scrutiny while the kernel of truth that it contains will be, hopefully, extracted.

There is a significant role for philosophy and philosophy of education in particular in enabling us to get clearer answers to these questions. Philosophy enables us to tackle such vital questions as what makes an education a good education and the role of teachers in providing a good education, however the latter is conceived. However, even more than this, it has a critical responsibility to engage with questions concerning the nature of teaching, the kinds of knowledge, know-how and personal characteristics that make good teachers and teaching, and the broader role of teachers within a society. It thus has a crucial role to play in framing the kinds of empirical questions that we should be asking about teachers and teaching, questions that are often taken to be obvious when they are not actually so, unless one takes certain presuppositions about the aims of education and teaching for granted.

Philosophical work on teaching and teachers has been carried out since antiquity and includes such notable contributions as Plato's *Meno* and Rousseau's *Émile ou de l'Education*, works that continue to exert enormous indirect influence on thinking about the nature of teaching. More recently, the topic has received a lot of attention in the analytical tradition since the 1960s. This chapter builds on work done in the 1960s, 1970s and 1980s (Hirst and Peters 1970; Kleinig 1982) on the nature of teacher ability and the relationship between teaching and learning. It also pays attention to the work of Passmore

(1989), which focussed particularly, but not exclusively, on the various kinds of matter that a teacher should teach and the different modes of teaching. This work will focus on the know-how involved in teaching in the broadest sense of 'know-how', which will include the knowledge as well as the various practical abilities that teachers require, including, of course, the way in which the knowledge is integrated and realised in their practical abilities. 'Know-how' will also include consideration of what, if any, theoretical knowledge teachers should possess in order to make their practice effective. This is a highly contested area to which I shall devote considerable attention. It bears strongly on the question of whether or not teaching is to be considered as a 'profession' as that term is usually understood. Inevitably, the enquiry will be directed at the role of the teacher in formally constituted educational systems where the school plays a central institutional role, but it will approach the role of the schoolteacher through consideration of universal issues concerning teaching and learning, while situating these within the contemporary institutional practice of public school-centred education.[3,4]

EDUCATION

It is possible to distinguish between a *categorial* concept of education and particular *conceptions* that reflect different perspectives on, or interpretations of, that categorial concept. The distinction, which owes much to Gallie's (1956) account of essentially contested concepts, focusses on the one hand on what is universal about education as a human practice, namely the bringing up of a society's young to be adults, and on the other hand on local versions of that human practice, which may be subject not just to the requirements of particular beliefs about learning and teaching, but also to the predominant values and social divisions within that society (Winch 1996a). This distinction was endorsed in the later work of R.S. Peters (1982) and has also received some more recent cautious support from adherents to Peters' categorial view of education (e.g. Barrow 2014).

---

[3] The important work of Higgins (2011) on the relationship between teaching as a profession and the possibility of the flourishing of those who practise it will not be ignored, but detailed discussion of Higgins' work would take us beyond the focus of this book.

[4] The focus of this book will be schoolteaching. It is recognised that teaching has many institutional forms and that conceptions of the teacher may vary accordingly. Space does not allow me to deal with other contexts of teaching than that of the school.

This study endorses the distinction, while also acknowledging that the boundary between the universal and the local in education is often difficult to keep in mind, even if one is constantly and conscientiously straining to do so. For the purposes of the argument, the categorial concept of education will refer to preparation for adulthood based on:

1. some processes of learning and teaching; and
2. the recognition that the preparation must be for something worthwhile for whom the person in question is deemed to be a suitable subject.

The first requirement is, perhaps, obvious but needs some comment. It is, of course, possible that one can learn without being taught. Could it not be the case that all learning could take place without teaching? This looks like a bare logical possibility, but I argue that on closer inspection it is not. We need to bear in mind that all aspects of human upbringing are to be considered, and that includes the period of great dependency of very young human beings. Young humans are to be introduced not only into a world of practices and institutions that are conceptually constituted but also into a normative order in which values and norms are part of the fabric of that conceptually constituted world. This means, as Baker and Hacker (1985) pointed out, that part of this induction takes place through *normative activities*, such as training, correction, encouragement, explanation, interpretation, instruction, exemplification and imitation (p. 47 ff.).

This cannot take place without the recognition of *authority* or entitlement, on the basis of not just knowledge and know-how but also position, of adults who have to take responsibility for ensuring that such processes, in whatever form, actually take place. The youngest of human beings cannot do this for themselves. Even a thinker about education like Rousseau, who believed that any such normative order had to be adopted without constraint and who regarded the role of the traditional pedagogue as subversive of the *psyche* of the young (see Dent 1988 for a very good account), had to posit a tutor who arranged matters so that his pupil was actually able to learn that which was considered worthwhile by his tutor for him to learn. Although such an individual would not be a teacher in the sense in which that term is commonly understood within our society, it would be nitpicking to say that he did not adopt a pedagogical role. We can conclude provisionally that the categorial concept of education, particularly in respect of condition (1), does seem to entail, at least loosely, that teachers have an essential role to play even if it is not the role that schoolteachers have generally been thought to play.

The second condition, although very important for the consideration of education more generally, has less importance in considering the place of teachers within the categorial concept of education. However, it is not completely without importance, as there are undoubtedly cases where the education of the children of some classes of people is not to be deemed suitable or in other ways desirable for children of others and *vice versa*. Thus, the pre-eminent role of the individual tutor of the children of an aristocrat may not be deemed appropriate to those of a day labourer, who may be thought to merit an education that would be regarded with horror by the aristocrat if applied to his own children. This issue will assume some importance when we come to consider different conceptions of the teacher in Chapters 6 to 8.

At this point, however, it is appropriate to address the question of whether education is necessarily a *good*. This issue was dealt with in some detail in *Quality and Education* (Winch 1996a), and there is only space to reprise the argument here. Briefly, the aspectual nature of the way in which education is regarded means that what may be seen as a good for some may well be seen as a bad for others. This could be because it will be seen as bad for them individually but also because it could be seen as bad for society that certain groups of children are educated in one way rather than another. It will not do, for example, according to an aristocrat, to educate the child of a slave in the same way as one would educate the child of an aristocrat. In our kind of society, there may well be agitated debate and campaigning about such issues. The important point for our purposes is that education is not to be seen merely as a private good (benefitting the individual and his or her immediate dependents) but also as a public good affecting the well-being of society as a whole.[5] It is thus important that the social effects of different kinds of education are taken into account when assessing what kind of education is important for whom.

---

[5] This is how I propose to talk about public goods. Economists tend to say that, in contrast to private goods, they are *non-rivalrous* (enjoyment by one individual does not preclude enjoyment by another) and *non-excludable* (enjoyment is available to all potential beneficiaries irrespective of whether or not they pay for the good) as a technical definition of the concept of a public good (cf. Varian 2006. I do not dispute the usefulness of these criteria but prefer to keep to the broader definition of a public good as one which has societal as well as private benefits. The point goes, of course, for public bads as well.

The second point above, about the aspectuality of education, suggests that we necessarily view education not just from the point of view of the educatee, but also from the point of view of those who will be affected by the education of that person. And, if this claim is correct, we must incorporate into our categorial concept the idea that education does not just impact on the interests of the educatee, but also impacts on those who will be affected by the individual being educated, whether for better or for worse. It seems, then, that the categorial concept will need to recognise a public dimension (in some broad sense of 'public') to education conceived of as a possible benefit.

A CATEGORIAL CONCEPT OF TEACHING

Having tentatively established that teaching and, by implication, teachers play a role in anything that we would call 'education', is there a categorial concept of *teaching* that could, to some extent, be filled out? Once again, at this early stage, the answers will have to be tentative, but they will point out part of the future direction of this enquiry.

The first point is a well-known one of logical grammar, namely that teaching involves a triadic relationship between teacher, pupil and matter taught. In any teaching relationship,

A (the teacher) teaches B (the pupil) about C (the subject matter).

We need to be a bit careful here, as Passmore (1989) pointed out that the triadic nature of the teaching relationship is often concealed within implicit locutions, which suggest that teaching is, in fact, a dyadic relationship.

After all,

A teaches B (pupil)

or

A teaches C (subject matter)

are by no means ungrammatical or illogical constructions. This brings us to an important methodological point. We are engaged in a grammatical exploration of the concept of teaching in order to gain clarification about what the expertise or know-how of a teacher consists. This involves considering the usage *in the widest possible sense* of a range of related concepts, such as *teaching, learning, instruction, training,* and *assessing.* We cannot rest satisfied with the surface grammar of particular sentences in particular episodes of use but need to be concerned with a grammatical investigation that involves a perspicuous overview of the conceptual field. This entails, in the example of teaching, that we need to look at how the concept is used, not only in various different contexts but as a whole, taking into account that a grammatical investigation has to be a broad one. We do not assume, for example, that because someone describes an episode of teaching as

A teaches B

that there is nothing that they are teaching them. We wish to look closer at what is actually going on and will establish on investigation that A is teaching B *something or other.* In such ways, the universal nature of the triadic relationship embodied within the concept of teaching will be maintained, through close attention to the detail of what is happening when such assertions are made within the context in which they are made. We can always ask 'What is A teaching B?' and expect an answer in terms of subject matter, know-how or whatever else it might be. Much the same point can be made about

A teaches C,

where C is the subject matter concerned.

The key methodological point about such a grammatical investigation into the concept of teaching is that it aims to go beyond the surface features of usage, not to engage in a logical analysis divorced from usage, but to gain a perspicuous overview of how the concept is used (Hacker 2011), by looking not only at the variety of usage but also at the contextual features of usage that give a particular utterance or conversation the significance that it has. We can conclude from this that it is quite proper to think of teaching as a triadic relationship between teacher(s), pupil(s) and subject matter.

The second point concerns another matter that preoccupied philosophers of education in the 1960s, 1970s and 1980s. This was the conceptual relationship between *teaching* and *learning*.[6] John Dewey contended that although the impulse to learn had to come from the learner, the teacher had to accommodate that impulse by facilitating the learning of the pupil and, if he failed to do so, could be said to be failing in the task of teaching (Dewey 1938, p. 40). This claim helped to raise the question as to what the conditions were under which teachers could be said to be teaching even if, despite their intentions to do so, not all or even any of their pupils were in fact learning.

It is perfectly true that while teaching is directed towards pupil learning, learning cannot take place without the engagement of the pupil. But Dewey goes too far in suggesting that the primary impulse for learning always comes from the pupil. Many a time, as teachers throughout the ages will testify, they will have been faced with reluctant or even hostile learners, as well as willing and energetic ones who fit the Deweyan mould perfectly. It is misleading to say that if pupils are failing to learn, then the teacher is failing to teach, since it will not always be the case that pupils are trying to learn. They may even be actively or passively resisting attempts to make them do so. This, of course, does not absolve the teacher of responsibility to teach (in the task sense); if anything, it makes the task of teachers more onerous since they are often called upon to teach unwilling or recalcitrant pupils. Inevitably, this makes the specification of success conditions more problematic. Suffice to say for now that I will argue that there is a categorial relationship between teaching and learning, such that teaching involves learning, even though there are different conceptions of teaching available in different times and places and these conceptions are not always consistent with each other. However, if no learning ever took place as a result of teaching, or even if it rarely and incidentally did, we would no longer possess the same concept of teaching as we do now.

Both the issue of the triadic nature of the teaching relationship and the conceptual connection between teaching and learning are

---

[6] 'Learning' is ambiguous between '*trying* to acquire knowledge, know-how etc.' and 'acquiring knowledge, know-how etc.' There is a similar ambiguity for 'teaching'. The philosophical discussion of the relationship between teaching and learning has focussed on the latter sense of 'learning' and the sense of 'teaching' that involves the *task* of trying to get pupils to learn in this latter sense. Of course, this is a more demanding condition for teaching than merely trying to get pupils to try to acquire knowledge or know-how, and rightly so. Likewise, if teachers are teaching in the achievement sense then necessarily pupils are learning in the achievement sense as well, but the converse does not hold, since successful learning does not necessarily require successful teaching.

important for this study. However, when particular conceptions of teachers and teaching are examined, it is much clearer that there are real differences of substance between the different and contestable conceptions. Discussion of these different conceptions will occupy Chapters 6–8.

AN OUTLINE OF THE REST OF THE BOOK

Chapter 2, 'Schooling and the Occupational Knowledge of Teaching', will thus pursue this issue of the relationship between teaching and learning in greater detail and will, in the course of this discussion, try to say something more precise about the teacher as an agent in the context of the occupation of teaching. While this will inevitably involve consideration of historical discussions of the presumed role of the teacher and the assumptions (often themselves contestable) that lie behind the descriptions of this role, it will come on to a consideration of teaching as a social practice within such institutions as schools. Thus, teachers have been variously described as midwives, facilitators and organisers, instructors, mentors, trainers and exemplars. While at least some of these accounts fasten on an important aspect of what it is to be a teacher, it is unlikely that any single one of them will be capable of capturing the whole truth of the matter. Getting clear about the nature of teacher agency will not be easy.

The question is further complicated by the fact that the actions that teachers perform are complex and that reductive accounts of teacher ability (e.g. in terms of skills) will fail to capture what is involved in the work of teachers. The so-called 'polymorphousness' of teacher agency will be raised, to be pursued in subsequent chapters. This entails that we take a closer look at the concept of practical knowledge and draw on some recent epistemological work. At this point, we will move from general categorial considerations to a closer examination of education as a formal practice within a social division of labour and within the framework of the institutionalisation of educational practices. It will also be necessary to say something about the success conditions for teaching and thus about the relationship, if any, between a teacher teaching and a learner learning. One challenge will be, however, to try to specify if the pupils are not always as Dewey describes them and as teachers would like them to be; what exactly is the agency of the pupil or student that responds to the intentions of the teacher, since if anything is clear, it is that pupils must play some role in their learning, even in conditions where they are reluctant or unwilling learners.[7] Short of being a purely passive recipient of brainwashing, there must be some assent and some effort on the part of an unwilling pupil if anything is to be learned. One of the challenges for understanding teaching as an occupation is the characterisation of their role in such conditions.

Chapter 3, 'Dimensions of Expertise and Their Relevance to Teaching', will examine the claim that teaching is an occupation in which it is possible to gain expertise. The related claim that it is a profession is also difficult to interpret, and to do so one needs points of comparison with other occupations in order to establish whether or not this claim makes sense and, indeed, whether or not it is helpful in understanding the role of teachers in contemporary societies. In order to do this, we will look at the epistemology of professional and vocational action, and try to map out what it involves and where teaching falls within this mapping exercise. It will be shown that there are some particular difficulties in tying down the nature of teacher expertise and consequently in characterising teaching as a typical profession. Does teaching fit the standard conception of the professions? *Inter alia* it will be necessary to examine what, if any, sense we can make of the profession–occupation distinction.

Chapter 4, 'Towards a Typology of Occupations', will look at different kinds of occupations – craftworker, executive technician and professional technician – and seek to establish what is involved in each and where teaching as an occupation might fit within these conceptions. It will be shown that a case can be made out for teaching belonging to any single one of these categories, and consequently even within a particular time and place there may exist vigorously contested interpretations of what a proper characterisation of a teacher might be. At this point, we have gone beyond what can usefully be said in a universal sense about teachers and teaching and have arrived at the point at which it is necessary to explore different, and in some cases contested, conceptions of what it is, or what it should be, to be a teacher.

This issue of classification is complicated by the fact that there are both compatibilities and incompatibilities between the different conceptions and that these need to be explored. For example, it is not clear that the craftworker and the professional technician conceptions are in all respects incompatible with each other. Neither is

---

[7] I use the term 'pupil' rather than 'student' to reflect the fact that the primary focus of this book is on schoolteaching. This is not just a matter of nomenclature since it can be argued that teachers have special responsibilities *vis-à-vis* pupils that lecturers do not have *vis-à-vis* students.

the role of educational theory irrelevant to the executive and professional technical conceptions, although it is relevant in very different ways in each case. Although the craft conception emphasises local knowledge, tacit practical knowledge, direct acquaintance with the materials of work, experience gained through some form of apprenticeship and the ability to make situational judgements, there are good grounds for supposing that these are also valuable attributes for the professional technical conception, even though they are not, by themselves, sufficient. On the other hand, the 'executive technician' conception, which involves teachers following mandated procedures which, at least notionally, have a research base justifying them, may well be incompatible with the first two conceptions. It should be emphasised that these three types are in fact theoretical constructs and constitute ideal types, which will be more or less realised in particular forms of education. Although critical of the 'pure' craft conception of teaching, the chapter will, however, emphasise the importance of craft in good quality teaching and will seek to understand its scope and extent. The chapter will go on to consider the role of teacher as a *professional technician*, namely a teacher with the ability to form judgements and to act based on understanding of a body of systematic (theoretical) knowledge (a 'technician' in the sociological literature on professionalism), as a *technologist*, or someone capable of contributing to the development of the application of the underlying theory, and as a *researcher*, someone contributing to the core areas of the underlying theory.

Chapter 5, 'The Elements of Teacher Knowledge and Know-How', examines the elements of teacher expertise, here taken to mean also the knowledge, know-how and personal characteristics that are required of an effective teacher. The dimensions covered include the subject knowledge that a teacher requires, usually the subject studied at secondary or tertiary level that the teacher intends to teach to pupils, but also the applicable knowledge of, for example, applied linguistics that it may be necessary for a primary specialist in literacy to acquire. It will then go on to consider *applied subject knowledge*, or those subjects that involve the acquisition of know-how on the part of pupils rather than strictly academic knowledge. It is, of course, misleading to suggest that there are sharp distinctions to be made here, since even in practical subjects, pupils will need to acquire some factual knowledge in order to be able to operate and the teachers will require some such knowledge in order to effectively teach pupils. The issue of how much more such knowledge than a pupil's knowledge a teacher requires will also be addressed in this chapter. The chapter will next consider what Shulman (1986) has called 'pedagogic content knowledge', or the knowledge how to render subject knowledge into relevant curricular structures and effective pedagogic strategies. It is argued that the complexities of this topic have not been sufficiently addressed in the extant literature.

Knowledge of how to teach effectively and how to enable pupils to learn effectively is also thought to be part of a competent teacher's repertoire. Such knowledge, rightly or wrongly, is thought to be derivable from systematic empirical enquiry. However, claims to such knowledge are notoriously unreliable, and not just the specifics of knowledge claims but the very possibility of acquiring such knowledge is often contested. This chapter will, among other matters, examine whether such claims can be justified. At this point, some of the more intuitive elements of a teacher's know-how will be introduced. The idea of developing a conception of oneself as a teacher and of thinking about one's strengths and weaknesses as a member of the profession will be distinguished from theories about how teachers teach and pupils learn. Finally, the sense in which an important part of teacher knowledge is based on the ability to size up complex situations and to make effective *in situ* judgements and the sense in which these can be said to be moral judgements will also be considered.

In Chapter 6, 'Teaching as a Craft Occupation', the popular and influential idea of teaching as a form of craftwork along the lines of pottery, smithing or carpentry is considered in detail. There are powerful (and, in my view, unassailable) reasons for thinking that there is a significant craft element in teaching. However, it does not follow from the fact that it is a craft that it does not rely on systematic or theoretical knowledge in making some professional judgements. In order to examine the cogency of this idea, it is necessary to look at what is involved in a traditional craft, in contrast to what we would now call a 'technical occupation', which explicitly depends on systematic knowledge as a support for and legitimation of professional judgement. It is then possible to get a better idea of the extent to which teaching can plausibly be said to fall into this category. One clear point where examination is needed is in considering the extent to which the teacher's subject knowledge can be effectively deployed in the context of purely craft know-how. We will consider an illustrative example to bring out what is at stake in this debate. Anyone who wishes to take the idea of a craft seriously needs also to acknowledge that the practice of a craft involves more than skill. We will therefore need to carefully consider the other kinds of know-how which we might reasonably expect from teachers and the extent to which they can meaningfully be developed as part of a craft. Such know-how, sometimes described as 'adverbial verbs' (Ryle 1979) or 'transversal abilities', will need to be considered in relation to the skills that are also an essential part of the repertoire of the teacher as craftworker.

In this connection, it is also necessary to consider the role of situational judgement and the moral responsibilities of the teacher in the classroom, not just in terms of a general occupational instruction to benevolence but also in the fine-grained detail of everyday classroom interaction. It will also be necessary to consider what is meant by the claim that a craftworker is in possession of a particular kind of knowledge, namely 'tacit knowledge', which is essential to their overall know-how. While not denying that there is such a thing, a generally deflationary and demystifying account of it will be given, which will make use of what Luntley (2012) has termed 'activity concepts'.

Finally, in dealing with the craft conception, it is necessary to deal with the often-made and superficially persuasive claim that it is simply commonsense that teaching is a craft. This will entail both an examination of the 'commonsense' claim and the view that there is a popularly validated conception of teaching that commonsense can yield for us. This will involve using the Gramscian distinction between *good sense* and *common-sense* and examining the ways in which commonsense views about teaching masquerade as good sense when in fact they are very often distillations and simplifications of highly theoretical and contestable views.

Chapter 7, 'The Teacher as Executive Technician', deals with the currently popular 'Taylorised' conception of teaching. Contrary to the craft view is the perception that there is a body of systematic knowledge about learning and pedagogy that can be pressed into service in the practice of teaching. However, since it is not practical (or perhaps even desirable) that teachers be acquainted with this body of knowledge, there needs to be some form of translation that allows the deliverances of theory to be reconstituted into empirically mandated normative procedures for realising the desirable outcome of teaching, namely pupil learning. On this conception, there is a division of labour between, on the one hand, the policymaker and the researcher who interrogate the research and devise optimal procedures for realising the ends of teaching based on that research, and on the other hand the teacher, whose job it is to put those procedures into effect without necessarily having much appreciation of their underlying justification. The judgement of the teacher, on this conception, consists of the ability to put such procedures into effect in an appropriate way so as to realise the aims of a lesson or scheme of work. In Oakeshott's (1962) terminology, *technical knowledge* is to be applied without any admixture of *practical knowledge*. Situational judgement is minimised, making compatibility between the craft and executive technician conceptions of teaching problematic. Lest this be thought an unlikely model of teaching, illustrative examples from both developed and developing countries will be given, including the English literacy and numeracy strategies and the concept of a 'parateacher' increasingly popular in some quarters in India and other countries.

Chapter 8, 'The Teacher as a Professional Technician', tackles the issue of what it is to be a 'professional' teacher. It is routinely claimed that teachers are, or should be, 'professionals'. There is less clarity concerning what this should mean in practice. One difficulty is that teaching is often characterised in ways that make it difficult to effect a direct comparison with other occupations described as professions, which lay claim to a systematic knowledge base on which professional judgments are formed. On the face of it, teaching should fall comfortably into this category, but the claim that there is such a systematic knowledge base is vigorously disputed, both within and outside the occupation. Certainly, it is very often claimed that teachers should not be reduced to the role of 'technicians', which rather begs the question as to exactly how they should be characterised.

This chapter will examine this issue, paying particular attention to the claim that teaching has a knowledge base that is capable of informing professional judgements. It will distinguish between conceptual, normative and empirical theory and also take account of the ethical commitment and personal development of teachers as part of their occupational make-up. The conclusion will be definite. Teaching is capable of being a profession along the lines of other traditional professions, in virtue of its possession of a knowledge base. However, care must be taken to give an accurate account of just what this knowledge base consists. It turns out to be highly complex and to have considerable implications for the initial and continuing education of teachers, a theme that will be taken up again in Chapter 10. No one should underestimate the challenges involved in giving a coherent account of the systematic knowledge that underpins teaching, and there are powerful arguments against such a position, to be found, for example, in the work of Wilfred Carr and Anthony O'Hear, not to mention more implicitly in the work of Robin

Barrow, David Carr and even Donald Schön. These arguments will be addressed in the course of the chapter.

Chapter 9, 'Teaching as an Occupation', considers the nature of teaching as an occupation in a broad sense. The literature on teaching has been perhaps excessively focussed on work in the classroom. This is undoubtedly the core of teachers' work and is seen to be so by them. However, school-based education is a complex area with an elaborate division of labour within it. There is a real question as to whether or not teaching should be 'Taylorised' with the essential division of labour giving way to a fragmentation of function, leaving teachers in the classroom but largely without a role in the broader business of teaching and education. Therefore, this chapter will address the issue of teaching as a career and the extent to which a career path can be developed that encompasses engagement with the broader functions of teaching.

There are two important issues to be considered when trying to get clear about a career in teaching. The first is concerned with the knowledge, know-how and practical characteristics required to assume roles beyond that of classroom teacher. The second is that of what might broadly be called the 'civic' role of teaching, by which I mean those aspects of teaching that involve both intra- and inter-occupational discourse and negotiation, including the governance and the management of educational institutions. These two functions are both very important but need to be kept conceptually (and probably, to some extent, functionally) distinct. It is a commonplace but nevertheless important observation that expertise in teaching children in a classroom does not translate readily into expertise and virtue in dealing with adults, including one's colleagues in teaching. Yet the profession of teaching needs to be led,[8] and it needs people who can lead it. I will not take the view that teachers should be the exclusive group who do this but will maintain that they form a very important 'college' of expertise and experience within the wider society on matters of teaching and education, who should always have an important role in curriculum development, inspection, assessment, governance and even policy making. An outline of what teacher careers might look like were such considerations to be taken seriously will be given. Finally, consideration will be given to the stability and continuity of the teaching corps, and it will be argued that a high degree of both is necessary for the health of a public education system.

---

[8] I hope to have shown by this point that teaching should indeed be recognised as a profession in an important sense of that term.

In Chapter 10, 'Teacher Education', consideration of the education of teachers brings us back to the core issues of teacher knowledge, know-how and expertise, which were the substance of Chapters 4–7. At the time of writing, the education (or, as some would prefer, the training) of teachers is a matter of lively political debate in many countries including the UK. There is little consensus on what it should consist of, and this lack of consensus reflects the lack of agreement about what kind of occupation teaching is. This chapter will make use of the results of the discussion in Chapters 5–7 and the conception of the teacher as a professional that was developed in Chapter 7 to outline what an appropriate form of teacher education for such a professional would look like were it to be thoroughly addressed, taking into account also what we can safely consider to be the principal characteristics of a good teacher.

Comparison will be made between the ways in which teacher education is conducted in various countries, including England, Finland, Germany and India. Three issues of particular importance emerge. The first concerns the relationship between teacher preparation in the workplace, practicum and classroom. Closely entangled with this is the question as to whether or not the intending teacher is best placed as an intern (supernumerary) or as a junior employee (an apprentice). The second concerns the relationship between the initial stages of teacher education, the consolidation phase of the early years of a teaching career and continuing education throughout a career, related to the taking on of further responsibilities as outlined in Chapter 8. The general form of the argument will be that there should be not only a careful articulation of the different loci of teacher education at each phase (internal articulation) but also a careful articulation of the initial, consolidation and career elements of teacher education (external articulation), taking into account the importance of stability and continuity in teaching argued for in Chapter 8.

The third issue concerns the balance between practical and academic preparation within the overall programme, particularly of initial teacher education. The argument here is that there should be an analytical separation between the apprenticeship versus internship question (which certainly does raise questions of quality) and the nature of the academic contribution to the programme. It will be maintained that there are considerable potential advantages to intending teachers becoming employees, provided certain other conditions are met, but there may well be considerable logistical and financial problems with 'massifying' an apprenticeship system of this kind. On the other hand, whether a society opts for apprenticeship or internship (where the intending teacher is supernumerary to the staff establishment of the school and is not an employee), the question remains as to the balance of theory and practice within the phase of Initial Teacher Education (ITE).

The argument of the chapter is, then, drawing on the argument presented particularly in Chapters 8 and 9, that teacher education should be of reasonable length and should consist of closely integrated periods of academic study of pedagogic content knowledge, and educational theory, both philosophical and empirical, culminating in more lightly supervised probationary practice. Continuing Teacher Education (CTE) should continue the academic rigour that ought to be found in ITE, but the balance between time spent on academic work and on school-focussed work should be tilted to the latter provided that the practice-based element is at all times informed by and interwoven with a high level of academic content. It will be argued that amongst the advantages of conducting teacher education in this way will be the reduction of attrition and the development of experienced teachers capable of assuming significant leadership positions within the profession and also of playing a significant role in the education of new generations of teachers.

It is quite legitimate and indeed natural to ask whether such an extended discussion sheds any light on the question of what makes a good teacher. The general argument in Chapter 11, 'A Good Teacher', drawing on the discussion in previous sections, will be that it does. It is evident that there should be a healthy relationship between the teaching that teachers do and the learning that pupils succeed in accomplishing, even if the exact nature of this relationship is at times difficult to pin down with complete precision. But most questions in life cannot be answered with complete precision, and we should content ourselves with achieving the greatest precision possible with the subject matter with which we are dealing, itself no mean achievement.

We cannot address the issue without considering the aims of education systems, bearing in mind that these will, inevitably, reflect the conception of education embodied in them and the perception of what it is morally acceptable for a teacher to do in pursuit of the goal of pupil learning. Another issue that deserves great attention is the often-misunderstood relationship between the practice of teaching and the use of assessment. The centrality of teachers assessing pupils as part of their practice will be argued for, and it will further be argued that the assessing that teachers have to do as part of their work should be kept distinct from the assessment of teachers themselves, their schools and the education systems within which they work. Strong philosophical and empirical considerations are brought to bear in support of this contention, and the implications of the argument for the education and professional development of teachers are drawn out. This discussion will itself shed some light on the question as to whether, if a teacher is teaching, a pupil should be learning. The inclination and ability to assess whether or not a pupil is learning are, as Flew (1986) argued, indicators of the seriousness with which teachers approach their work.

The final chapter, 'Some outstanding Issues', will deal with a number of outstanding issues that affect the nature and perception of teaching in the early-twenty-first century: discipline, reward and punishment as a system for managing the teaching force; retention and attrition of teachers; the allure for policymakers of the idea of 'charismatic' teaching and educational leadership; and the problems of teaching in a consumer society. These issues will not be dealt with completely *de novo*, but will draw considerably on the arguments of previous chapters. Thus, the treatment of discipline will draw on the arguments of Chapters 2 and 8 but will also consider the role of contemporary society and culture in assisting or impeding teachers from their role of ensuring that their pupils learn. No easy answers will be suggested, but the nature of the problems with indications of the direction of solutions will be offered. It will also be pointed out that certain currently favourite policy ideas, such as strict teacher accountability and the casting of teachers as providers of services, will actually be contributing to rather than reducing such problems.

This completes a synopsis of the book. It is not intended as a completely comprehensive account of teachers' knowledge. In particular, it does not dwell in detail on the ethics of teaching, not because this is not an important topic but because to do so properly would have extended considerably, if not doubled, its length.

2
Schooling and the Occupation of Teaching

INTRODUCTION

The main aim of this chapter is to consider teaching as an occupation in contemporary societies. It has already been noted that teaching (and learning) happen in any society as the young need to be prepared for adult life. However, how this happen varies enormously from historic period to historic period and from society to society. One finds, for example, societies that do not depend on formal structures for teaching and learning to take place, but which place emphasis on learning non-formally or informally through interactions with individuals whose claim to authority in any teaching role is nothing more than their expertise in a particular area (Sarangapani 2013). At the other extreme, there are societies in which teachers play a preponderant role in teaching and learning and where the role is formally enshrined in institutions such as the school and through a distinct occupational status for teachers. Thus, in our society teaching has come to be a distinct role within the overall social division of labour, particularly connected with formal institutions of education such as schools, colleges and universities. We shall find that teaching is an occupation, but that due to the different ways in which occupations are conceptualised in contemporary societies, this fact leaves a very large degree of freedom as to how in fact teaching is conceptualised and organised and leaves open the possibility not only for the co-existence of different conceptions of the teacher, but also for conflicts about what should be the correct interpretation of what it is to be a teacher.

Teachers' Know-How: A Philosophical Investigation, First Edition. Christopher Winch.
© 2017 Christopher Winch. Editorial Organisation © Philosophy of Education Society of Great Britain.
Published 2017 by John Wiley & Sons, Ltd.

OCCUPATIONS

Before we discuss teaching as an occupation, it is worthwhile saying something first about the concept of an occupation. Philosophical
discussion of the nature of occupations is relatively sparse but rather
more has been written about *practices* in recent years, notably by
MacIntyre (1981), and MacIntyre's work has led to an extensive literature on the nature of practices, some of which will be helpful to
our discussion (e.g. Hager 2011; Higgins 2011). Nearly all societies
have a division of labour whereby different social needs are attended
to by different individuals: agriculture, manufacturing, construction,
retail, extraction, education, health and so on all have labour forces
who concentrate their effort principally in these areas. These *sectors*
as they are called are fairly permanent features of the socio-economic
scene and reflect a fundamental need, in any complex society, to
organise the availability of their complex requirements.[1] As these
sectors are broadly based, it is not usually possible for any one individual to have a sufficient practical grasp of any of them to engage in
the production of all their characteristic products and services. This
division of labour, although necessary in complex societies such as
ours, also has potential negative consequences as the impossibility
for any one individual to cater for his needs leads to dependence on
others for doing so, which leads to the potential for abuse or exploitation of this role. The potential for conflict and exploitation also arises
through the necessity for co-operation and co-ordination between
sectors and occupations in order to develop complex products and
services through disparities in power between different occupations.
There is thus a double-edged aspect to the division of labour; on the
one hand, the complexity of society imposes a need to co-operate
and co-ordinate, and, on the other, it brings in its train the potential
for dependency and exploitation. However, as a condition of existence of societies such as ours, the division of labour, with its potential problems, is unavoidable. As we shall see, this aspect of the
division of labour has important consequences for the occupation of
teaching.

This *division of labour*, found in all societies of any complexity, whereby individuals specialise in certain activities, should
be distinguished from the *fragmentation of the labour process*,
whereby an articulated sequence of activity can be broken down into

---

[1] There is a philosophical tradition that sees this as an evil, albeit a necessary one. See Weil,
Oppression and Liberty (1955)

parts (Williams 2000). The *division of labour* would involve, for example, some individuals specialising in woodwork (carpenters), others in clay (potters), some in farming (farmers) and some in hunting (hunters). The division of labour is compatible with considerable autonomy on the part of the worker concerned. Thus, a product, service or something else that is valuable (such as an educational experience) is conceived, the conception is put into effect and the result evaluated. It is important to note that this can itself be done co-operatively or individually, although it is unfortunate that much of the literature sees it as a purely individual activity (e.g. Marx 1887, vol. 1, p. 178; see also Arendt 1958; but, by way of contrast, Weil 1955; Kerschensteiner 1906, p. 16), rather than as potentially social. The *fragmentation of the labour process*, on the other hand, involves taking the operations of an occupation such as carpentry and assigning each single, on its own simple, step to a different individual. Fragmentation thus involves different individuals, all performing simple tasks in sequence, each requiring relatively little in the way of independence or know-how, co-ordinated by a 'line manager'. But the fragmentation of the labour process has a consequence that, although to an extent unavoidable, has had if anything more baleful consequences than the division of labour. This fragmentation was drawn attention to by Adam Smith (1776, 1981), although as Williams points out, he misleadingly refers to it as the division of labour from which it is conceptually distinct. It is quite clear, for example, that one could have an extensive division of labour without fragmentation of the labour process as in the examples above.

Smith argues, using the example of pin making, that fragmentation of the process of production, assigning a simple role to each individual in sequence, results in far greater productivity per man hour than an arrangement whereby each individual completes a product. In a fully articulated pin-making sequence, you might get the following fragmentation of the labour process. A plans the sequence whereby the pin is made; B supervises the production process; C, D, E, F and G carry out different actions in the sequence and H assesses the quality of the finished products. Numerous commentators have drawn attention to the psychologically, socially and politically deleterious consequences of this way of organising economic activity (which is now commonly known as 'Taylorism' after the management specialist Frederick Taylor; Taylor 1911). Smith himself commented on the bad effects on the mental state of those involved in the routine elements of these processes, and others have continued to do so. Teaching itself has not been immune to such fragmentation, and there have been some who have advocated its extension. It is a difficult and contentious point as to whether or not individual teachers can or should undertake all the roles involved in formal education, and there are no easy answers to such questions, which we will return to in subsequent chapters.

Typically, economic sectors are subdivided into *branches* and beyond that into *occupations*. Take the case of construction. Construction can be divided into the branches of, for example, house-building, commercial building and civil engineering. Within these branches, but also cross-cutting them in many cases, are occupations such as bricklayer, carpenter, electrician, scaffolder and so on. In addition, there are occupations which, although they might belong to a particular sector themselves, are also to be found within other sectors. Thus accountants work in financial services, but they can also be found in construction and other sectors. In education we can find administration, curriculum design, assessment, inspection, ancillary work and teaching itself, some of which, arguably, cut across the sector. Just as the boundaries between what a bricklayer is supposed to do, as opposed to, say, a carpenter are malleable and vary from country to country (Brockmann *et al.* 2010), the same is true of teaching and we will have cause to consider these boundaries in more detail and, in particular, what the proper scope of a teacher within the overall sector of formal education should be. And, as we shall see, there are no easy or universal answers.

Occupations do then have a socio-economic reality grounded in the ways in which society's work is organised. This is not to say of course that their social and economic strength, malleability or institutional support may not vary greatly across different societies. One only needs to compare, say, Germany and the UK in order to appreciate this (see e.g. Hanf 2011). Nonetheless, it remains true to say that the concept of an occupation is fundamental to our understanding of the division of labour in the sense that the provision for different kinds of human needs is functionally specialised and that individuals tend to specialise in the provision of certain needs rather than others. So far, I have sketched out a case for the recognition of the concept of an occupation as an analytically useful category, but as yet have made no judgements about how well rooted as a social category it is or indeed should be. Can one then arrive at a view of what the strength of the category should be, that is, make a *normative* judgement about its value? How would one go about this? One approach would be to look at the question on economic grounds, another on social grounds and yet another on moral grounds.

In contemporary societies, there is usually a sector recognised as *education*, the principal workers in which are teachers and lecturers. Teaching is usually considered as a distinct occupation, while lecturing and, more generally, teaching adults are considered to be distinct, although closely related ones. The social need to which the existence of the occupation of teaching is said to respond is not merely a general need for children to learn in order to participate in society as adults, but the need to have structured means of learning so that:

- The mass of the population learns what society deems necessary for its well-being.
- This learning is systematically organised so that all possible do undertake it under the supervision of specialist workers whose job it is to teach so that the young population can learn.
- This organisation takes a distinct institutional form, the school, which in an economical way provides a uniformity of conditions of teaching and learning in a collective form, through the organisation of the learners (pupils) into *classes* or manageable groups organised by age and/or ability to permit optimum use of the specialist worker (the teacher) who is charged with their learning.
- There is also organisation of the content and know-how through systematically organised subject matter.

Not only is the school an institution whose framework and also very often its detailed financing and organisation are undertaken by the state but the state also, in most developed contemporary societies, ensures that attendance for a number of years is compulsory.[2] Teachers who work in schools that cater for young people whose attendance is compulsory thus have a special role in carrying out a function that the state deems essential to its well-being and to that of the society that schools are meant to serve.

Teachers of young people are agents of compulsion in a number of senses, and this has a profound effect on the nature of the occupation. First of all, as remarked, it is very often the case that young people have no choice but to attend a school in which teachers have the function of teaching them and getting them to learn, but also of ensuring that they stay at school for the requisite period and learn in a way that is not disruptive to the working of the school. This can

[2] This book will focus principally, although not exclusively, on education directly funded and controlled by the state, bearing in mind that the state bears different kinds of relationships with educational provision, including allowing non-state schools complete independence.

impose a difficult burden on teachers, particularly in relation to those young people who do not wish to be in the school for whatever reason (see Willis 1977). The burdens of compulsion do thus not fall only on pupils, but on teachers as well. Even where schooling is not compulsory or where it does not take place in an institution that is owned and controlled by the state, pupils will usually not be there because they want to be there (although they may indeed not mind being there) but because their parents have deemed that they should be there. In this case, teachers are the agents of parents. They find themselves very often to be the agents of *both* the state *and* parents, a role that can lead to acute conflict. It should be pointed out as well that there is a limited sense in which the state is the indirect agent of parents who contribute through the election of politicians to run the legislative process that determines the structure and functioning of schools and through the provision of resources through taxation. The lines of accountability for teachers become complex, and this has a profound effect on the nature of their occupation and how they see it and how they are seen by others.

Finally, they are agents of compulsion in that, in nearly all cases, they prescribe on a day-to-day basis what is to be learned, the way in which that material is organised, how it is taught and learned and how learning is assessed. They may, in some systems, have a larger role and determine the broader outline of the curriculum and the way that it is organised on a year-by-year basis within a school. They may themselves have a hand in determining it, or, more likely, they are the agents of those who determine it and are thus under a form of compulsion themselves, having a delegated responsibility to prescribe the material on a day-to-day basis. In some cases, even this possibility may be taken away from them, and they may be obliged to teach according to a pattern prescribed day by day or even minute by minute. It can be seen then that teaching has the potential for being an onerous occupation, regarded on the one hand as essential for the well-being of society, but also as an agent of the compulsion that society and parents bring to bear on the learning of young people. Young people do not, and cannot be expected to, have the decisive say in what, how and when they should learn in order to become full members of society, but those who do have that say place a burden on those charged with carrying it out. This burden is all the greater in those circumstances where society is unsure about what the aims of its education system are and also when it is unclear about the degree of autonomy that teachers should have in carrying out its wishes. We can safely conclude that the compulsory nature of education in contemporary developed societies not only provides vast opportunities to enter the occupation of teaching but also has the potential for placing large and sometimes conflicting burdens on the shoulders of teachers, which they have little option but to bear.

THE RELATIONSHIP BETWEEN CONCEPTS OF *EDUCATION* AND *TEACHING*

We now turn to the relationship between education and teaching. It has already been observed that although there is a 'thin' categorial concept of teaching, there are different interpretations of this categorial concept, some of which are in conflict with each other. As a first point, it is worth looking at the way in which the Germanic countries conceptualise the categorial concept. German makes a distinction between *Erziehung* (upbringing) and *Bildung* (education), which we would normally both include as aspects of education in the English language.

Erziehung mainly takes place in the home, starting at birth, while *Bildung* is associated with formal education, but by no means exclusively so. Thus, we find that *Grundbildung* corresponds with what we might call 'grounding' (Letwin 1986) or primary education and *Allgemeinbildung* with general education, what you would need to become an 'educated person' in everyday parlance (see Hintz *et al.* 2001). *Ausbildung* refers to the educational processes through which one is prepared for an occupation that will normally take place at least as much within the workplace as within a school or college. We should note that even within a process of *Bildung*, there may well be elements of *Erziehung* and *vice versa*, together with more formal academic instruction (*Unterricht*), so these categories should not be treated as if they were hermetically sealed from each other. Finally, there is what is perhaps the most interesting element in the Germanic categorisation, namely the category of *allgemeine Menschenbildung* or general human education. Although this is itself subject to different academic interpretations (see Benner 2003, ch. 1, in particular pp. 20–21), a reasonable interpretation would be to describe it as a continuing process of personal growth and self-discovery that has no necessary endpoint. Thus, although one may have to undertake an *Ausbildung* in order to become a useful citizen, that *Ausbilding* should do much more than prepare one for a mere job or even an occupation. It should also equip individuals with the means for self-reflection and the possibility of continuing learning in such a way that they have the possibility to develop as a unique individual during the course of life. In terms of our categorial concept of education, then, we need to acknowledge that preparation for life is not something that necessarily comes to an end on reaching adulthood but continues as long as one is in a position to reflect on one's position in the world and to have an influence on it.

Obviously only some of these processes will be supervised by early childhood educators, schoolteachers and university lecturers, but *Ausbildung* and *allgemeine Menschenbildung* are of potentially the greatest importance for the education of teachers themselves, a point to which we will return in Chapter 10. It is also evident that although teaching, whether carried out formally or informally, has an important role to play even in *allgemeine Menschenbildung*.[3]

Teaching, especially teaching in formal education (such as schooling), is especially salient in processes of education, even if it belongs only loosely to the concept of education itself.[4] So our concern will be largely restricted to the role of teachers in formal educational processes, bearing in mind that teachers are not and cannot be superintendents or participants in many necessary educational processes.

SCHOOLING: THE INSTITUTIONAL SETTING FOR TEACHING IN MODERN SOCIETIES

In industrially developed societies, formal, compulsory education regulated and often run by the state has come to be organised in schools. A school in this sense is an institution whose primary purpose is the education of young people. Its operations are typically carried out by teachers, whose job it is to oversee the education of the young people in it and mostly to do this by teaching them (in what sense of 'teaching' we shall presently investigate). There are good reasons why education in these societies has used the school as the main institutional instrument for education. They bring with them economies of scale in the deployment of physical and intellectual resources, including the efficient deployment of teachers. They are also a specialised environment in which young people spend a considerable part of their days away from influences other than their

---

[3] See for example *Der Grüne Heinrich* (Green Henry) by Gottfried Keller (1951), which describes such informal teaching in a variety of contexts in relation to the troubled *Ausbildung* of the hero of the novel, Heinrich Lee.

[4] 'Education' is here being referred to as the *process* of education, rather than the *outcome* of educational processes.

teachers and each other. This gives the school ample opportunities for influencing the character and outlook of their charges through the development of its own aims, moral outlook and procedures. This in turn leads to the possibility of different schools specialising in curricula, in type of character formation and in preparation for the destination in society of the young person. It is important to understand that these functions (often the result of the implicit adoption of certain aims) are often conducted informally through the creation of an internal culture within the school.[5] The teachers who work in a school are essential agents in the maintenance of a school culture as well as in teaching and assessing the curriculum, and no serious consideration of the nature of teaching can be undertaken without careful consideration of this role.

Although the role of teacher had been well-established well before the advent of schooling, different kinds of teacher have always co-existed with and probably predate the schoolteacher. The informal guru (e.g. Socrates), the sophist, the tutor and the governess are all examples of such teachers, and they figure significantly in some classic works of philosophy of education, such as *Meno* and *Émile*, as well as in literature. This is a matter of importance for our enquiry as the example of such teachers looms large in philosophical discussions of teaching, and there is a danger of pressing the analogy of the guru or the tutor with the role of the modern schoolteacher too far. On the other hand, of course, such works give us a great deal of food for thought about teaching and certainly cannot be ignored.

School teaching appears as a recognisable occupation on a large scale from the eighteenth century onwards and as an employee of the state from the early-nineteenth century (Green 1990). The schoolteacher is a salaried employee who may or may not have undergone a postsecondary education (and sometimes not even a complete secondary education) and may or may not have had formal preparation for his role. Teacher training institutions did not become well-established in the UK until well into the nineteenth century. Even now, attendance at one is not compulsory for entry into teaching in many countries, including the UK. In contemporary developed societies, the typical teacher has received education at tertiary level in the material that he is supposed to teach (and 'supposed' is not an idle word here, as many teach subjects for which they were not

---

[5] See, for example, the culture of minority non-conformity described in Rudyard Kipling's (1999) 'Stalky and Co.' and its connection with careers in the British secret service.

explicitly prepared). Usually he or she will have undergone some formal preparation for taking up the role of teaching, which may be short (e.g. 10 months of a PGCE in England) or lengthy (e.g. 7 years for a secondary school teacher in Germany).

Is the teacher an independent worker? We have already noted the role of compulsion both on and by teachers as important characteristics of their working conditions. In many cases teachers work in highly regulated frameworks, both within and beyond the school itself. This often leaves them with limited scope for independent action, except perhaps in the confines of their own classrooms and in some cases not even there. This lack of power, both in the immediate work context and within the school and the larger society, regarding educational matters is well-established and the negative effects continue to be referred to (e.g. Pring 2012). Whether it should be changed in the teacher's favour is an issue that we will need to seriously consider.

Taking the usually accepted traits of a profession (Freidson 1986), it is difficult to characterise teaching as being one. These are the commonly accepted traits of a profession:

1. Practice underpinned by well-established body of abstract and difficult-to-master systematic knowledge.
2. Expertise consisting in application of this knowledge in complex and often unpredictable situations.
3. Mandatory licensure connected with achievement of tertiary or post-tertiary level occupational qualifications.
4. Control of entry and exit from the occupation through a self-governing occupational body.
5. A specific ethical mission. (cf. D. Carr 1999)

It is not difficult to see that teaching does not fulfil even one of them in many countries. Failure to fulfil some of the criteria reflects the political power of the occupation and uncertainty about the nature of teachers' expertise, and there is a good case to be made out that uncertainty about the latter has effects on the former, usually negative. This uncertainty about the nature of teacher know-how and the role if any which a knowledge base plays in it is one that will be a preoccupation throughout this book. Writing about this topic in England in 2016 is particularly interesting as we are currently living through an attempt, which is not unique to England, to redefine the nature of teaching and in particular to downplay the role of underpinning knowledge and the connection with higher education certification that underpins it.[6]

This uncertainty about teaching as an occupation is reflected in the ways in which teachers, politicians, parents and the public view it. Although the term 'professional' is often used by teachers as a descriptor of their occupation, they often do not mean what the term is taken to mean by academic commentators, for example that teachers are technicians who put into effect in judgement a systematic body of knowledge (cf. Hoyle 1974). There were protests in England when the National Curriculum was introduced in 1988, to the effect that it reduced teachers from professionals to technicians by providing them with a structure (the prescribed content in the curriculum) that they had to interpret in their planning and teaching. As we shall see, the 'craft' conception of teaching is often associated with the term 'professional' by teachers, even though most professionals (other than teachers) would not see themselves as craftworkers.

Another way (at least until about 25 years ago in England) in which teachers think of themselves as 'professionals' lies in their preparedness to carry out unremunerated extra contractual work like supervising school dinners or coaching and refereeing games at weekends. Ironically, some of the established professions such as lawyers prefer to bill by the minute to ensure that they are properly remunerated. It is sometimes said that the professions are distinguished from other occupations by the ethical commitment that is intrinsic to the core of their work. Thus they provide valuable civic goods and cannot do their work unless they are motivated by an ethic of benevolence rather than financial reward. In Lynch and Walsh's (2003) useful classification, they could never be more than weak lucrephiles and certainly not lucrepaths (pathologically addicted to financial reward). Some professions, the clergy for example, would even be expected to be lucrephobes (averse to more than minimal remuneration).[7] It is difficult to escape the conclusion that British teachers have historically regarded themselves as 'professionals' in

---

6 Some adherents of the craft conception of teaching would deny this and claim that they respect the role that research should play in teaching. However, their anxiety to distance teachers from higher education and systematic study of educational research makes this a largely empty claim (see DfE 2016).

7 According to Lynch and Walsh, we can distinguish attitudes to remuneration on a scale ranging from *lucrepathia* (a desire for remuneration which has few moral and possibly no legal side-constraints), through various forms of interest in remuneration – from *lucrephilia* (a positive attitude towards remuneration), which can range from strong to weak, to *lucrephobia* (aversion to remuneration other than what is strictly necessary to keep body and soul together).

the sense of practitioners of a craft with relatively little theoretical underpinning (despite the emphasis on this in teacher education from the 1960s onwards), but with a distinctive kind of ethical mission that involves the well-being of their pupils.

A DISTINCTIVE ETHICAL MISSION?

It is worth spending a bit more time on this issue as it raises larger questions about the relationship between ethics and occupations. I do not mean by this merely whether or not there is a 'professional ethics' connected with the conduct of members of the occupation (although this is part of the issue), but also a question about the moral dimension of the occupation and what its practitioners are supposed to achieve. An influential paper by David Carr (1999) argued that the ethical dimension of professions was what distinguished them from other occupations.

Professions, according to this view, are concerned with providing both goods pertaining to life and death (e.g. medicine) and goods pertaining to civilised living (e.g. law relating to justice), and these aims are partly constitutive of what they are as professions. It follows that someone ostensibly practising such a profession could not be evaluated positively if he did not strive to achieve the ethical aims of the profession. One cannot be a good lawyer if one cheats one's clients. By contrast, *trades* such as that of butcher or baker do not depend on such ethical aims. Indeed, Adam Smith suggested that we supply our needs from the butcher or the baker not through their benevolence but through our attention to their needs (Smith 1776, vol. 1, bk. 1, ch. 2, pp. 26–27). Consequently, the excellence of a non-professional occupation does not depend on the adherence to ethical occupational aims: a good butcher might cheat his customers and still be a good butcher. According to this model, teaching would look much more like a profession in this sense than like a trade, since it is founded on the idea of benevolence, specifically the welfare of the pupil who is being taught.

Carr's model certainly deserves further examination. It seems to rest on the idea, persuasive in itself, that there are two kinds of virtue associated with the practice of any occupation. First, *technical virtues* associated with the ability to generate the products and services characteristic of the occupation: cuts of meat for the butcher, a journey for the bus driver, a vase for the potter, crops for the farmer. These might include: patience, self-mastery, diligence, attention to detail and flexibility. It is then suggested that there is a further set of *civic virtues* that the practitioner may or may not exhibit: honesty, fair-mindedness, benevolence, compassion and courage, for example.[8] However, the very claim that there are two different kinds of virtues connected with the practice of an occupation can also lead us to think that the same distinction can be made in relation to those occupations known as professions. A good lawyer in the technical sense will have abilities associated with deep knowledge of relevant parts of the law, ability to master a brief and to assess the relevance of evidence, together with rhetorical skills and confidence associated with effective performance in a courtroom. The acquisition and practice of such abilities might include: diligence, self-mastery, patience, attention to detail and open-mindedness. But just as it seems to be true for the butcher or baker that one can possess these virtues without being honest, benevolent or courageous, it seems just as true for the lawyer, the doctor and, dare we say it, the teacher.

Neither does it seem clear that the kinds of goods that the professional is asked to create (justice, health, knowledge and spiritual well-being), desirable though they undoubtedly are, are any different in this respect from those of the practice of other occupations. Without bricklayers we would have no shelter and would die, without plumbers no water or sanitation and would also die, without the manufacturers of cars and buses we would not be able to travel and so much of the quality of our lives would be restricted, and so on. Of course there are occupations that do not contribute in any obvious way to our well-being, without necessarily being criminal: cigarette manufacturer or croupier, for example. But there are also branches of medicine and the law that have a tenuous claim to be tending to individual and social well-being: certain types of cosmetic surgery in the case of medicine and claim-chasing in the case of law for example.

So, is there no difference between occupations in ethical commitment? Lynch and Walsh's already-mentioned scale of attitudes towards occupational remuneration might be helpful here. Do the professions tend to the lucrephobic end of the spectrum while the other occupations in various degrees shade off towards the lucrephiliac or even lucrepathic end? It is difficult to see how this would work in a consistent fashion. True, one would expect lucrephobia from the clergy, but it is by no means uncommon to find strong forms of lucrephilia within the law and medicine. There are certainly cases of

---

[8] See also Kerschensteiner's (1901) distinction between *bourgeois* and *civic* virtues, which is very similar to the distinction made above.

teachers who are 'in it for the money' even though, on the whole, it is not a lucrative occupation. These reflections give us good reason to believe that, although Carr is right in identifying general moral orientation as an important characteristic of occupations, he is not correct in identifying the professions necessarily with benevolence and other occupations with being only contingently so related. Perhaps it is a mistake to think of occupations in these terms if we wish to distinguish categories of occupations. However, the question "for whose benefit occupations are being conducted?" is very important and merits further examination.

FOR WHOM IS TEACHING DONE?

In the previous chapter, the categorial triadic relationship of the verb *to teach* was discussed. *A teaches B to C*. While teaching has been often discussed in these terms, it is arguable that there is a fourth term in the relationship, namely *on behalf of D*, so that a complete unpacking of the concept of teaching would involve: *A teaches B to C on behalf of D*. It is perfectly natural to assume that C the pupil, and D the beneficiary, will necessarily be the same person, in which case it looks as if it is superfluous to spell the relationship out as a four-part rather than a three-part one. Unfortunately, however, it is not quite that straightforward. It is assumed here not only that D has some interest in the outcome of C's education, but also that D, through committing resources to the education of C, has some claim on the nature and quality of the outcome. We noted in the previous chapter that there is a perspectival element to the concept of education. Although the object of educating someone is necessarily worthwhile, we cannot assume either that the same education will be worthwhile to everyone or that everyone will have the same view of what is worthwhile for whom.

This consideration has a direct impact on how we view teaching. We cannot *assume* that A teaches B to C on C's behalf. This is not just because C may not wish to be taught B. It may be in C's interests to be taught B even if C does not consider this to be the case. The problem goes deeper than that. Let us suppose that D, the beneficiary or one of the beneficiaries of C's being taught, is not C himself. Furthermore, let us suppose that D does not identify his interests with those of C or even that D has no interest in furthering the interests of C (not just as C might see them, but in the sense that D is not interested in maximising C's well-being, or sees it in different terms from his own). It is not difficult to imagine such a possibility. D may wish *C* to be an unskilled menial worker and provide an education for *C* appropriate to such a role. It is not difficult either to imagine that on an alternative view, this is not the best outcome that *C* could have in terms of his well-being. *D* might be a politician or civil servant concerned with the efficient or at least the customary running of the economy and sincerely consider that *C*'s receiving an education adequate for preparation to be an unskilled worker might be in the best interests of society if not so much for *C* himself. We might also consider that people or groups other than *D* may also have a stake in *C*'s education and take a different view from *D*. These might be, but need not be restricted to, *C*'s parents and *A* the teacher.

However, the general scenario suggests that *A*, the teacher, who is supposed to provide benefits from teaching *C* might find himself in a situation fraught with conflict, where accountability to the provider of resources for *C*'s education (and his own salary) conflicts, or has the potential to conflict, with the views of others concerning what they regard as a legitimate stake in *C*'s education, not least *C* himself. These considerations suggest that teaching as an occupation has an irreducibly *civic* role (it concerns a public interest in the nature and quality of *C*'s education) and a *political* one in the sense that different views concerning the nature of the education that *C* is to receive need to come to some kind of resolution. One view of course is that such considerations are no part of a teacher's business, but that is scarcely a plausible position to take if it is true that there is a moral dimension and a *prima facie* duty of benevolence on the part of teachers for the people whom they are responsible for teaching. Although there are powerful arguments for thinking that this is so, advanced by Carr among others, it is a particular interpretation of the role of teachers and cannot be extracted from an analysis of the concept of education itself. It needs, in other words, a particular ethics and political theory to underpin it. It thus turns out that the moral position of teachers, particularly in education funded and/or regulated by the state, is more complex than most commentators acknowledge. One of the claims of this book is that this is a situation that teachers, and those responsible for educating them, cannot ignore.

TEACHING AND AGENCY

It is categorically true of teaching as an occupation that it involves agency on the part of the teacher. This, however, does not take us very far. The form of this agency has been interpreted very differently by different philosophers and in different societies. As well as the to-be-expected interpretations of the teacher as a trainer or as an instructor, there are influential conceptions of the teacher as a mentor, sage or guru dispensing wisdom, whether it be theoretical or practical. Philosophers have tended to downplay the agency of the teacher relative to that of the pupil. Thus, Socrates in *Meno* compares the teacher to a midwife, bringing forth latent knowledge within the pupil. For Rousseau, the imperative for the teacher was to harness the pupil's natural *amour de soi*, but in a way so as not to unbalance his self-esteem or *amour propre* (cf. Dent 1988). Socrates thought that his aim could be achieved through dialogue with the pupil, Rousseau by manipulating situations that would engender appropriate learning or, as we would nowadays say, by 'facilitating learning'. In both of these examples, a debateable metaphysics or moral psychology lies behind the prescribed method for teachers. In the case of Socrates, it is the doctrine of transmigration of souls and consequent recollection of what has been learned in past lives. In the case of Rousseau, it is the speculative moral psychology of the innate *amour de soi* (or impulse to well-being) within the context of a need to maintain an always-fragile self-esteem or *amour propre*.

Even if we reject these views of teacher agency in favour of something that looks more 'common sensical' such as the teacher as trainer and/or instructor, this cannot absolve us from the obligation to give an account of what assumptions we think that the teacher's agency rests on. This, needless to say, is no easy task. It seems safe to say that if we are to make any sense of teaching as an occupation, then it must involve some agency on the part of the teacher. Even those who, like Rousseau and Dewey, place great emphasis on pupil agency do see a quite specific role for the action of teachers. A major problem is, however, in determining what this agency consists of and how it relates to its mirror image, the agency of pupils.

One possible line of objection to the positions of philosophers and educators such as Socrates, Rousseau and Dewey is that they over-emphasise the possibilities of pupil agency and under-emphasise those of the teacher. However, this raises the question of the extent to which one can expect agency from the pupil and what the proper relationship of the teacher's agency with that of the pupil will be. A categorial answer to this question cannot be given, but nevertheless it is possible to say something of philosophical significance about the matter. This is that teaching is not possible if there is *no* agency on the part of the pupil. One can mechanically transmit beliefs and abilities through processes such as hypnotism and brainwashing, but these are not regarded as forms of teaching as they involve no or minimal agency on the part of the taught. Even a process such as indoctrination involves agency by the learner. We consider that learning by a conscious and rational being demands some effort to learn and the direction of attention to what is to be learned. Very often, what is to be learned requires repetition, practice and conscious memorisation. Routines to be learned require repetition and correction. Instruction will be unsuccessful without attention, mentoring without participation from the mentee and so on.

Assume the contrary. The pupils learn (i.e. achieves an increment in knowledge, ability or understanding) through a process of teaching, but the pupil, apart from his physical presence, plays no part in the process. This can only be done through some process generally accepted as by-passing agency such as hypnotism or brainwashing, which, it is generally accepted, are not forms of teaching but rather of doing something to someone in order to cause learning by deliberately by-passing the agency of the learner. A successful process of teaching without some degree of pupil engagement is, therefore, not an intelligible proposition. This result raises two questions: first, what is the minimal degree of pupil agency that is to be expected? Second, to what extent is the teacher responsible for ensuring that this degree of pupil agency is present in the learning situation? We often hear the cry 'Make your lessons interesting' (a cry beloved of inspectors) as if this is enough in itself to evoke the agency of the pupil in such a way that the pupil will attempt to learn what the teacher intends that he should learn. But the 'Make your lessons interesting' cry also suggests that there is little or no responsibility on the part of the pupil to be engaged unless he is interested in what the teacher has to offer. And, as many commentators have pointed out, much that is of interest to the pupils is not necessarily in their interests and much that is in their interests is not necessarily interesting to them. Maybe it is part of the job of teachers to make their pupils interested in what is to be learned even if they are not inclined to be interested.

This question of pupil interest raises another question about teacher accountability. It has become more or less accepted wisdom in the Anglophone countries that teachers are responsible for the learning of their pupils. While this position is quite unobjectionable, it becomes problematic as soon as it is interpreted as 'teachers are *solely* responsible for the learning of their pupils.' While teachers may be responsible for getting their pupils to be interested in what they are teaching even if the pupils are not inclined to be interested, there are clearly moral and practical constraints on what they can do to achieve this, and these constraints are set by those to whom they are accountable for the learning of pupils. If they are solely responsible, then they are in an impossible position and the only way in which they can seek to salvage some success is by doing as much of the pupils' work for them as they possibly can, minimising pupil effort and maximising teacher effort. Needless to say, this is likely to have a demotivating effect on pupils, who cannot expect any sanction on themselves for failing to engage, but who can confidently expect that their teachers will be sanctioned if they fail to learn.

One way of looking at the civic role of teachers, together with the accountability that they should be subject to, is to regard them as a social service, 'delivering' benefits to their clients (Hinchliffe 2011). If these benefits are to be counted as items of knowledge or skills, then they are to be held accountable for not delivering them, just as a bus driver is accountable for not getting the bus he is driving to its destination or a social worker for not giving correct advice to a client. That this situation is not a philosopher's nightmarish fantasy, but a reality in some schools in the UK, is evidenced by, for example, Kathryn Birbalsingh's account of a year's teaching in a London comprehensive (Birbalsingh 2011).

These reflections suggest that, although it is dangerous to regard teaching as a social service, it is a kind of public service in the sense that it can benefit not only pupils themselves, but also society by providing educated individuals who are themselves a public good. But it is unlikely that we will arrive at an adequate conception of teaching in a developed society by thinking of teachers either only as providers of a private good to be enjoyed solely by the individual who is taught or only as providing a service to society. It is likely, in other words, that we will need to think of teaching as an occupation in *sui generis* terms, accepting that there is a close relationship between teaching and other occupations, but also resisting the idea that it can simply be subsumed into some other occupational category (for more on this issue, see also Carr 2003). We can only do this by taking a much closer look at what teaching involves, which is one of the principal tasks of the chapters that are to come.

3

Dimensions of Expertise and Their Relevance to Teaching

INTRODUCTION

This chapter will consider the kinds of knowledge and know-how that practitioners of occupations are expected to possess. It will begin by reviewing the literature on know-how and attempting a conceptual map of this terrain, showing where teaching or, rather, various conceptions of teaching are located on it. The endpoint of this investigation will be the development of a typology of teachers and their know-how, which will then be examined in more detail in subsequent chapters. By looking more closely at know-how and its relationship to knowledge, we can prepare the ground for a more detailed investigation of what is involved in being an effective teacher, an investigation that will concern us more closely in Chapter 5.

THE 'KNOW HOW'–'KNOW THAT' DISTINCTION

We owe to Gilbert Ryle the modern distinction between two kinds of knowledge, knowing how and knowing that.[1] As well as distinguishing between the two, Ryle was concerned to show that knowing how should in no way be considered inferior to knowing that. Ryle's

---

[1] I have chosen to frame the distinction in Ryle's terms rather than in Aristotelian ones. This is because it allows for a directly accessible entry into the subject matter without beginning with a number of subtle distinctions. Needless to say, there are subtle distinctions to be made within the field of both know-that and know-how, but I would like to develop these distinctions in the course of the argument. In addition, the contemporary epistemological debate on the nature of know-how opens up a number of important issues which would not otherwise be raised.

Teachers' Know-How: A Philosophical Investigation, First Edition. Christopher Winch.
© 2017 Christopher Winch. Editorial Organisation © Philosophy of Education Society of Great Britain.
Published 2017 by John Wiley & Sons, Ltd.

well-known distinction between knowing that (KT) and knowing how (KH) (Ryle 1946, 1949) has come under critical scrutiny in recent years, in particular from a school of philosophy known as *intellectualism*, which holds that knowledge of how to do something is invariably a special case of knowledge that something is the case (Stanley and Williamson 2001; Bengson and Moffett 2007, 2011; Stanley 2011; White 1982 are all good examples of this school). Intellectualism does not come in just one variety. Stanley and Williamson, for example, express KH as KT in a practical mode of presentation, Bengson and Moffett as reasonable conceptual mastery, Carr (1979, 1981) as mastery of a mode of practical reasoning and White (1982) as ability to give an account of how something is done.

There are some problems, both with Ryle's account of KH and with the various forms of the intellectualist position. I will briefly set out what I take to be the problems with the various forms of intellectualism that are currently influential, and then examine Ryle's position and show where it needs supplementation. My general approach will be to distinguish between KH and KT and to hold that KH is a distinct although closely related epistemic capacity to KT, but that a clear view of the relationship between them is important for our understanding of occupational ability. Stanley and Williamson defend a view of KH as an agent's knowing that there is a way to carry out an action in a practical mode of presentation in a contextually relevant manner (Stanley and Williamson 2001, p. 430). There are two major problems with this approach. The first is that it reduces KH to the position of technique (*w* is a way to perform *A*) when it remains to be established by them that KH is nothing more than the practice of a technique, and thus seriously undermines a full understanding of KH, and the second is that it fails to account for the evaluative nature of ascriptions to agents of KH, that is, the fact that we can say *how well* someone knows how to do something, whereas we cannot say how well someone knows that something is the case. This is a problem shared by all intellectualist accounts, and although there have been attempts to circumvent it (e.g. White 1982, p. 24), they are not particularly successful (on White, see Winch 2010b).[2]

The intellectualism of the other authors discussed labours under another difficulty. Since they attempt to characterise KH as a kind of ability, they cannot escape the charge of circularity. Thus, the reasonable conceptual mastery of Bengson and Moffett, the mastery

---

[2] A recent very detailed defence of the intellectualist case for know-how (Stanley 2011) does not deal systematically with this issue.

of practical reason of Carr and the ability to give an account of White are all forms of ability; furthermore, they are forms of ability that have the characteristics of KH. They are forms of ability that can be learned and are subject to normative appraisal. Bengson and Moffett's account suffers from the further disadvantage of failing to distinguish between know-how as the ability to describe a procedure and know-how as the ability to perform a certain kind of action. Arguably, this is also a problem with the Carr and White accounts as well. Ability to describe a procedure is an example of KH and thus cannot serve as an account of what it is. Somewhat implausibly, Bengson and Moffett (2007, 2011) claim that there is no conceptual difference between these two forms of knowing how and that this can be demonstrated through linguistic evidence (for a critique, see Winch 2010a).

Another line of intellectualist thinking can be found in Luntley (e.g. 2012), where it is denied that there is any conceptual element to action concepts such as skill and any conceptual element to attributions of ability is to be necessarily considered as an example of KT. This is an important point, as it will be argued in this and subsequent chapters that conceptual understanding is an important element in many if not all forms of KH and is particularly important for the ability to teach. In general terms, this particular intellectualist move is open to criticism as it presupposes what it seeks to prove, namely that action is non-conceptual in nature. This does not even apply to skill exercised in routine situations, which is assumed to be paradigmatic of KH (for a restricted range of examples, see also Stanley and Williamson 2001). This points to another difficulty with the ways in which intellectualism is usually presented. The assumption is too readily made that KH is about the exercise of technique or skill (the two are distinct, it will presently be argued). Although these are undoubtedly important elements of KH, they do not exhaust our understanding of it, and an exclusive focus on these not only helps to present intellectualism in a favourable light, but also distorts our understanding of the variegated and interconnected nature of the different forms of KH, an understanding particularly important for giving an accurate account of teaching as an occupation.

By contrast, anti-intellectualists like Ryle argue that KH and KT are distinct.[3] Ryle's arguments are largely motivated by the idea that were one to characterise KH as a form of KT, one would be trapped

---

[3] Although Ryle (1945, pp. 224–225) argues that possession of KT is dependent on certain forms of KH.

into a vicious regress, unable to explain what KH is or how someone possessing it could act. If KH was a form of KT, then no one could be said to 'know that' anything. Put succinctly, Ryle's thinking is that if one presents the intellectualist case in the following way, as one must, he thought, then the regress arises.

1. If A knows how to F, then A knows that w is a way to F. (Compare Stanley and Williamson (2001), who assume that knowing how to do something is knowing that w is a way to do it.)
2. If A knows that w is a way to F, then A can avow that w is a way to F. (This is not a premise generally shared by modern intellec- tualism, but it is pervasive in the Cartesian tradition.)
3. If A can avow that w is a way to F, then A knows how to avow that w is a way to F. (The idea is that being able to do something entails knowing how to do it – in many cases this is not controversial, but not in all.)
4. If A knows how to avow that w is a way to F, then A can avow that w^* is a way to avow that w is a way to F.[4]

It can easily be seen that this reasoning can be replicated *ad infinitum*, leading to the uncomfortable conclusion that an agent would never be able to act. It is not, however, a decisive argument. Thus, Stanley and Williamson point out, reasonably, that (2) is hardly true in general. Ryle's arguments seem to be most damaging against Cartesians, who arguably need to hold to (1), (2) and (3) jointly. Anti-intellectualists would deny that (1) and (2) are true in all circumstances. There is also a good case for denying (3). It simply does not follow that, for any KH that we may possess, we are able to give an account of what that possession consists of. Although the term 'tacit knowledge' is often used in misleading ways, for example, to suggest that there is an ineffable form of propositional knowledge that we cannot articu- late, it is not at all problematic to claim that we cannot always give an account of what we know how to do, let alone a complete and exhaustive account.[5]

This is a very important point as (3) if accepted appears to claim far too much. Now of course Ryle presented the argument as a *reductio ad absurdum*, to show that intellectualism was incoherent,

---

[4] Ryle (1949, pp. 30–31) and Stanley and Williamson (2001, pp. 413–414); see also Winch (2009, pp. 88–90).
[5] But see Gascoigne and Thornton (2013) for the claim that a context dependent articulation of KH is possible.

and he is hardly committed to any of these premises himself. On the other hand, although it is perhaps obvious that he would reject (1) and (2) himself, it is hard to find within his writings a specific rejection of (3). Instead, he was sceptical of the view that an act of judgement could lead to an action (a central claim of the Cartesian form of intellectualism) and appears to have thought that commitment to that view entailed a commitment to (3). Ryle is thus put in a somewhat paradoxical position of appearing to endorse a view that is an essential component of a philosophical thesis that he rejects. This has the important consequence of entailing that if one accepts the 'package' of (1) to (3), one is led to deny that action can be preceded by judgement, because of the regress argument. But Ryle has no need to accept any of (1) to (3) and consequently has no need, either, to deny that there is any paradox involved in the view that sometimes knowing how to do something has to be explained in terms of an agent forming a judgement that F is the way to proceed and then acting on it.

This matters because Ryle is clearly uneasy about accounts of KH which suggest that, in some circumstances, agents form non-verbalised judgements or engage in processes of non-verbalised reasoning that then result in action supported by those judgements or that reasoning. Yet such practices are essential to any realistic account of professional judgement and action. But they contain no Cartesian commitments of themselves. One can affirm the importance of professional judgement and the use of bodies of knowledge (KT) to arrive at a view on a correct course of action and not be committed to any of (1) to (3) as true of every action. It may seem odd to deny (1) as always true, but as we shall see, it is false in certain important cases (cf. Winch 2010b). Thus, although Ryle is correct to make a clear distinction between KH and KT and to deny that the former is an instance of the latter, there is a limitation to his account that makes it look as if his account of KH is purely dispositional and takes no account of episodes of judgement (but see Ryle 1949, ch. 5) on heed concepts where he wrestles with this issue; see also Geach (1957, pp. 2–4) for criticism of Ryle on this point). My suggestion is that if we give due account to the role that tacit knowledge (as an aspect of KH only) plays in action, we can dispel the fear that an account of judgement in and preceding action leaves us prey to an unacceptable metaphysical thesis.

The implication of this analysis for our understanding of teaching as an occupation is significant. The know-how of teachers is to be understood as their ability to act as teachers, not to entertain propositions about teaching even in a practical mode of presentation. But it is to be understood not only as the ability to act (which itself needs fuller explanation), but also as the ability to make judgements and to act on those judgements. Indeed, it will be argued in subsequent chapters that this is a fundamental feature of teacher know-how and expertise. The point that I wish to make here is that there is no philosophical objection of the kind that Ryle feared to the adoption of this position and that we can give full credit to the episodic nature of much professional judgement even if 'precise clockability' may remain something of a chimera (Winch 2009, 2010b).

EVALUATION AND VARIETIES OF OCCUPATIONAL KNOW-HOW

The strengths of non-intellectualism in helping us to understand occupational knowledge do not, however, just rest on the weaknesses of the intellectualist case. Ryle's discussion is also extremely helpful in understanding other important aspects of know-how. First, his account of what he calls 'intelligence epithets' is very important for understanding occupational ability. Second, his later work on thinking (Ryle 1979) is essential in helping us to understand certain forms of KH, which are not technique or skill but which play a vital role in professional action.[6] These are relevant to discussions of expertise as opposed to know-how *tout court* and fall outside the direct scope of this study.[7]

Intelligence Concepts

Ryle emphasises the fact that attributions of KH can be accompanied by a rich array of evaluative vocabulary, encompassing technical, aesthetic and moral attributions. Most of what we can do can be appraised in terms of its appropriateness or the quality of its execution. In making such appraisals, we draw on criteria for what counts as the right thing to do in certain circumstances and what counts as a praiseworthy or substandard performance. Thus, to take the first case, we may comment on the aptness of performing a certain kind of

---

[6] Ryle does not directly discuss tacit knowledge, nor does he discuss *phronesis* or the moral dimension of action, but these concepts can be readily accommodated within the 'portmanteau' conception of KH offered here. See the paragraph directly below.

[7] See Winch (2010a) for a more extended discussion of expertise. Dreyfus and Dreyfus (1996) is a very influential text, although their apparent dismissal of the use of theory by the expert practitioner goes against the approach adopted in Chapter 8 of this book (see also the discussion of Dreyfus and Dreyfus in Winch 2010a).

action at a certain time or on the moral quality of what was done, very often taking into account the particular circumstances in which the action was performed and the way in which it was done in those circumstances. Such judgements on our part may also take into account the character and attributes of the individual performing the action (cf. Winch 1964).

In the case of actions subject to appraisal, we are prepared to use, for example, the terms 'ably' or 'skilfully' to characterise an action or judgement. But these are only placeholders for a much more subtle and variegated set of concepts that draw on detailed and intimate knowledge of what it is for a performance to be good or excellent. Thus, we talk in terms of 'petty' virtues using terms such as 'carefully', 'persistently', 'with attention to detail' and so on, and we also use terms that in part characterise what a praiseworthy action of that type is like. 'She danced gracefully', 'He summed up succinctly', 'He fished cunningly', 'She introduced the speaker tactfully', 'She cooked imaginatively', 'He taught the lesson with flair and pace' and so on. Such adverbs and adverbial phrases go together with singular KH attributions in a way that they do not with singular KT ones. 'She knows how to sing Schubert songs very movingly', 'He knows how to measure with accuracy' and so on.

Learning how to perform various kinds of action and learning to take part in practices that involve such actions involves learning to use such vocabulary. We are usually not inclined to rest content with actions that satisfy a bare minimum needed to make them constitutively that kind of action, but, to the extent that we are able, we want to perform according to standards of excellence and for others to do so as well. Ryle rightly identifies the use of such 'intelligence epithets' as characteristic of our talk about judgement and action and also as characteristic of talk about qualities of mind (1949, pp. 25–27). Such attributions are not appropriate to KT in the same way. We cannot say, '*He knows that the capital of the UK is London thoroughly', for example. It has been pointed out that such evaluative vocabulary can, however, be used of bodies of knowledge for example 'She has a very good grasp of the French Revolution' (see White 1982, p. 24) This is perfectly true and a very important observation. Teachers, for example, are expected to have a good grasp of the subject matter that they are responsible for teaching.

However, when this kind of remark is examined, something interesting emerges. To say of a teacher that she knows her subject well is not to claim that she believes many true propositions about the subject, although her knowledge of the subject may well involve this.

It is rather that she knows her way around the subject, understands the main principles and concepts and the connections between them, can make inferences rapidly and accurately within the subject matter, is able to assess and validate knowledge claims by others and so on. In other words, a good grasp of a subject involves a great deal of knowledge how, which makes the true beliefs within the subject matter much more than inert, but useable in various ways including, in the case of teachers, as a means for getting others to learn about the subject.

Intellectualism has yet to find a way of giving a satisfactory account of the applicability of intelligence concepts to KH attributions, including singular ones such as 'He knows how to drive safely', given that they are a central feature of the way in which we talk about KH in a way that is just not the case with singular KT attributions such as '*He knows that eggs boil in three minutes accurately' (for a more extended discussion of this issue, see Winch 2010b). We can conclude that there is little temptation to adopt intellectualism as a conceptual framework for thinking about teacher knowledge and expertise, without being drawn into broader metaphysical debates about the relationship of KH to KT, and that we should work on the assumption that they are distinct although closely related epistemic capacities.[8]

Technique, Skill and Transversal Abilities

A lot of discussion about KH, particularly perhaps within the intellectualist tradition, tends to conceptualise KH as *technique*. Stanley and Williamson (2001) are good examples, characterising, as we saw, 'A knows how to F' as 'A knows that w is a way to F in a practical mode of presentation' (p. 430). Much know-how involves the deployment of technique as a *way of doing something*, which can be exhibited through description or demonstration. But, although necessary for many kinds of performance, demonstration of technique is usually not sufficient for an attribution of know-how. The clue as to why this might be so can be found in the next qualification of Stanley and Williamson's definition, that w be carried out in a 'contextually appropriate manner' (2001, p. 430).

This means that the practice of technique must be done in such a way as to conform with minimal criteria of competence in those

---

[8] Acquaintance Knowledge (KA) is also a closely related epistemic capacity to the other two. It is not treated at any length in this book, as it is not centrally involved in the detail of the arguments. It is, however, an important aspect of teachers' subject knowledge (see Chapter 4).

situations in which the relevant know-how is called for. Thus, one may have acquired the technique of laying bricks in a college environment, intending to be a bricklayer. However, laying bricks in the construction industry requires attributes that go well beyond the mastery of techniques. These include being able to handle constraints of money and materials, the demands of employers and colleagues and the exigencies of height, temperature and weather conditions, which all have to be accommodated if one is to be said to possess the *skill* of a bricklayer.

One can easily distinguish between certain *techniques* employed by teachers which they might practise in controlled conditions and the *skills* that they employ in the 'operational conditions' of the classroom and school spaces. The space where teaching takes place is often characterised as a complex and rapidly changing environment, which gives rise to often unexpected situations. Thus, what may be practised in controlled conditions may only with difficulty be transferred into the conditions of a large and boisterous class with the kinds of operating exigencies of time, space and limited resources that often characterise the working conditions of teachers. However, there are good reasons for thinking that although the possession of an array of skills is extremely important for successful teaching, it is a serious mistake to think that the ability to teach consists in the possession of nothing more than an array of skills. Why is this? To answer this question, we need to go back to earlier discussions of the 'polymorphousness' of teaching and the neglected work of Ryle (1979) on thinking and 'adverbial verbs', as well as concepts widely used in European Vocational Education and Training (VET). Answering this question will also give us a possible answer to the question raised in Chapter 1, 'If a teacher is teaching, must a pupil be learning?'

When observers look at a teacher in action, they see someone engaged in teaching in the task sense, that is, they are engaged in attempting to get pupils to learn what it is that the teacher intends that they learn. But, as has been pointed out, there are no specific actions that the teacher performs that count as an action called 'teaching'.[9] Neither is it the case that the cumulation of observable actions (which will involve the exercise of skills) amounts to an action called 'teaching' even in the 'task' (attempting to get pupils to learn) sense. In fact, it is misleading to talk of the practice of teaching solely in terms of the exercise of skills. This, incidentally, is a point not just

---

[9] For example, Hirst (1974, ch. 7).

about teaching, but about many professions and occupations in which the worker concerned is meant to exercise a degree of independence and judgemental discretion in the workplace (cf. Brockman *et al.* (2010) for the case of European bricklayers).

How then should we characterise teachers' actions and the abilities that they manifest when they are teaching, if not as the exercise of skills?[10] Ryle (1979, ch. 2) argues that there is a category of verbs whose manifestation may take different forms, and which are characterised by the *way* in which specific actions are undertaken. To take one of Ryle's examples, one can *obey* in many different ways, performing actions and exercising skills that, depending on context, may or may not count as obeying. The context of the action is important in determining whether or not it constitutes obeying. Second, and this is perhaps more difficult to appreciate, not every action that has the semblance of obeying actually constitutes an act of obeying. One can 'go through the motions' of obeying an order (i.e. one's action is contextually appropriate to be a *prima facie* candidate for obeying but may ultimately consist only in a semblance of doing so). One may be invited by one's superior to prepare a meal and go through the motions, but fail to come up with something that is actually of such a standard as to constitute a meal, without actually disobeying the order to prepare a meal. Some of the comic literature on soldiering, for example, Hasek's *Good Soldier Schweik*, illustrates this (Hasek 1923). And, of course, there exists a range of possible cases that lie somewhere on the borderline between outright disobedience and sullen and minimal obedience.

However, the cases that are of particular interest to teaching are a range of actions that are often mentioned in relation to the specification of occupational capacity in countries like Germany (cf. Brockman *et al.* 2011). These include: planning, controlling, co-ordinating, communicating and evaluating. The ability to carry out these kinds of actions is central to successful teaching. A little reflection shows that they cannot be reduced to 'planning skills' 'communicating skills' or the like any more than obeying can be reduced to 'obeying skills'. There may well be such things as planning skills, such as drawing a flowchart or briefing one's colleagues, but these do not of themselves constitute planning. So what is the difference

---

[10] To simplify for the moment, I will restrict this discussion to action in the classroom, but I do not wish to convey the impression that a teachers' professional sphere of action is confined to the classroom. See, for example, Chapter 8–10 and 12.

between exercising, say, a planning skill and actually engaging in planning?

A preliminary observation is that what counts as planning or communication in one context such as teaching is unlikely to be the same as planning or communicating in another context. Second, in teaching as in numerous other activities, the manner in which one goes about exercising the skills associated with the activity (and we should certainly not assume that there is a set of necessary skills associated with the action in every case) is critical to our preparedness to attribute planning or co-ordinating to the agent. The care and attention (aspects of the way in which specific, maybe skill-based, actions are performed) that are exercised are constitutive of those actions as the kinds of actions that they are. One can 'go through the motions' of planning, co-ordinating, controlling, evaluating or communicating without actually doing so, while all the time exercising relevant skills. What makes the difference is the manner in which the relevant abilities are exercised. Thus, someone who is exercising planning or communicating abilities is not just exercising skills such as preparing flow charts or briefing staff (although he may well be doing these things), but also doing so in a way that makes the action more than just the exercise of skill. He is doing so with a degree of attention and seriousness that is criterial for our being prepared to say that planning or communication is actually taking place, *irrespective* of whether the goal of the action (the action that is planned, the type of communication to be achieved – to convince, amuse, move etc.) is actually achieved. Being engaged in planning, evaluating, controlling and so on does not entail that one succeeds in doing what one sets out to do.[11] It does entail that one approaches the matter with the manifest intention to do so, being appropriately serious and paying the appropriate degree of attention. Such abilities then have a moral dimension to them that is present to a more salient degree than is the case with skill exercise which, although it can involve aspects of character, can also be done with a greater degree of automaticity.

This discussion is highly relevant to the case of teaching. First because teaching is an occupation that centrally involves such

---

[11] To take another example of an adverbial verb very relevant to this discussion, one can try to do F but not succeed and still be deemed to be trying. However, one can 'go through the motions' of trying to do something (exercising skills relevant to trying to do F) but still not be trying. But see also the discussion in Hasselberger (2014), in which it is claimed that very often we cannot tell whether someone has, for example, carried through a plan until we see the results of their actions.

abilities as planning, communicating, controlling, co-ordinating and evaluating. Second, because the ability to teach is itself polymorphous in this sense, it involves various kinds of skills and second-order abilities in different ways and in different combinations. Third because there is a real distinction between 'going through the motions' of teaching and actually teaching (even if one is not succeeding in getting all one's pupils to learn what one intends that they should learn). This discussion suggests that the ability to teach is highly complex, involving skills and the kinds of transversal abilities that have just been discussed. It also implies that teaching, as opposed to seeming to teach, involves going about one's work with a degree of seriousness (including moral seriousness) that is partly constitutive of teaching.

Of course, one might contend that if one's pupils fail to learn what one intends that they should learn, then one is not carrying out activities that constitute teaching with the appropriate degree of attention and seriousness. In many cases this may be correct, but it does not follow that the fulfilment of one's intentions is a criterion for one's being able to teach. We are also in danger of losing sight of the distinction between the ability to teach as a task (which is what teachers are exercising in the classroom) and the ability to teach as an achievement (achieving the goals of the task sense of teaching). They must be related, but it is not particularly illuminating to precisely specify when teaching as a task is constituted as such by teaching as an achievement. The important point is to identify the manner in which the task of teaching is carried out (which in the normal course of events will result in teaching in the achievement sense) rather than a tight specification of the task–achievement relationship.

HIGHER ORDER KNOW-HOW: PROJECT MANAGEMENT AND OCCUPATIONAL CAPACITY

It is easy to assume that a teacher's work consists in nothing more than the performance of tasks. Of course, it is true that teachers perform innumerable kinds of different classroom tasks in the course of their working day, but there is much more to their work than that. Obviously, of course, they have to plan, evaluate and assess the work that they carry out in the classroom. In this sense, their work is more extensive than the performance of classroom-based tasks, complex and interconnected though these may be. We may note in passing that this sequence of *before-during-after* a classroom sequence already involves actions describable as 'adverbial verbs'. However, nearly all teachers who exercise a degree of professional independence are expected to plan whole sequences of work, covering a year's teaching or more (sometimes called *syllabuses* or *schemes of work*).

Project Management

It would be misleading to call the planning, carrying through and evaluation of a year's work a 'task' if one were to imply by this that there were only a difference in length between this kind of activity and that of taking a lesson. It is difficult to find the right word for this extended kind of activity, but the term 'project' might do better than most. In this sense, then, a teacher is not only a carrier out of tasks, which often involve a good deal of independence, but also something like a *project manager*, who has to take responsibility for a temporally extended sequence of complex, interrelated and articulated activities that in a sense involve a cycle, starting with planning the year's activities and ending with their evaluation and the recursive recommencement of the cycle (i.e. using the end point of one cycle as the starting point of the next).

Typically, the transversal abilities already mentioned (planning, pursuing, controlling, communicating, co-ordinating and evaluating) will all be involved, sometimes sequentially, sometimes simultaneously, in the carrying out of the project. Project management thus builds on not only skill but also transversal ability, which, as we saw, is involved in classroom practice.

The ability to engage in project management (in the sense described here) is very important in any account of the work of teachers that seeks to describe them as having control over their own work and a degree of independence in their professional judgement. As a minimum, this ability is needed in order for it to be possible for teachers to set objectives over a period of time, to plan extended sequences of work and to carry them out, to adjust and control the details of what they are doing, to co-ordinate where necessary different elements of the programme and to evaluate the outcomes either during or at the conclusion of an extended sequence of activity.

However, this is to think of a teacher's project management abilities in only one dimension. It is evident that a teacher could plan a programme of work for a term or a year within a framework such as an examination board syllabus or National Curriculum framework. It is important not to underestimate the degree of expertise that is involved in 'putting flesh on the bones' or adapting prescribed material to the needs of particular classes and circumstances. The ability to carry out this kind of work effectively presupposes considerable subject knowledge, knowledge of how to present the subject in a pedagogically effective way and, arguably, some technical knowledge about teaching and learning. Some, however, would argue that this is far too mean an account of the proper expertise of the teacher. Teachers, it is argued, should be designers or creators of the curriculum, not just technicians putting in filigree work on a large-scale structure. This claim raises very important issues concerning the civic role of teachers and the responsibilities and duties that they have in the wider society in which they work.

Teachers are in a very important position in relation to curriculum design. Above all, they should be in a position to say what it is plausible that should be taught, when and in what sequence, through their own extensive collective knowledge of what is practical and possible in teaching. It is arguable that, at the largest scale of educational endeavour, the expression of the values underpinning an education system and the aims that give expression to such values should have important roles to play. However, to make this point, and it is one that will be defended in the course of this book, is implicitly to suggest that there are limits, not only to teacher expertise but also to what it is right to expect from such important servants of society. Although there was not the space to argue the point in detail, the claim was made that education is a public as well as a private good, and it follows therefore that the public has an interest in the structure, content and process of education, and, therefore, a *prima facie* right to a say how education is organised and conducted.[12] If this is right, then teachers cannot be the sole determinants of those values and aims and the curriculum that is to put them into effect. However, for reasons mentioned above, their role needs to be central and should best be expressed as a kind of partnership with the other major parties interested, however these are represented within the polity. We shall have more to say about this in Chapter 9. We can conclude this part of the discussion by noting that the project management abilities of teachers, especially more experienced and senior teachers, should involve co-operating with other interested parties and appropriate technical experts in such projects as macro and meso design of the curriculum, the design and commissioning of school buildings, the preparation of pedagogic materials and the construction of evaluation and test materials. More will be said about this in Chapter 9.

---

[12] See Raz (1986, chs. 7, 8) for further explanation.

Occupational Capacity

Occupation in the Anglophone countries does not have the same con-
notation as it does in, for example, the Germanophone ones. There,
the concept of *Beruf* carries much more conceptual, legal and social
freight than it does in, say, the UK (Greinert 2007; Hanf 2011). The
nearest we have is the concept of a *profession* as a legally and socially
recognised occupational category, but there are also significant differences. Although countries like Germany recognise a distinction
between professions and other *Berufe*, in particular in terms of regu-
lation and an entry route through a higher education qualification, in
other respects the difference is smaller than that between the English
profession and other occupations, including what we call 'trades' (cf.
Clarke *et al.* 2013).

Key to understanding the German concept of *Beruf* for our purposes is that it is supposed to embody *berufliche Handlungsfähigkeit*
or 'occupational action capacity' that, however, includes a significant reflective element. *Berufliche Handlungsfähigkeit* is conceived
as a unitary capacity, the intended outcome of a vocational education programme (Hanf 2011), but this does not mean that it is
not made up of identifiable subcomponents. These include various
other kinds of competences, which should not be understood merely
as skills, but which also include what have, in this chapter, been
described as *transversal abilities* and *project management abilities*
or combinations thereof, not to mention what are perhaps more properly described as virtues. Thus, the German Vocational Education
and Training regulations distinguish between *technical, method, personal* and *social competences*, which each contribute to the overall
occupational capacity.

It is important to understand that the Dual System qualifications[13]
are not just vocational but educational as well and that civic education is an essential element in them. This draws on a long philosophical tradition of thinking about vocational education in Germany
that recognises the important role that reflection on the consequences
of occupational practice has for those affected, not just clients and
consumers but the broader public as well (Kerschensteiner [1906]
1964). *Berufliche Handlungsfähigkeit* also encompasses an understanding of the impact of practice on society. Within the German
industrial and artisanal system, this is given further purchase through
the widespread system of *Mitbestimmung* or co-determination within

---

[13] The Dual System is the German system of apprenticeship through which more than 60% of
16–25 year olds in Germany eventually progress.

the economy, through which employees have a significant role not only at the plant level but also at the level of the supervisory board (*Aufsichtsrat*) of their firms, thus giving them a civic and political role in their capacity as workers.[14]

These reflections are highly relevant to the consideration of teacher ability since, quite apart from the economic and ethical desirability of individual employees exercising civic responsibility as part of their role, the public goods nature of the teachers' work renders understanding of the role of teaching in the society and an ability to respond constructively to that wider role highly desirable for teachers to acquire. We will return in greater detail to this in Chapters 8 and 9. But occupational capacity in this sense is significant for the 'inward facing' aspect of the occupation as well, as this capacity is considered to be something whole that is more than a sum of the skills, transversal abilities and so on that it includes. It signifies an ability to operate independently within the occupation, to have a communicative, integrative and evaluative role and to understand the technical, economic and social evolution that the occupation undergoes. As we shall see, this capacity is also something that teachers should have.

THEORY AND PRACTICE; THEORY–REFLECTION–PRACTICE

Much of the sociological literature on the professions characterises them as having, among other traits, the command of a body of systematic relevant knowledge (the theory), which they are capable of putting into practice through the formation of judgements leading to action in the often complex and unpredictable working environment in which they operate.[15] Workers with these attributes are often referred to as 'technicians', although none of these commentators suggests that being a technician in this sense precludes one from making use of *tacit knowledge* in the more detailed working out of professional judgement in the context of particular situations.

One of the intriguing features of the debate about teaching and the question of whether or not it is a technical occupation in the sense mentioned above is the widespread scepticism about whether there is actually such a body of theory to which teachers can appeal in their day-to-day action. It is well known that those who would like to

---

[14] This, of course, is in addition to their extra-enterprise role of citizens within their society, which is also taken care of through vocational qualifications.

[15] Eraut (1994), Freidson (1986) and Etzioni (1969).

see teacher education detached from higher education are sceptical about whether there is such a thing as a theoretical background to teaching that can justify professional action (e.g. O'Hear 1988), but the scepticism can be found within the teaching profession itself (see the account of the 'restricted professional' in Hoyles 1974) and even within the philosophical establishment of teacher education (e.g. W. Carr 2004, 2005, 2006; Hogan 2011). This view is usually combined with scepticism about the possible useful deliverances of educational research, which could be used to inform the professional judgement of teachers (D. Carr 2003; Barrow 2014). This topic requires a whole book in itself in order to receive adequate treatment, but a few observations are in order at this stage. First, I will defend the idea that teachers can learn from empirical educational research as well as from conceptual work on educational theory (Chapters 5 and 8). Second, I will show that the view that teachers can learn nothing from educational theory is itself incoherent. This task will be undertaken now in order to show that some engagement with educational theory, both conceptual and empirical, is necessary in order to give a complete account of teacher know-how. In doing so, it can be shown that teaching should belong with the other professions that share this trait and indeed with the German *Berufe*.

Few would deny that there is such a thing as a world in which educational institutions or practices have their place (what we might call, for present purposes, 'educational reality'). Neither would they deny that our understanding of educational reality depends, among other things, on an adequate grasp of the concepts that constitute those institutions and practices. It is just as unlikely that a sceptic would deny that we could know anything about such institutions and practices, since that would entail that judgements made about educational matters were based on belief and prejudice rather than on beliefs underpinned by a justification of some kind. What the empirical research sceptic seems to be denying is that systematic investigation of educational reality can lead us to any knowledge worth having. This is not just a claim about our inability to attain *certainty* in such investigations (which few would deny), but our inability to know (that is, attain something like justified true belief about such matters).[16]

---

[16] I do not mean to endorse a particular (and much debated) account of knowledge by putting the matter in this way, but to point out that, in contexts such as these where it is reasonable to ask for justification for beliefs, this can form a working account of what we mean by 'knowledge', without suggesting that it will work universally (for further discussion, see Hanfling 2000).

Does the sceptic mean that such investigations never yield anything of value, either true or false? Hardly, since if this were to be so, we would need to accept that either the referents of names and descriptions in propositions about education were non-existent or that the concepts employed were always incoherent. This seems implausible and, to my knowledge, has never been maintained by a sceptic. It is much more likely that the sceptic maintains that the deliverances of educational research are false (see the comments of D. Carr 2003, ch. 4). Another position, which we will look at more closely in Chapter 6, is that educational theory of any sort is simply irrelevant to what teachers do (W. Carr 2004, 2005). Unfortunately for the proponents of this position, however, it is never discussed in relation to the kinds of examples that would allow us to determine whether this was in fact the case. However, if all the deliverances of empirical educational theory are false (to a certain degree of certainty), then whether or not they are irrelevant has to be decided on its merits.

If one takes this position, then the consideration of examples will quickly show that it is highly implausible. Consider some more recent examples. The theory of intelligence quotients is clearly relevant to the kind of education that a normative theory would claim that children should receive. If such a theory is incoherent, then we are entitled to ignore it on the grounds of its incoherence, which might arise from an inadequate conceptualisation of 'intelligence'. But this consideration does not make it irrelevant; it tells us something very important about the conceptual field of education in which we are operating, which should inform practice. Or consider verbal deficit theory, as formulated by theorists such as Basil Bernstein (Bernstein 1973, 1975, 1977). It is more plausible in this case to maintain that verbal deficit theory, although in some formulations coherent, is nevertheless unlikely to be true (Tizard and Hughes 1984; Winch 1990). This is hardly irrelevant either to the practice of teaching. In both cases it is possible to infer, from the incoherence of the one and the falsity of the other, the maxim *do not base your practice on either intelligence or verbal deficit theory*, and such a maxim is very far from being irrelevant to the practice of teachers. More formally, if we know that a proposition *p* is false, then we also know that its contradictory, *not-p*, is true. And *not-p* is an important piece of knowledge that will inevitably have a bearing on the conduct of education. Likewise, if it can be shown that *p is irrelevant to educational practice* is true, then one would be in error in supposing that it was relevant and in acting upon that putative relevance. Or again, if *p* cannot be demonstrated to be true, then we are not entitled to act as if p were in fact true, and this too is an important maxim of educational practice. In other words, the deliverances of educational theory, whether they be good, bad or indifferent, have to be taken seriously and judgements have to be made as to how they should be reacted to. This in turn implies that teachers have to be aware of theory, including empirical theory, and take account of it in their practice, even though this may entail that they cannot accept it as true. They will thus need the wherewithal for deciding whether it is true, false, unproven or irrelevant.

However, we may wish to maintain that commonsense is the most reliable guide to our practices as teachers (Barrow 1976; Barrow in Barrow and Foreman-Peck 2005). Furthermore, we may also wish to claim that in addition to commonsense, something called 'tacit knowledge' is the other main epistemic asset that a teacher needs to rely on. The response to these claims is necessarily complex and nuanced. The issues will be dealt with in detail in Chapter 6. It will be maintained, however, that whatever role they play, commonsense and tacit knowledge cannot be the sole knowledge-based pillars of a teacher's expertise. Enough has been said in this chapter to establish that teachers' expertise, broadly conceived, is complex and cannot be reduced to skill or technique. We have also established that the occupation of teaching shares many features in common with a *Beruf* when it is considered expansively. We have yet to show that it should be considered as a profession. We must now go on to look at other features of teacher know-how by considering different kinds of occupations and how they relate to teaching.

4

Towards a Typology of Occupations

INTRODUCTION: TOWARDS A TYPOLOGY OF OCCUPATIONS – WHY DO THIS?

In Chapter 3, the different dimensions of know-how relevant to teaching were examined. It is now time to see how these different dimensions are incorporated into different conceptions of occupations. The procedure will be to develop 'ideal types' of each, without a commitment to the existence of any in their pure form, to begin a brief description of their characteristics and their relationships with each other and, finally, to relate them to different conceptions of what it might be to be a teacher. It will be acknowledged that there are different ways of conceptualising teaching as an occupation, and the advantages and disadvantages of each will be discussed in the light of the typology presented here. At a later stage in the book, a preferred model of teaching will be argued for, consonant with the kind of society in which we live.

Why would one wish to do this? The reason is that within debates on the nature of teaching, different models are in play and terminology such as 'craft', 'technician' and 'professional' are used without sufficient examination as to what they mean. This lack of clarity makes it sometimes difficult to see what is at stake in these debates. Thus, we are told that 'teaching is a craft, best learned on the job' (DfE 2010), or that the National Curriculum reduced teachers from being professionals to being 'mere' technicians. Hoyle (1974) noted the distinction between 'restricted' and 'extended' professionals. We need to understand better what this terminology means and how the

Teachers' Know-How: A Philosophical Investigation, First Edition. Christopher Winch.
© 2017 Christopher Winch. Editorial Organisation © Philosophy of Education Society of Great Britain.
Published 2017 by John Wiley & Sons, Ltd.

different conceptions are related to each other. This is the task of the present chapter.

THE CRAFTWORKER

It is fair to say that the craftworker or 'craftsman' has become a kind of vocational icon in recent years, with books such as 'Shop Class as Soulcraft' by Matthew Crawford (2009) and 'The Craftsman' (Sennett 2008) attracting a great deal of attention. It is hardly surprising that, in a society characterised by Taylorised forms of commodity production and the pervasive influence of an ever-changing technology on all forms of work, there should be a yearning for the ancient and mediaeval idea of the craftsman. It is not just that the craftsman seems to embody an ideal of individualised production, whose outcomes are, in our society, preponderantly the preserve of the wealthy. It is also that craftworkers are thought, through their work, to have access to a spiritual realm that is beyond the reach of most who have to work for a living. This not only involves the exercise of the virtues associated with craftwork such as patience, persistence, attention to detail, aesthetic sensibility and the like, but also is because craftwork is thought to provide access to self-knowledge, which is difficult to obtain elsewhere. It is no coincidence that the classic *Bildungsromanen* of the German-speaking countries had sustained occupational engagement at the heart of the hero's search for himself. Thus, Heinrich Lee in Gottfried Keller's 'Green Henry' (1951) attempts to become an artist through various forms of induction into the occupation, which ultimately prove unsuccessful, and Wilhelm Meister in 'Wilhelm Meister's Apprenticeship' engages with the craft of acting and producing plays before deciding that the life is not for him. Craftwork is thus thought to be a form of *self-exploration* as much as it is an exploration of an occupation and the materials and techniques that it makes use of.

Although craftwork is thought to be a form of exploration of one's individuality, there is a social aspect to it that is also found to be intriguing and attractive. The work of the craftsman is associated with the idea of the guild (the key institution in mediaeval urban life), with apprenticeship (a powerful image for the transition from childhood to adulthood) and last, but not least, with the idea of learning by osmosis through watching and, little by little, doing until one becomes a master of a craft. Associated with this is the idea of picking up the 'mysteries' of a trade, the techniques and knacks that mark out the expertise of the craftsman and exclude those who are not in the know. This aspect of the work of the craftsman has received particular attention from the work of Jean Lave and Etienne Wenger (1991) in their idea of a 'community of practice' (picking up on the social dimension associated with craftwork), and the idea of learning by 'legitimate peripheral participation' whereby an initiate is legitimated to appear at the boundaries of the practice (apprenticeship in the traditional sense) and is gradually drawn in towards the mysteries at the centre, all within a comparatively unstructured process of participation. The idea of craftwork thus combines a vision of growing individuality and at the same time a story about moving to the centre of a human practice. It is not surprising that the practice of crafts is thought to be a characteristically human way of becoming creative. It goes well beyond Arendt's (1958) notion of man the maker as *homo faber* (also found in some of Marx's formulations), an essentially solitary figure who puts plans generated in the imagination into effect.

However, there are five further (prominent but not exclusive) features that figure in most accounts of craftwork which deserve attention: *experience, tacit knowledge, phronesis, commonsense* and *tradition*. Although the techniques employed in crafts might, in some cases, have ultimately arisen as a result of scientific investigation, they are not formally transmitted in a school environment. They are passed informally from person to person and generation to generation. They are based on the experience of workers who have, through long practice and trial and error, developed and perfected the techniques that characterise the craft. Generally speaking, craftwork is talked about in terms of the skills of the craftsman, but to the extent that he is a creator as well as a producer it is arguable that he is a 'project manager' in the sense of the previous chapter as well. Experience, albeit *active* experience, is the main mode of learning for a craft. At first the experience is vicarious, then it involves assistance to a journeyman or master. Moving on, the apprentice learns skills and finally acquires the ability to manage a project on his own, but not without the assistance of the 'community of practice' in which the craft has its life.

Tacit knowledge, an epistemic category we owe to Polanyi (1958), to Oakeshott's (1962) discussion of practical knowledge and to Chomsky's (1965) discussion of personal linguistic knowledge, is almost always considered to be a key component of the armoury of the craftsman. Rather than get into a discussion of what is often a deeply confused concept underlying the phrase 'tacit knowledge' (see Baker and Hacker 1984; Read and Hutchinson 2012),[1] I will confine the use of the phrase to that element of practical knowledge that cannot be reduced to describable procedures. Tacit knowledge is a key element in almost all occupations but is particularly prominent in crafts or occupations that rely on craft-like activity. The way in which the craftsman acquires the ability to carry out complex and intricate tasks often involves the observation and imitation of procedures that are far from fully describable (for a good account from the trade of the wheelwright, see Sturt 1923). He, in turn, can only pass these on through practice and very limited explanation.

Phronesis is concerned with situational judgement; doing the right thing at the right time in the right way. In its non-moral aspect, it involves judgements as to, for example, how to handle a particular piece of stone, wood or clay or how to respond to the exigencies of weather or the pressure of time. In this sense, it is perhaps better characterised as an element of tacit knowledge. However, there are also very often aesthetic and moral aspects to the work of the craftsman that go beyond the purely practical and are of particular relevance to the work of the teacher. These concern the way in which the craftsman responds to the wishes of the customer or to the needs of a supplier or an apprentice, paying regard not only to considerations of private morality but also to the values of his own occupation. Sometimes this aspect of phronesis has an aesthetic element, and the craftsman must judge on what is fitting for this customer's home or for a public space. Sometimes the aesthetic and moral aspects of phronesis come together, as is beautifully described in the work of the monumental mason in Siegfried Lenz's novel 'Die Klangprobe' (1989), where the needs of one afflicted by grief are rendered into a public memorial that celebrates a departed loved one in a way that is both appropriate and ennobling rather than tawdry.

The importance of *tradition* is another feature of craftwork that arouses a great deal of interest. Institutions, customs and practices that have endured for long periods of time and which have, perhaps, evolved slowly in response to developments within the society have evoked a positive response from those who value gradual change. Crafts, embedded as they have historically been within stable institutions such as the guilds, seem to embody the mixture of change and continuity that allows for both stability and adaptation to

---

[1] See also the discussion in Gascoigne and Thornton (2013).

changing circumstances. Both Burke (1790) and Oakeshott (1962) lay stress on the ability of institutions that live according to customary allegiance to adapt piecemeal to change, drawing on Hume's ([1739–1740] 1978, bk. 4) psychological account of the strongest source of allegiance being long association. In this account, 'prejudice' (Burke 1790) and 'practical knowledge' (Oakeshott 1962) provide the unreflective but situationally sensitive capacity to respond to change while preserving what is valuable in institutions (see also Popper 1965). In this account, tradition sustains the role of tacit knowledge in allowing for responses to changing circumstances.

Central to the working of tradition is the role of *commonsense*, often appealed to by the proponents of teaching as a craft. This is a complex and ambiguous term, widely appealed to in accounts of teaching but in need of some careful unpicking. There appear to be two ways of thinking about commonsense. The first appeals to the idea of sound judgement, usually informed by experience and reflection. In this sense, commonsense is a species of capacity for situationally appropriate and sometimes critically reflective judgement that combines tacit knowledge and phronesis; it is what Gramsci (1975) called 'good sense'. Good sense does not rely in any obvious way on the deliverances of theory but is indispensable to the everyday conduct of life and sound dealings with one's fellow human beings.

The other sense of 'commonsense' (what Gramsci calls 'commonsense') is the idea that there is a set of ideas that one can appeal to in everyday reasoning, which is capable of providing a guide for action. Thus, Vico ([1725] 1968) invokes natural law or the idea that we have a God-given faculty of reason that allows us to determine what is right as the basis of commonsense.[2] Gramsci developed this line of thought in a different way. Commonsense is embedded in our everyday actions, attitudes and judgements in the way in which good sense is, but unlike good sense, it is the sedimentation and simplification of ideas that originally had a theoretical or ideological provenance, but which have become popularised and incorporated into everyday life as attitudes, actions and judgements. They seem so obvious to those who hold them that they are in fact difficult to distinguish from good sense. On the whole, though, Gramsci considers commonsense

---

[2] See also Hobbes ([1651] 1904) on natural law or the law of God in *Leviathan* for development of a similar idea. It is at least arguable that the Gramscian notion of good sense has some affinities with Vico's account of commonsense.

to be an obstacle rather than an aid to coherent action. Thus, he writes that:

> its most fundamental characteristic is that it is a conception which, even in the brain of one individual, is fragmentary, incoherent and inconsequential, in conformity with the social and cultural position of the masses whose philosophy it is. (Gramsci 1974, p. 419)[3]

Keynes too has this idea in mind when he writes of the way in which economic ideas enter the bloodstream of contemporary thought:

> Practical men, who believe themselves to be quite exempt from any intellectual influences, are usually the slaves of some defunct economist. Madmen in authority, who hear voices in the air, are distilling their frenzy from some academic scribbler of a few years back. (Keynes 1936, p. 383)

Given that commonsense with its inbuilt ambiguity plays a central role in some accounts of teacher know-how, it should be clear that it needs careful handling when used as a tool for describing teacher expertise (for a fairly recent example of its use in this way, see Barrow 2005).

Keynes had in mind such economic ideas as monetarism and free trade, but it is not difficult to see 'commonsense' at work in education and hence in the work of teachers through the sedimentation of ideas about intelligence, verbal deficit or development, to name but three.

THE EXECUTIVE TECHNICIAN

One way in which theory comes to play a role in the work of teachers is via the sedimentation of theoretical ideas into everyday practice and judgement through the popularisation and simplification of ideas that have a theoretical or scientific provenance. It should not be forgotten also that such ideas in their systematic form often also resonate with ideas already influential within the society. See, for example, Desmond and Moore's (1991) account of the way in which

---

[3] My thanks to Geoff Hinchliffe for drawing my attention to this passage and for clarifying the positive and negative aspects of commonsense as Gramsci understands the term.

'social Darwinism' actually had an effect on the formulation of 'bio-logical Darwinism'.

But there is another and more direct route through which theory can come to be embodied in practice. Theories invariably suggest ways in which changes may be effected in the world. They may be constructed to do this explicitly, or they may be adapted for such a purpose. A theory whose propositions have a bearing on how action may be taken to reach a desired goal may generate precepts that, if followed, will lead to the desired goal. Thus, if theory T is taken to be true, it will generate a proposition of the form:

1. In order to do A, do B.

where the following is true:

2. B is a procedure mandated by T.
3. So, given that you wish to accomplish A, do B.

Thus, if a theory (in this case, an empirical theory) suggests that a certain method of teaching reading is more effective than alterna-tives (perhaps as a result of extensive experimental investigation), then the theory will mandate the procedure that has emerged from the experimental work.

It is quite possible to detach B from T by simply recommending (1) without any further reference to (2). In this case, the justification for B is removed and B stands as a recommendation for action. B of course may be further decomposed into subprocedures that have to be followed closely in order to achieve the desired result, but the point remains essentially the same.

Not everyone will be able to understand T, let alone carry out the work necessary to discover or validate it. Because of this, it will be necessary to train operatives in B. Those adept in T will devise the necessary procedures, no doubt taking advice on the practical-ity of those procedures for those who are charged with undertaking them. The end result will be a 'manual' of procedures that can then be applied in mass production. Adam Smith describes the process clearly:

The first invention of such beautiful machines, (clocks and watches CW) indeed, and even that of some of the instruments of work employed in making them, must, no doubt, have been the work of deep thought and long time, and may justly be considered as among the happiest efforts of human ingenuity. But when both have been fairly invented and are well understood, to explain to any young man, in the completest manner, how to apply the instrument and how to construct the machines, cannot well require more than the lessons of a few weeks; perhaps those of a few days might be sufficient. (Smith [1776] (1981), pp. 139–140)

Thus was born the 'executive technician' or the carrier-out of procedures devised by a scientist or an intellectual. The 'young man' need not understand the theory of how watches work or of the machine tools needed to manufacture them. Instruction in a *technique* ('perhaps those of a few days might be sufficient') will suffice in order for the operative to carry out the procedures that lead to the manufacture of watches.

Key to understanding the role of the executive technician is that this individual's discretion in the workplace is recognising the circumstances and applying the appropriate procedures to them. The executive technician must go through a three-stage process of identifying what the circumstances are, selecting the appropriate procedure and then applying it. Judgement is required in the first two steps of the procedure. For the executive technician model of work to be applicable, variation in the environment in which the procedure is to be applied must be minimised. If not, then the operative will need to take account of these changes and perhaps even have to modify the procedure in order to accommodate them. The possibility of operator error is correspondingly increased. In order to further minimise error, it is also desirable that the procedure be broken down, as far as possible, into simple steps whose misinterpretation and hence misapplication are minimised. The fewer judgements that the executive technician has to make, the fewer errors are likely to be committed. The executive technician, in order to be successful, needs to work in a simple and easily segmentable environment. Conceiving teachers as executive technicians will necessitate configuring their teaching environments in such a way as well.

THE TECHNICIAN

The technician, properly so called, needs to be carefully distinguished from the executive technician above. The executive technician does not need to have any grasp of the theory underlying his practice. It is the mark of the technician, on the other hand, that he does and is able to apply his knowledge of the theory to the circumstances of his work. This makes a profound difference to the way in which he carries out his work.

What does it mean to say that the technician understands the theory and can apply it? The executive technician is handed theory-derived procedures that he is trained to put into effect. The technician has to devise those procedures according to the circumstances in which he finds himself. In order to do that, he needs to be able to interrogate the relevant theory in order to devise a procedure to act in the here and now. The procedure is thus not a general one applicable to a range of simple types of situation, but one applicable to the particular circumstances in which he finds himself.[4]

It follows that the vocational education of the technician needs to be quite different from that of the executive technician. The latter's vocational education could fairly be described as 'training', while training in procedures will not do for the former. The technician needs to have some considerable acquaintance with the relevant theory and maybe with the disciplines that underlie that theory. He needs to be able to apply that theory to practice by devising and executing procedures that are mandated by the theory. But there is a further point about the technician that merits attention. The technician is expected to make judgements *in situ* in the workplace or before or after entry in the workplace. This requirement will be particularly important where the workplace is complex and unpredictable (at least to a degree). The theory acquired cannot be the sole guide to action in these circumstances.

The technician needs to recognise the requirements of the situation in relation to the goals that he is pursuing. He needs to be able to assess the ability of the theory to mandate a procedure to deal with these circumstances. But, since the procedure has to be put into effect in circumstances over which he has incomplete control, the procedure itself may need to be adapted to take account of these circumstances. The expertise of the technician, then, which marks him from the theoretician or the executive technician, is that he devises and utilises procedures that are apt for particular circumstances, often of a complex and unpredictable nature.

---

[4] This does not mean that the technician never finds himself in recurrent kinds of situations that require repeated application of the procedure. Indeed, fluency in applying such procedures repeatedly may be one (but by no means the only) mark of the expert (Dreyfus and Dreyfus 1996).

It follows therefore that learning the relevant theory is not going to be nearly enough to become an effective technician.[5] Crucially, procedures for applying the relevant theory will need to be devised, which are apt for operational conditions, where mistakes may have serious consequences, where judgements often need to be made rapidly and where exigencies of time and resources, as well as the needs of clients, employers and workmates, have to be taken into account in the application of procedures. It is not difficult to see that the technician will need to have some of the attributes of the craft-worker in order to be successful *as a technician*. In particular, he will need to be able to make judgements and to take actions that make use of the relevant theory as well as other factors, which include the particular circumstances in which he is placed.

We have noted that the technician needs to have access to the relevant theory before he can judge and act. But what does this mean? By 'theory' is meant a body of systematic knowledge relevant to the occupation. This can be philosophically based, normatively based, mathematical-logically based or empirically based, or some combination of these four in the case of, for example, medicine or engineering. Empirically based theories range from the natural to the social sciences and encompass different areas of study and different methodologies. There is no reason to suppose that the theoretical basis that underpins an occupation has to be confined to one subject or one type of theory. It is becoming increasingly common to combine different theoretical frameworks in the systematic knowledge underpinning an occupation. The social sciences, for example, play an increasing role in subjects that previously perhaps only relied on one or more of the physical or biological sciences. The 'theory' with which a technician works should not then be necessarily thought of as acquaintance with either a single subject or empirical material. Very often, the systematic knowledge underlying an occupation will be drawn from a range of different subjects with different fields of interest and methodologies.

This observation raises in turn a question about what exactly 'acquaintance' should mean. There must be a balance in the education of a technician between the requirements of the occupation and the requirements of mastery of relevant bodies of systematic knowledge. If excessive emphasis is placed on the latter, then it is difficult to see how the emergent technician will acquire the ability to make

---

[5] 'Learning the relevant theory' is an expression that cries out for expansion. This will be provided in Chapter 8.

sound professional judgements. Lack of theory on the other hand will push him towards either a craft style of work or that of an executive technician.

It is evident therefore that the education of the technician is going to involve compromises. There is no ready *a priori* answer to the question as to how much theory a technician is going to need. There will be some occupations for which little or no theoretical preparation is required. On the other hand, how an occupation is designed will itself have considerable consequences for our understanding of the nature and degree of systematic knowledge required to practise it. This brings us to an interesting observation about the design of occupations that require technical ability. We noted a form of 'epistemic Taylorism' in the case of the executive technician, whereby the theoretical development of the occupation was entirely removed from the control of the person practising the occupation. There can be degrees of occupational disengagement from underlying theory, and the question is about the extent to which the practitioner should have a sound grasp of the theory. It is not enough to say: 'The technician needs enough to do the job properly', since the issue is in large measure about what precisely 'the job' consists of.

This brings us to a key point about the technician. He or she is a person who emerges as the result of designing work in a certain way. The design of the job will depend to some extent on whether it is envisaged that it will form part of a well-defined occupation.[6] Whether the category of activity considered should constitute a well-defined occupation will depend on many factors, but among these will be social and political as well as economic considerations. The reader of Adam Smith and Karl Marx will be likely to conclude that job and hence occupation design is the result of remorseless economic forces alone. In the case of Smith, this is the imperative of the employer to increase productivity by fragmenting the labour process into ever smaller and more discrete tasks. In the case of Marx, this imperative is aided and accelerated through the employment of technology, resulting in what are sometimes called 'Fordist' production methods.

But this view is at best a large oversimplification. Whether or not the fragmentation of the production of a good or service into multiple discrete tasks takes place depends to a large extent on economic

---

[6] By 'job', I mean specific tasks or projects defined in the work contract of an individual. By 'occupation', I mean a defined area of economic activity in which particular jobs can be identified. For more on this, see Winch (2013b).

considerations, but not in quite the way in which Smith and Marx envisaged. There may be very good business reasons for thinking twice about going in for full-blooded Taylorism, particularly, for example, if the business concerned involves what is known as 'diversified quality production' (Streeck 1992) where the value of the product or service depends in no small degree on the ability of the producer to adapt to the needs of the customer by the ability to (1) manage a project (in the sense outlined in Chapter 3) or to (2) make changes suited to the individual needs of the customer (see also Greinert 2007).

But reasons for designing jobs that depend on technical ability in well-defined occupations may go beyond the technical requirements of the field of activity concerned. They may also result from a decision to design work in such a way as to give workers a degree of independence and discretion in order to make work satisfying or to accord it a worthwhile status within the society. Technical kinds of labour are most likely to achieve prominence in a society when the economic imperative of moving up the 'value chain' and producing skilled-labour-intensive goods and services is combined with an idea of making the dignity and worth of labour a political and social priority (see Glasman 1994).

The question then arises as to the extent to which the technician, in order to work independently and to produce goods or services of a high standard, needs to engage with relevant systematic knowledge. That extent will be to no small degree determined by the design of the occupation. For example, if it is determined, as it is in the case of the French *maçon*, that such a person should be capable of building a two-storey structure, then a considerable degree of systematic knowledge will be required in order for the *maçon* to be able to do this. The relevant academic disciplines will need to be identified and curriculum design will need to ensure (1) that the worker is capable of attaining a sufficient degree of understanding of the underlying principles of the subject and can use those principles in practice and (2) that those areas of the subject that he studies contain material that is relevant to the work that he is expected to undertake.

The technician needs to be able to understand the underlying theory in order to form sound judgements about how to apply it in the range of activities that he is expected to undertake. This will mean much more than an ability to recall propositions within the subject; he will also need to be able to find his way around it, that is to understand the basic conceptual structure and to make material inferences and, where relevant, calculations that allow him to infer what is required in the range of relevant situations he will encounter. It follows that a 'learning outcomes' (Coles 2007) approach, that involves nothing more than recall of a range of relevant propositions, will be inadequate for such a purpose. There can be no substitute for understanding the conceptual structure of the subject to the extent necessary to work independently within the occupational field. Furthermore, it is likely that he will need to have some practical experience of some of the key findings, which may include experimental findings that define the field and to have the ability to replicate, to a limited extent, those findings in order to gain a more practical understanding of the principles underlying practice (Winch 2013a). Above all, the technician will need to be capable of making judgements that include premises about what the theory mandates in a particular situation with a judgement about what are the key features of the situation in which he is operating. There will need to be the capability of a kind of dialectical working between the theory and the work situation in order to arrive at a sound judgement or legitimation (Luntley 2012) for a judgement. The education of a technician will be different from that of either an executive technician or a craftworker in that it will need to combine both theoretical instruction and practical experience and, quite possibly, further elements. We will return to this issue when discussing the education of teachers in Chapter 10.

THE TECHNOLOGIST

The technician needs to establish a dialectical relationship between the relevant theory on the one hand and the practical necessities of the occupation on the other. Theoretical knowledge, to be useful, has to be tempered to the requirements of particular work situations. This entails that the technician must judge whether, when and how theory is relevant and how it should be applied. Although nothing precludes the possibility, the technician is not expected to contribute to the theoretical understanding of the occupation but to nuance its application. Is there, however, another category of occupation, part of whose brief is to modify theory in the light of practice or of the changing requirements of practice? Such an occupation would be that of a *technologist*. The technologist would have, as a major part of his professional task, the development of theory-based approaches to the solving of practical problems. The problems will be set by practice, as is the case with the technician. However, the technologist will be expected to develop new approaches to the solution of these problems, which might include the invention of the machinery for making watches that

Adam Smith refers to in the passage quoted above, or the adaptation of such machinery or the development of new techniques that may or may not involve new equipment. To take an example from civil engineering, a tunnel-boring machine, equipped to handle clay soils, might not be able to cope with wet and chalky soil. The civil engineering technologist would be capable of modifying and adapting the original design to cope with such conditions.

It might look as if the technologist does no more than adapt existing theory to new conditions by making more detailed and extensive use of the theory than would be expected of the technician. This may, on many occasions, be the case. However, the case should not be excluded where the modification of equipment or approach required by a practical problem has an implication for the theory, at least for the situational implications of the theory. This can, perhaps, be best illustrated through consideration of the engineering example above. The technologist encounters a problem for which there are no obvious ready solutions available within the underlying discipline. It is possible to form hypotheses about what those solutions might be and to test them to see whether they can provide a solution to the problem. If not, then the hypothesis may be discarded or further modified. On the other hand, construction of equipment or development of a procedure on the basis of the hypothesis might lead to a solution. The hypothesis and its consequent procedures and equipment are accepted into engineering practice and are used to deal with cognate problems in the future.

At first, the theory T was unable to suggest a solution to problem P.
Using T and possibly other knowledge, a solution to P is found.
The technologist now knows of T that it is capable of suggesting
    (even if not entirely on its own) a solution to P.
The understanding of T for its relevance to practice is therefore modified.

It is usually unlikely, but by no means impossible, that central elements of the theory will be greatly modified by a procedure like the above, but those parts of the theory that concern its applicability in certain contexts will be, thus contributing to overall understanding of the theory. This is the territory of the technologist. It is likely that technologists will not be so intimately involved in the day-to-day practice of the occupation as the technician. They will need the opportunity to interrogate the theory more deeply and to spend time in controlled conditions devising equipment and procedures that can then be tested in realistic conditions. Their education may overlap, but not be identical, with that of the technician working in the same field. It may well be possible and desirable for there to be routes that allow the technician to progress to the role of technologist within the sector in which he is working. Therefore, the education of the technician will need to be considered with that of the technologist in mind as well. It is likely that a fruitful working relationship and mutual understanding of each of their respective roles will prove beneficial to the sector in which they are both working. Thus, one of our lines of enquiry will concern the extent to which, during the course of a career, a teacher can adopt the technological role.

THE RESEARCHER

The theory that informs an occupation or group of occupations within a sector was constructed through research according to appropriate methods. Assuming that the theory is not static, we may imagine it undergoing incremental growth, whereby elements are discarded or added and on occasion major changes occur when central assumptions, principles or comments come under scrutiny. This may all happen without any intention to apply the theory, although such changes will very often have important implications for various practices that depend on the theory for their success. Researchers have the job of modifying a theory, very often a well-established 'non-applied' (although not non-applicable) subject such as physics or mathematics, the law or sociology, by conducting investigations that aim at validating claims made within the theory. This is usually a highly specialised type of occupation that requires extensive education in the theory.

It is sometimes claimed that anyone learning a subject should do so by conducting research in it and also that practitioners of an occupation should be researchers in that occupation, a claim often made about teaching (e.g. Hargreaves 1996). The suggestion is that research is something that can be undertaken at an elementary level and then be pursued at progressively more advanced levels as the individual's education progresses. Such claims rest on a misunderstanding about what research consists of and hence of the occupational category of researcher. Subjects such as mathematics, chemistry, philosophy, law and sociology do not just have a field of investigation but also underlying conceptualisations of what the discipline is and a range of methodological approaches to the development and validation of knowledge claims within the subject.

The effective use of the methods mandated by the methodological approach requires a deep understanding of the philosophical underpinnings, the principles and the central concepts of the subject, not to mention a very extensive understanding of its content. In addition, expertise in the use of the characteristic methods of the subject is required. This is often acquired through the use of those methods to, for example, replicate and validate already validated knowledge claims or to do so in different circumstances (as the technologist might do). But in working like this, one is not, for example, forming and testing hypotheses or pursuing a new line of enquiry. This makes the work of someone who is using existing methods to replicate findings quite different from the work of someone who is carrying out research.

To take the example of experimental research, a critical requirement is the ability to form relevant, useful and testable hypotheses. These cannot just be plucked out of the air, but must arise within the tradition of enquiry within the subject. The selection of a hypothesis for further investigation is a crucial activity for the researcher and requires deep knowledge of the subject, which will normally include a developed expertise in actually applying the methods of investigation to be employed. This cannot be the province of someone who is in the process of acquiring mastery of the subject (Winch 2013a). A researcher who is leading and designing a substantial piece of research has to be an expert in the subject or field of knowledge under investigation. The occupations of teacher and researcher are distinct, and the implications of this distinction are important.[7]

RELATIONSHIPS BETWEEN THE ELEMENTS IN THIS TYPOLOGY OF OCCUPATIONS AND THEIR RELEVANCE TO TEACHING

Unclarity about the relationship between a craftworker, an executive technician and a technician properly so called has been a problem in discussions of teaching, where distinctions are not always examined with the care that they deserve, particularly in the philosophical literature on the subject. The first point to note is the radical disparity between the craftwork and the executive technician conceptions of

---

[7] It is very important to bear in mind that this claim by no means excludes the possibility that those less well briefed in the methods, principles and presuppositions of the subject cannot play an important role in such investigations. Indeed, this may well be a requirement in the case of research into teaching (see Chapter 9 for further discussion).

an occupation, it being assumed that they are not dissimilar (this seems to be the view in government publications, for example). A craftworker (as an ideal type) does not engage with theory and has to use his own expertise to work effectively within particular situations, using experience and acquired ability, including the ability to devise appropriate procedures when required. The executive technician, on the other hand, is constrained by the rules that the underlying mandating theory prescribes and which he has to follow. In its most extreme form, this results in so-called 'teacher-proof' lesson plans that must be followed without deviation. It is a moot point, and one which we will investigate further in Chapter 7, whether this prescription can actually be followed and whether any substantial modification means a lapse into incoherence of the 'pure' executive technician model of the teacher.

The technician, although dependent on theoretical knowledge for the formation of professional judgement, does not have to eschew the craft element of his or her work. Indeed, it can be argued that the power that theory is said to confer on the formation of professional judgement necessitates that there be a craft element if the technician is not either to succumb to helplessness or to be little more than an executive technician. Theory, on this model, does not directly mandate action; it provides the material for both the formation of judgement and the legitimation of action. The technician-teacher finds himself in circumstances in which judgement as to the best course of action is required. The resources that he has to drawn on include relevant theoretical considerations but also experience and good sense, as well as the ability to assess the relevant features of the situation in which he finds himself. In addition, as argued in Chapter 3, he needs the ability to form and put into effect long-term plans of action and to be aware of the civic dimension of occupational capacity. Here again, theoretical resources will be important for the formation of judgement. The ability to draw on all of these resources according to the demands of the situation, particularly the classroom situation, is precisely the craft element that the technician-teacher needs, albeit that the craft element is transformed and made more complex through the perceived relevance of theoretical considerations.

Implicit in this characterisation of the technician is that he is not a researcher, but a user and interpreter of research. But these are abilities, indispensable not only to his role but also to his potential development as a researcher, be it as a technologist in the above sense or as a researcher in the full sense, although in this role, his experience and expertise as a teacher is a potentially powerful resource for understanding the scope and limitations of academic research into educational practice, about which we will have more to say, especially in Chapter 9. The technologist, on the other hand, is someone whose engagement with educational practice has to be fairly close, and the work of the technologist is likely to be improved through an understanding of the constraints of work in the classroom and through an ability to validate new approaches, techniques or tools through practice in realistic conditions.

In this chapter, three broad approaches to the work of teachers have been presented, together with their relationships with each other. Each is in a sense capable, if properly executed, of providing 'good enough' teachers for an education system at a given level of development.[8] The key point that I wish to make, however, at this stage is that those responsible for the way in which teachers conduct their work have critical choices to make concerning the type and degree of expertise that they wish the occupation to have. Do they want depth of ability to act wisely in classroom situations, or accuracy in carrying out theoretically mandated instructions, or a breadth of understanding of the possibilities of a broad and independent role for teachers? And, given these choices, are they prepared to commit the appropriate resources required to realise the type of teacher that they wish for? It is better that such choices are made explicit and decided on their merits rather than that a pretence be adopted that there are no such choices to be made.

---

[8] Meaning, among other things, what its aims and values are and the ability of the resources available to it to realise those aims and values (cf. Naik 1975).

5
The Elements of Teacher Knowledge and Know-How

The focus of this chapter's discussion is on the specific nature of teacher knowledge, including KT (propositional knowledge), KH (know-how), KA (knowledge by acquaintance) and their interrelationship. There are features of teaching that it may share with other occupations, namely those associated with craft, executive technician and technician occupations. There are also features of teacher knowledge that are specific to teaching, which receive attention in the literature. It is with these specific features that this chapter is principally concerned.

At this point, it is worth reminding ourselves briefly of the important relationships between our three epistemic powers. First, KT can inform KH (see discussion in Chapter 3). Second, KT understood as knowledge of a field of enquiry or a subject does in fact involve a form of KH (see discussion below). Third, KA is an important resource for both KH and KT. This will be explained in terms of teachers' ability.

SUBJECT EXPERTISE

In one sense, a subject exists when it has official recognition of some kind within a curriculum. But, in another sense, it is supposed to designate an area of conceptual and epistemic unity – but just how is quite hard to describe precisely. A starting point is to suggest distinguishing between organised and non-organised knowledge, although the boundaries between the two are not always clear and systematic enquiry can arise where previously there was only unsystematic

Teachers' Know-How: A Philosophical Investigation, First Edition. Christopher Winch.
© 2017 Christopher Winch. Editorial Organisation © Philosophy of Education Society of Great Britain.
Published 2017 by John Wiley & Sons, Ltd.

enquiry. The distinction is not so easy to capture precisely, since there are conceptual connections within all fields of knowledge, whether organised or unorganised. A subject, however, depends on a degree of *formalisation*, whereby what is known is set out explicitly and at least some propositional and conceptual relationships are set out. A further stage would be when a form of hierarchical structure is introduced, in which some propositions are central or even take a normative form, and where conceptual relationships can, in some cases, be quite precisely defined.[1] The reverse process may also happen whereby systematic knowledge or belief is sedimented into 'commonsense' belief (see Chapter 3).

How does one talk about the emergence of systematic knowledge? First, a field of concern emerges from the direction of human interest. Examples include the study of pattern in quantity, space and number and distinctive methods of inquiry, such as calculation, algebraic manipulation and deductive proof in mathematics.[2] More generally, from these fields of concern arise characteristic methods of acquiring, validating and reviewing knowledge. It is important to note that knowledge is not to be equated with *certainty* except in some areas of some subjects and that what counts as knowledge within a subject may change over time. Both fields of concern and methods of enquiry may be disputed, for example, whether modern literature and film belong to the study of literature in the first case, or to different paradigms of investigation in economics or psychology in the second. Some methods may become 'paradigmatic' in Kuhn's (1962) sense. Not all subjects can be expected to yield knowledge as their only product, for example, philosophy.

This can be drawn out in more detail, using the pioneering work of Paul Hirst (1965) on forms of knowledge as a starting point. It is thus useful to distinguish between fundamental concepts, fundamental principles and conceptual relationships in describing the particular features of individual subjects. One can distinguish between:

1. *Fundamental concepts*: causality, matter, energy, time and space, for example, in physics. There is a conceptual link to these concepts in everyday use, but they often assume a clear definition within a subject such as physics while they remain undefined in non-subject use.

---

[1] For a helpful discussion, see Young and Muller (2014, pp. 18–30).

[2] Comprehensive definitions of the content and methods of mathematics are difficult to come by.

2. *Fundamental principles*: One example is Newton's laws in physics; another example is arithmetical laws in mathematics. They can also be axioms or quasi-axioms as in geometry or physics, or laws of inference (e.g. principles of natural deduction).
3. *Conceptual relationships*: Principles make use of concepts, including fundamental concepts. Concepts invariably exist in related fields (antonymy, hyponymy, relations of transitivity etc.); these conceptual relationships can be expressed implicitly through conversation and action through which grasp of the relationships may be inferred, but also through specific forms of material inferential relations. Another way of putting this is to say that conceptual relationships are primarily manifested *propositionally* in judgements and suppositions, for example (Mackenzie 2016). Sometimes it may be appropriate to express such relationships in terms of formal inference, for example, displaying the law of non-contradiction in the case of formal logic. 'Making it explicit' may be an assessment strategy when assessing a novice's grasp of a systematically organised field. It can also turn out that some subjects or elements of their fields and methods are embedded in others, as is the case for mathematics in physics and other disciplines.

Not all subjects show the same degree of systematicity. It is possible, for example, to ask whether history is a systematically organised discipline compared with physics. It has a reasonably well-defined field of concern (the recorded human past), fundamental concepts such as cause, reason, chronology and narrative, plus various institutional concepts such as monarchy, legitimacy and so on, which have more well-defined uses than they have in everyday usage. Methods of enquiry are more rigorous than in everyday usage. There are, for example, canons for making inferences from traces, inferential warrant from evidence for: the motivation of agents, justification for the narrative account offered and so on.

We can also distinguish between subjects that are relatively free-standing (what Bernstein calls 'singulars' and others that are more obviously composed from other subjects ('fields'), even though the distinction need not be a rock solid one). Most subjects, although they have distinct fields of concern, may borrow elements of methods from other subjects, like mathematics in physics or experimental methods in psychology. Those most heavily used and borrowed from are, in a sense, more fundamental than others, since mastery of elements of them is to a larger extent necessary in the pursuit of systematically organised knowledge.[3]

New fields of concern may emerge or a larger field of concern may combine more than one in what Hirst calls *fields* of knowledge (e.g. geography and politics).[4] Subject boundaries may also intermingle, for example, theology and philosophy, or mathematics and physics.

In addition, subjects have their own character, determined in part not only by the ways in which they are organised, but also by their traditions and histories, not to mention within-subject debates about philosophical presuppositions, methodologies and the scope of fields of interest. These subject characters are important for teachers and often form a significant part of their own professional identities.

Two Ways of Looking at Subject Knowledge
Up until this point, the organisation of subject knowledge has been considered as a whole, as someone who is 'subject-omniscient' might see it, with the relationship between concepts, principles and key propositions rendered transparent. In such a perspective, it is possible to judge, for example, what is fundamental to a subject, whether it has foundations and if so what these are. It is a point of view that will also take as transparent the different kinds of KH involved in validating, acquiring and discarding items of knowledge and also what KA is necessary to secure conceptual grasp. It is a point of view open to one who is already an expert, and, arguably, such an overview could only belong to someone possessed with superhuman epistemic powers, particularly if that overview is thought to be comprehensive. However, such a perspective could usefully be seen as a regulative ideal for someone aspiring to be a subject expert, even if it is not a state that they will ever realise.

There is, however, another way of looking at subject knowledge which is not so much concerned with the subject in its entirety but with the point of view of someone who is seeking expertise but is, as yet, only a novice. A pupil will be such a person, and the perspective suggested is the one that confronts the learner. By its nature, such a perspective cannot consider the subject as a whole, but will at the outset consider it from a single or limited number of points (granted perhaps by general knowledge and relevant fragments from other subjects). Pictorially, the difference is between seeing the

---

[3] However, it is useful to caution against disciplinary arrogance. See, for example, Gould's (1989, p. 281) remarks on a disparaging comparison between palaeobiology and stamp collecting.

[4] See Oakeshott (1962, ch. 5, 'Political Education') for a detailed treatment of politics as a subject.

subject as a room from the ceiling downwards on the one hand (as a putative expert) and opening a door slowly onto the room on the other (as a novice aspiring to greater expertise). This latter perspective will be particularly important in considering the role of the teacher. The process of moving in terms of knowledge from novice to expert I will call Epistemic Ascent (EA), and it involves an understanding of the structure of systematic knowledge from the point of view of the learner rather than of the expert.[5] The concept of EA involves an understanding of the conceptual structure of a subject from the point of view of someone acquiring expertise in it, and the study of EA within any subject will be a kind of conceptual exploration, albeit somewhat different from that which the expert might conduct. It involves the study of conceptual dependence and interdependence from the point of view of learning about existing claims and connections, rather than from the point of view of validating and acquiring new subject knowledge. It will be argued that possession of such a perspective is indispensable for a teacher of subjects, whether academic or applied.

APPLIED SUBJECT KNOWLEDGE

Although the distinction is not always clear, there are some subjects whose matter is more obviously KH than KT, where what is to be learned are forms of know-how rather than bodies of propositional knowledge (in the sense of propositional knowledge argued for in the previous section).

Among other subjects, these include: physical education, dance, design and technology, literacy, art and, arguably, mathematics. Teacher expertise in these subjects consists more in developing KH than KT. While it is usually necessary that teachers have (or, in some cases, have had) the know-how necessary to perform well in the subjects that they teach, it is also usually the case that this know-how does not exhaust what they need to know in order to teach the subject effectively. This point is not always fully understood by the lay public.

It is worth taking an extended example to make this point clearer. The teaching of the ability to read is considered one of the core tasks of primary education and is notoriously one that many schools and education systems fail to adequately develop in all their pupils. There

---

[5] These are perspectival differences. It is important that teachers are able to switch between both perspectives.

is a complexity about the teaching of reading that requires systematic knowledge, not only of some areas of applied linguistics but also, arguably, of applied psychology. Furthermore, it is arguable that for many teachers, important aspects of the teaching of reading are not understood, and indeed there are academic disputes as to what exactly the problems of teaching the subject are. For example, it is widely but controversially held that *dyslexia* is not a distinctive learning disability, but rather a section on a continuum of difficulties in learning to read (for examples, see Bryant and Bradley 1985; Elliott and Gibbs 2008; Elliott 2016). More generally, there are debates about what methods are most suitable for the teaching of reading and in what combination (Mackay 2006). The position is further complicated by the fact that the debates about these issues are not merely empirical but also include a considerable conceptual element. Thus, the definition of dyslexia is in some ways problematic (Elliott and Gibbs 2008; Elliott 2016). More generally, the relationship between the spoken and written forms of language is debated (Winch 1990), and even the nature of reading itself is disputed (Winch 1989). There is thus a theoretical complexity to and convergence of disciplinary approaches appropriate to understanding the teaching of literacy, which includes contributions from psychology, linguistics and philosophy, and this is not fully appreciated in most programmes of teacher education.

How much should teachers understand about these often complex and difficult topics? An obvious response might be to urge that the education of teachers in such areas should take the *executive technician* route (see Chapters 4 and 7) and that teachers should merely be trained in procedures derived by others (Mackay (2006), Clay (1979), and Miskin and Archbold (2007) all provide examples). This is one possibility. On the other hand, teachers who are able to form independent professional judgements based on relevant knowledge and understanding will not be well served by such programmes, although they may have something to offer as part of teacher education. In particular, as Hattie (2009) has argued, a crucial element in a teacher's ability is to appreciate the difficulty that a pupil may be experiencing in their learning. This should include not just empathy with the problems the pupil is encountering, but also a detailed understanding of where the intellectual and/or emotional problem with the subject matter may lie. A good grasp of what EA occurs within the subject (see previous section) is important, as well as a good understanding of the relevant research. The fact that some of this knowledge may be controversial does not absolve teachers of the need to make their own judgements, relying on other than *commonsense* as described in Chapter 4, and on a measured view of the relevant research together with reflection on their own experience of teaching.[6]

These abilities are closely connected with what is sometimes called 'formative assessment'. Appreciation of pupil difficulties depends on the ability to accurately diagnose what they are likely to be. But that is only a first stage, since teachers need to be able to devise ways of addressing those difficulties that are appropriate to the needs of the pupil. This in turn depends in large part on the understanding of EA within the subject and the ability to develop ways of recording, procedures and materials for enabling pupils to overcome difficulties and to progress. Similar considerations apply to the requirement for knowledge of mechanics and anatomy in physical education or of aesthetics and elements of chemistry in painting.

In this connection, it is also necessary to add, as it is in the case of non-applied subject knowledge, that the philosophical foundations and conceptions of the subject to be taught should also be within the grasp of the teacher. The issue is one familiar in professional work, namely the question of how and to what extent theoretical considerations need to be taken into account in the formation of professional judgement and the justification of professional action. The theoretical element of applied subject knowledge needs to be integrated into professional know-how and action, and this can only be done through practice, reflection and re-iteration and, last but not least, processes of conversation and discussion with colleagues. The general point is that the applied subjects should not be treated as if they were qualitatively different from the more conventionally academic ones, as being purely concerned with the transmission of know-how from one individual (the teacher) to another (the pupil) but with the systematic knowledge, both conceptual and empirical, that provides justification for procedures adopted within the subject and which needs to be drawn on for effective teaching. This may be disputed by the advocates of the executive technician approach, and this issue will be addressed more fully in Chapter 7.

PEDAGOGIC CONTENT KNOWLEDGE

Pedagogic content knowledge (PCK) is a category introduced by Shulman (1986) and concerns the knowledge (or, perhaps better,

---

[6] See Shalem (2014) on the construction of possible subject frameworks for teachers' professional judgements.

know-how) needed by a teacher in order to re-organise her subject knowledge in a form fit for learning by her pupils. Having good subject knowledge in the expert sense (see above) is a prerequisite of gaining effective PCK, but teachers will also need to have a good grasp of the nature of EA within their subject if they are to do so. Indeed, it can be said that grasp of EA is a major element of PCK, since a good sense of how the subject is likely to appear from the perspective of the learner is an important prerequisite for the successful reconfiguration of subject knowledge for pedagogic purposes. The other important element of PCK is a grasp of the needs of the particular pupils whom one is teaching. If this analysis is correct, then subject knowledge is very important for the teacher, who needs to have a good grasp of her subject. But it is not sufficient; indeed, a case can be made out for saying that possession of expert subject knowledge on its own might be a hindrance to teaching for some teachers compared with others with less subject knowledge but a better grasp of PCK and, indeed, of EA. This issue is connected with a good understanding of the philosophical underpinnings of subjects. EA is concerned with the philosophical analysis of how learning should take place by investigation of the epistemic (rather than logical) prerequisites of advancing in knowledge within a subject.

How, then, should EA be characterised? A helpful place to start would be to consider the fashionable approach of specifying 'learning outcomes' as a way of structuring teaching and learning. Coles (2007) argues that one may approach the assessment of a subject in two ways. One is through the specification of standards, and the other through the specification of learning outcomes.

> For example a module of learning on Roman history will include many objectives concerned with timelines, major events, significant rulers, transport systems, social developments and so on. Assessment may sample across these aspects and will allow a general judgement of the level of knowledge of the Roman era to be made. On the other hand, the assessment of learning outcomes will usually be inclusive of all outcomes and will be based on assessment criteria relating to each outcome, for example the ability to describe the advance of the Roman army in Europe, or the ability to identify the distinguishing characteristics of the architecture of Roman public buildings. (p. 13)

Coles refers here to objectives (learning objectives) that I, following Pring (1992), call 'standards'. Standards are a waymark within a curriculum, and by using them one can design assessment instruments in order to determine the extent to which these standards have been acquired by a pupil. They are usually stated at quite a high order of generality (see the discussion in Winch 2013a). The Attainment Targets in older versions of the English National Curriculum are a good example of standards in this sense. Learning outcomes, as the quotation above makes clear, are particular propositions or sets of propositions that the pupil must articulate in some way (through multiple choice or statement, for example) in order to demonstrate knowledge. We can see the problem raised in Chapter 4, that the ability to articulate propositions is not sufficient to demonstrate knowledge (or even, in some circumstances, true belief) as it is difficult to capture the element of understanding that stands behind knowledge through this form of assessment.

Assessment through instruments based on standards takes another approach. It assumes that knowledge of a subject matter must require that the pupil understand it, and in order to do this the pupil needs to understand that the subject matter is ordered in various ways: conceptually and empirically. The subject is conceived of, not just as sets of propositions more or less loosely grouped together, but also as a related conceptual field in which concepts, principles, key propositions and, where relevant, empirical findings all contribute to the field of knowledge. If a pupil can state that Napoleon was made Emperor in 1804 but cannot infer that in 1804 France ceased to be a republic, then it is reasonable to suppose that the pupil does not properly understand the proposition that Napoleon was made Emperor in 1804 since his grasp of the concept of an Emperor is incomplete. In other words, a conceptual field concerned with the governance of states must be grasped to a large degree before one can attribute knowledge. This in turn implies not only that subjects build upon pre-existing knowledge on the part of pupils but also that they need to develop concepts jointly so that, in a sense, 'light dawns over the whole' (to use Wittgenstein's (1969) phrase) rather than over one proposition at a time.[7]

Ensuring this poses a considerable challenge for a teacher, who must make judgements both about what the pupil can reasonably be supposed to already know and about what concepts should be jointly

---

[7] See Tizard and Hughes (1984) for good examples of this.

introduced in order to ensure that understanding (a prerequisite of knowledge) is gained. The example above suggests that the pupil needs to find his way around the subject that is being acquired inferentially, using what Brandom (2000) calls material rather than formal inference.

> The kind of inference whose correctnesses essentially involve the conceptual contents of its premises and conclusions may be called, following Sellars, "*material* inference." (Brandom 1998, p. 97)

The ability to make inferences, whether it be in the formal or material mode, is a kind of know-how, arguably one that in its more basic forms lies at the foundation of the ability to use language. It involves the ability to make connections between conceptually related material, in speech and later in thought, and it is a condition of understanding in a subject area, 'finding one's way about' or 'knowing how to go on' with respect to a conceptual field.[8] One of the things that one learns as one acquires one's native tongue is a grasp of the conceptual structure of the language (which is no doubt to a large degree shared with that of other languages). Although one may perhaps refer to such abilities as mastery of a technique, it is often the very basic kind of technique that is largely inseparable from one's ability to speak, at least as regards basic, non-subject-specific conceptual structure. The teacher presupposes pupils to have such abilities and proceeds to build on them.

An important point here is the observation that the growth of expertise in a subject, and this includes both 'academic' and 'applied' subjects,[9] does not involve accumulation of knowledge of more and more propositions or even groups of propositions, but the growth of ability to grasp the relationships between propositions within a subject, in other words, the growth of understanding in the subject. Growth in subject knowledge is thus actually inseparable from growth in understanding, which among other things involves inferential ability. It is therefore mistaken to think of subject knowledge as a property distinct from the practical ability to find one's way around a

---

[8] For a recent defence of understanding as ability, see Brandt (2014).

[9] A somewhat arbitrary distinction, as the example of mathematics makes clear. There are elements of 'know-how' and 'know that' in intimate combination in mathematics. For example, 'I know that $7 \times 8 = 56$ and I know how to work it out', through, say, iterated addition. I am very grateful to Dr R.C. Solomon for this and other, much more complex, mathematical examples.

subject. This point has an important bearing on the abilities of teachers, as we shall see later in this book.

Subject expertise involves practical knowledge or KH in other ways as well. Pupils need to understand that a subject is a living field of human endeavour in which knowledge is being tested, validated, accumulated and even at times rejected.[10] In order to do this, there are procedures characteristic of each subject that allow this to happen. Thus, in mathematics there is calculation and proof, in the natural sciences experimental procedures and systematic observation, in history the study of documentary and archaeological evidence and so on. It is also desirable that acquaintance with these procedures is, at some stage, a practical one so that pupils do not just learn about them but understand what using them involves, including the practical difficulties involved in doing so. The example of astronomy in the natural sciences is a good one. Giving someone the opportunity to use a telescope to make observations of the heavens allows them to understand the problems involved in setting up the telescope, identifying where a celestial object is likely to be, making accurate observations and recordings and keeping track of the object. In this way, knowledge by acquaintance (KA) plays an important role in securing EA. Of course, instruction and practice in these matters do not preclude a beginner making new observations, but this would not be the primary object of the exercise, which is to introduce the pupil to practical acquaintance with procedures and objects of study in order to understand some of the way in which knowledge is acquired within the discipline of astronomy.

Through such practices, pupils are helped to understand a subject as a living institution and something of the nature of the achievements of those who have made significant contributions to the subject. The kind of know-how developed is replicative rather than discovery oriented and should not be identified with the ability to make a meaningful contribution to the subject, but rather should be seen as a necessary prerequisite for doing so. In order to make this clearer, it

---

[10] This may sound paradoxical, but the term 'knowledge' does not imply timeless certainty. Our knowledge is what we currently have sufficient grounds for believing to be true, not an immutable body of truth that we can never fully access. If it were the latter, then it is difficult to see how we could know very much. Procedures, too, can undergo change, a point important in the practical as well as the academic subjects. See Ellenbogen (2003) for a more extended discussion. See also Mackenzie (2016) for a more sceptical view of the role of knowledge in the curriculum.

is necessary to point out that 'to know how to …' is, in English in at least one sense, ambiguous.[11] On the one hand, it can mean 'is able to F'; on the other, it can mean 'is able to give an account of how to F'.[12] In terms of this discussion, pupils need to know how discoveries are made and tested without being expected to know how to do such things themselves.

But although such a distinction seems clear enough, there is nevertheless a further ambiguity embedded in the second sense of 'know-how' which is pedagogically very important.[13] It is important to realise that 'giving an account of how to F' can mean that one is able to do so verbally, or it could mean that one is able to do so *enactively*, that is, by enacting the procedures involved without actually carrying them out. To give the example of a crucial experiment, a pupil might be able to describe, perhaps even in some detail, how that experiment is carried out. But he or she might also be able to set up the equipment, carry out the tests and record the results. This would show that they knew how to carry out the relevant procedures but would not necessarily entail that they knew how to carry out the crucial experiment in the sense that the original researchers did. To successfully conceive and complete to fruition a crucial experiment involves far more. It involves subject expertise in the 'panoramic' sense described earlier, an appreciation of gaps in knowledge and weaknesses in justification, an ability to formulate a research question and a hypothesis that address such gaps and weaknesses, and the ability to persist in the face of previously unmet difficulties in set-up, recording of observations and interpretation of findings. Such work normally requires great subject expertise, great insight and great persistence as well as a good grasp of the technical requirements of running an experiment. Therefore, the enactive 'giving an account' of how an experiment is conducted, even if it replicates many of the obstacles originally faced, does not amount to knowing how to carry out a crucial experiment in the relevant sense.

---

[11] See Brogaard (2011) for another philosophically significant sense.

[12] German makes this distinction explicit between *können* and *wissen wie*, while French contrasts *savoir faire* with *savoir comment faire* (see Rumfitt 2003).

[13] It should also be noted that the second, 'giving an account' sense of *know-how* is itself derivative of the first 'ability' sense. Giving an account of how to F is itself an ability. Any account of know-how that seeks to explain it in terms of giving an account of how to F does not succeed, therefore, in explaining what it seeks to explain, a problem with, for example, A.R. White's (1982) account of the nature of practical knowledge.

Teachers who are expert in their subject will often quite rightly wish to acquaint pupils with the practical procedures involved in validating and gaining knowledge. Such requirements are often written into curricula, for example, the English National Curriculum. There are good arguments to suggest that this is a powerful means of learning. However, the ability to replicatively conduct (for example) experiments, astronomical observations, surveys or complex proofs is not the same as the ability to discover in the relevant field. It is important for teachers to understand the scope and limits of what they are trying to do by developing a proper sense of what is the pedagogically most appropriate ordering to strive for in one's planning of schemes of work. The interplay between empirical and conceptual considerations is complex here and lies at the heart of what is called PCK. Thus, the distinction between 'ability' and 'account' forms of know-how and the logical relationship between them are conceptual matters, but the question of judgement as to whether and when to introduce the one in preference to the other depends on factors like the ability of individuals in the class and background knowledge of what the class has already learned. The acquisition of PCK is, therefore, complex and depends on a blend of subject knowledge in both panoramic and epistemic senses and at least a reasonable amount of practical experience and reflection. It would also be a mistake to assume that fully formed PCK is acquired relatively quickly; its coming to fruition could conceivably take years.

KNOWLEDGE OF LEARNING AND TEACHING

In many ways, this is the most controversial of the categories of teacher knowledge at the time of writing. Although not by any means just a matter of empirical study, knowledge of how individuals learn (including children, who are usually held to be a special case) is thought to heavily depend on what the facts of the matter are concerning human abilities to learn and teachers' capacity to effectively exploit those abilities. Indeed, some are inclined to maintain, as we noted in Chapter 4, that empirical data on such matters are irrelevant or necessarily false. It is well worth pointing out that our knowledge of learning and teaching is highly sensitive to philosophical considerations. Hamlyn (1978) has pointed out that conceptual relationships place limits on what sequences learning can take place in. The rule-following and private language considerations of Wittgenstein (1953) are, if cogent, important limitations on what we can coherently expect individuals to learn on their own (see also Bakhurst

2011). Whether or not theories of learning are coherent and whether they meet reasonable standards of epistemic probity are also matters of legitimate philosophical concern (see e.g. the discussion in Winch 1998). Finally, the fact that such empirical investigations may also be investigations into concepts in use should also heavily influence the nature and direction of inquiry into teaching and learning.

Once all these reservations have been made, however, it remains the case that facts about human abilities and the possibilities for their acquisition are important. The example of the careful research into the nature of reading difficulties described above is a good illustration of this point. And here we undoubtedly face a difficulty, as it seems as if our desire to establish such facts and to encode them in large-scale explanatory frameworks that would be useful to educational policy-makers and teachers far outruns our ability to actually do so. It is only necessary to look at attempts made to do so in the twentieth century to appreciate this. Thus the work of Galton, Burt and their numerous followers to identify and measure innate ability has been plagued by deep philosophical questions about, for example, whether intelligence is a unitary and measurable quality and about whether the nature–nurture distinction is really helpful in enabling us to understand human ability (see Cooper 1980; Bakhurst 2011).[14] Likewise, psychological developmentalism of the kind advocated by Piaget is vulnerable to questions concerning the relationship between normative and empirical theoretical elements, the metaphysics of human growth and Wittgensteinian worries about an excessively individualistic account of learning. Verbal deficit theorists should be worried about definitions of what verbal deficit amounts to, conceptions of rationality encoded in language and the nature of the evidence that would count as 'verbal deficit', not to mention confusion over the relationship between orality and literacy.[15] And these problems have to be adequately considered before we can even begin to worry about the nature, validity and warrant of whatever empirical evidence might be gathered.

Nevertheless, even when all these very considerable reservations about the possibilities of enquiry into teaching and learning have been quite properly taken into account, it remains the case that empirical enquiry is and always will be central to our ability to

---

[14] More recently, attempts have been made to circumvent these difficulties, but these attempts bring to the fore further difficulties about the conceptualisation of the relationship between heredity and environment (Shakeshaft *et al.* 2013; Rose 2014).

[15] See Winch (1990) for further discussion of intelligence and verbal deficit theories.

understand learning and teaching better. Why is this, and how can teachers equip themselves with useful knowledge of such matters? A starting point is to accept that in areas of human endeavour and relationships, understanding has to involve the supposition that the conceptual and the empirical are very closely related.

In other words, in order to understand the reasons that people have for their actions and their attitudes, we need to understand the concepts that lie behind them. It was already noted that there are differences in conceptions of education, and these differences affect the ways in which the central concepts of education are understood. We cannot assume, for example, that because we tend to identify education with formal schooling and conclude (in the main) that formal schooling is valuable in helping children to prepare for life, this is a view that would be shared by those who prefer (for very good reasons for them) to prepare their children for adult life through informal and participatory methods by working with adults in a form of apprenticeship, despite the fact that there is a formal requirement on their children to attend school. If we come across people who do this, then in order to understand their attitudes and actions concerning education, we need to engage with what they understand education to be and how it differs from how we take it to be. We simply cannot take it for granted either that their conceptions are the same as ours or that schooling plays the same role in their lives as it does in ours.

Such conceptual considerations do not receive sufficient attention in much empirical education research, and indeed more generally it is possible to maintain that insufficient attention is paid by researchers to the central concepts with which they work and of which they assume that they have a good grasp. If such considerations were taken more seriously, then there would be fewer problems with concepts such as *intelligence, verbal deficit, learning styles* and *development*, to take just a few examples from research in the twentieth century.

And yet, even when one has acknowledged all these points, it remains the case that empirical research is an important resource for teachers in gaining understanding of teaching and learning. Conceptual clarity is important, but in order to gain it, it is often necessary to conduct empirical enquiries into how people employ concepts and what they think they mean when they use them.[16] But when conceptual clarity is attained, there is still plenty of scope for investigating

---

[16] For examples relating to vocational education in Europe, see Brockmann *et al.* (2011).

for example the factors involved in difficulties in learning to read, or why some young people are reluctant to go to university. What the considerations above signify is, first, that some systematic empirical enquiries are enquiries into the ways in which concepts are employed and, second, that systematic enquiry cannot precede conceptual clarity but either has to seek to establish it or has to proceed only once it has been achieved. Such enquiries are potentially useful for teachers as they can help them to understand better the kinds of difficulties that their pupils may be facing in learning, whether these be intellectual, emotional or motivational. Whether or not teachers rely on such research, they still need such understandings and, as we saw, to rely on 'commonsense' will not be an acceptable substitute for systematic enquiry, not least because it is in many cases itself the result of simplified and badly digested empirical enquiry.

Having established the potential usefulness of empirical research, we can now ask whether or not it can actually be made use of by teachers in their work. And here too there are difficulties. If teachers are to use empirical research in the formation of their own judgements, then they need to be able to understand the research, what actions it is likely to warrant and how it applies to their own particular circumstances. In the case of the executive technician approach, this need not be a pressing issue as it will be the designers of the curriculum and pedagogy who will need to understand the research and then devise procedures for teachers to follow in order to realise the fruits of that research. And, as has already been pointed out, this is one possible way of realising the role of a teacher, and we will need to pay serious attention to its persuasiveness in Chapter 7.

For teachers who are technicians in the professional sense outlined in Chapters 4 and 8, however, their relationships with the relevant research will be much more intimate. They will need to understand it. This means that they will have to grasp the structure of the argument and the extent to which the conclusions rest reliably on the evidence and premises presented. In order to do this, they will need to grasp the research questions posed, the strategy employed to answer them and the particular methods used to answer those questions, which may often be technically quite demanding. It is likely that they will come across conflicting conclusions about particular topics (e.g. in the teaching of reading) and will find it difficult to choose between the competing conclusions of specialist researchers. They will also need to have a good appreciation of how such research might bear on their own particular circumstances as teachers and whether it bears on them and in what way. These are very significant demands to make of teachers, and the question has to be asked as to whether the challenge of doing so can be made less onerous than it appears in the remarks just offered.

Although empirical educational research is a comparatively young discipline and has suffered from excessive ideological influence and over-ambitious theory generation, a number of researchers have tried to make an assessment of what the cumulative nature of empirical research has to say to teachers and policymakers. This has been done through the creation of *metasurveys* of research into particular areas and even of *meta-metasurveys*, which attempt to provide a panoramic view of what cumulative research on a particular topic is able to say. Notable among these attempts is the work of John Hattie (2009), who has provided meta-metasurveys in a range of educational research, including the effects on learning of schools, teaching methods and teachers. School effects on learning are relatively modest in contrast to those provided by the quality of teaching methods and the quality of teachers.[17]

It is easy to be cynical about the findings of empirical research that tell us that effective schools are well-organised, assess well, are focussed on learning and so on, and that good teachers understand pupil difficulties and are well qualified. 'After all', it may be said, 'commonsense could tell us all this or maybe it is no more than tautological' (on school effectiveness research, see e.g. White 1997). My view is that this kind of response is much too glib. In the first place, as already noted, the deliverances of commonsense are often ideologically loaded and of dubious provenance. The second point is that such research is illuminating because, as well as suggesting what factors are effective it also indicates quite clearly what appears not to be effective, including some approaches that are fashionable and influential, such as neurologically based teaching (for a useful survey and critique, see Davis 2004) or the emphasis on learning styles (see also Coffield 2004). Third, we can learn where it may be more important to direct resources and efforts out of a range of possible alternatives. Thus, it may be more productive to concentrate on the selection and education of teachers rather than on internal school organisation and external inspection and other accountability measures. Fourth, and by no means least, learning which hypotheses and theories are almost certainly false is a hugely valuable outcome of educational research. If a theory P is known to be false, then its

---

[17]   OECD (2013a, 2013b).

contradictory not-P is known to be true.[18] Such results can be very important in clearing false and harmful theories out of the way of policymaking and teaching practice. Getting priorities wrong may lead to a massive misdirection of effort and inefficient use of resources. Such large-scale panoramic surveys of research have a potentially very useful role in helping us to determine where the thrust of policymaking and teacher effort ought to lie. It is certainly significant that the quality of teachers and their teaching rather than the organisation of schools, the alleged deficits of pupils and the adoption of particular kinds of teaching methods or of external accountability mechanisms seem to be of the greatest importance in promoting pupil learning. To claim that this is nothing more than 'commonsense' is to ignore the ways in which policy has been influenced by fashion and political prejudice (often masquerading as 'commonsense'), rather than by a careful and discriminating look at what the evidence seems to be suggesting.

So, such large-scale metasurvey work is potentially significant. But the fact is that it does not yield either teachers or education policymakers with ready-to-hand recipes for promoting effective education. Such metasurveys are, by their nature, large-scale in scope and general in their conclusions. They are of little value in, for example, enabling teachers to plan a good lesson. They can, however, direct attention in the direction most likely to bear fruit in effective teaching. It is the responsibility of university departments, research institutes and policymaking bodies to identify specific research within such large bodies of research that teachers can actually study with a view to understanding the nature of the processes by which, for example, certain teaching methods are effective. When they have looked at such research, teachers still have the responsibility for deciding whether it should impact on their own practice and, if so how, in their own particular circumstances, it should.[19] Whatever the quality of educational research, its quality cannot absolve teachers from establishing what its significance for their own practice is. This

---

[18] This case should be distinguished from one where a false theory does not necessarily validate a contrary theory (one that advances an incompatible but not comprehensive alternative to the one considered). In such cases, both P and its contrary, Q, may turn out to be false. For example, both Piagetian and Vygotskyan forms of developmentalism may turn out to be false. But if they are false, then we know that the negations of both Piagetian and Vygotskyan forms of developmentalism are true.

[19] It is also important to note that the efficacy of an educational intervention at place P does not provide an assurance that it will be efficacious at Q, since there may be variables operating at P unnoticed by the researchers that contribute to the efficacy of the intervention and are not present at Q.

has profound implications for the initial and continuing education of teachers, as we shall see in Chapter 10.

'A THEORY OF ONESELF' AS A TEACHER

The above section focussed particularly on the relevance of theory to practice. 'Theory' in this sense was seen as an objective and systematic set of claims (conceptual, normative or empirical, or all three) with a bearing on the conduct of teachers. I have argued that such theories are an important element in the knowledge of teachers. There is, however, a somewhat different kind of knowledge that is also important – a 'theory' of themselves as teachers. These two different kinds of theory are quite often confused with each other, particularly in some of the literature on the 'reflective practitioner' and 'reflective teacher'.[20] This literature has tended to take the concept of reflection ('What should I do?' 'What should I do next?' and 'Why did I do that?') as questions about the individual practitioner and their practice rather than as questions about the relationship between theory, the individual practitioner and their practice. The 'reflective cycle', as it is sometimes called, goes from practice to reflection on practice to further practice in a recursive three-stage pattern. If this is meant to be an account of the kind of thinking that conscientious teachers should be doing, then although it may well be necessary it cannot be sufficient, at least not for the conception of teacher that I have called the 'professional technician' (see Chapter 8). This version of the reflective cycle misses something that all technicians need to be able to do, namely to incorporate the theoretical underpinning of their occupation into their professional judgement and action. There is no doubt that they need to reflect on the relevance of that theory to their own personal practice, but reflection on theory needs to be a component of the reflective cycle.[21]

Having said this, however, the idea of reflection that focusses on the teacher's personal reflection *on their own practice* is very important. Teachers have their own capacities, limitations and potential for change. They need to know about themselves as teachers as well as about their subjects, their pupils and theories that may inform their practice. Such self-knowledge is not always easily come by.

---

[20] Cf. Schön (1987).

[21] Both in the sense that theory may inform *in situ* professional judgment (sometimes misleadingly called 'reflection in action') and in the sense that it may inform *post hoc* analysis with a view to improving practice 'reflection on action'. This is an important issue for the craft conception of teaching that will be further addressed in Chapter 6.

One needs not only to mature to acquire it, but also to have the relevant experiences (including significant experiences – in German *Erlebnisse* as well as *Erfahrungen*) to provide the material for such reflection. Such issues are the stuff of the traditional German *Bildungsroman* novel in which the hero acquires self-knowledge, including knowledge about himself as a practitioner, through extended occupational engagement.[22]

Teaching is a very demanding occupation, and the demands that it makes include those on the personal resources of individuals. It is well known that it poses particular challenges to the enthusiasm, self-confidence and resilience of teachers at different stages in their careers, and that in some countries, such as the UK and the US, the attrition rate from teaching is very high (more than 40% post qualification within five years in the UK).[23] Of course there are many different reasons for this, but one contributory factor one may assume with reasonable confidence is lack of preparation for the personal test that a career in teaching may be. The ability to reflect on one's own practice as a teacher in a positive way, in order to develop not just technical expertise but also enthusiasm and resilience through enhanced self-knowledge, is an important part of the knowledge, broadly conceived, that it is necessary for teachers to have.

CONCLUSION

There is no doubt that subject knowledge is important but not enough for effective teaching. Teachers need to combine panoramic subject knowledge with an epistemic perspective oriented towards pupil learning. They need to combine this with an appreciation of the kinds of problems that their pupils face in learning, which can be derived from pedagogic content knowledge, systematic knowledge about teaching and learning and personal experience, including personal self-knowledge. The knowledge needed by a good teacher is very complex.

---

[22] See Goethe, 'Wilhelm Meister's Lehrjahr', and Keller, 'Der Grüne Heinrich', as classic examples. More contemporary examples include Lenz, 'Die Klangprobe', and, in English, the ironic take on the *Bildungsroman* genre, Tolkien's 'The Hobbit'. For the philosophical background to the idea of *allgemeine Menschenbildung*, the Humboldtian conception of a form of education that facilitates both insertion into a socially valuable occupation and the continuing lifelong development of one's individuality, see Benner (2003) 'Wilhelm Humboldt's Bildungstheorie'.

[23] House of Commons (2010).

6

Teaching as a Craft Occupation

It is often said that teaching is a craft.[1] This claim commands widespread assent amongst teachers, politicians and the wider public. Furthermore, the craftworker is considered to be an exemplar of attention to quality, service to the public, personal satisfaction and the embodiment of tradition.[2] The teacher as craftworker can safely be seen as one of the three archetypes of the teacher described briefly in Chapter 4. Furthermore, it is perhaps the default conception of the teacher in recent philosophical treatments of the nature of teacher's work.[3]

It is reasonable to ask 'What is a craft?' in the relevant sense, since if we are not clear about that, then we will not make much progress. Craftwork is traditionally associated with small-scale commodity production by small, autonomous businesses and is usually thought to flourish in activities where large-scale industrial production either has not or cannot dominate. The typical mode of association is the craft guild, and the principal mode of reproduction is through a structure of apprentice, journeyman and master. Craftwork is principally associated with manufacture (e.g. the metalworking occupations) and to a lesser extent with services (butchers and bakers). Although the craftworker works with materials whose properties are apt for scientific investigation, which has the potential to drive

---

[1] For a recent influential example, see DfE (2010).
[2] Sturt (1923), Sennett (2008) and Crawford (2011).
[3] See D. Carr (2003), Barrow (1984), W. Carr (2004, 2005), and Dunne (1993) for different and sometimes opposing defences of this conception.

Teachers' Know-How: A Philosophical Investigation, First Edition. Christopher Winch.
© 2017 Christopher Winch. Editorial Organisation © Philosophy of Education Society of Great Britain.
Published 2017 by John Wiley & Sons, Ltd.

technological innovation, the craftworker in his pure form does not draw directly on such scientific knowledge,[4] nor does he particularly desire to do so. Craft knowledge is not systematically organised, does not apparently derive from scientific enquiry and is very often local rather than universal. It is transmitted informally within the workshop and within social activities connected with the craft. Thus, the type of knowledge that the craftworker relies on tends to be local and unsystematic (*Kenntnis* rather than *Wissen* in German), and the abilities of the craftworker have stronger affinities with the aesthetically attuned abilities of the artist rather than the technical abilities of the technical worker. Indeed, the artist and the craftworker were historically very closely aligned,[5] and part of the romantic appeal of the craftworker lies precisely in the strong association with aesthetically valuable creation.

One other feature of the craftworker needs to be mentioned. This is the requirement for the exercise of practical knowledge in a way that is alive to the particulars of the work situation: the materials, the needs of the client and indeed the mood of the craftworker. Associated with this is an ethic of concern for the reputation of the craft and the interests of the client, again situationally mediated.[6]

WHAT WOULD TEACHING LOOK LIKE AS A CRAFT?

On the face of it, teaching looks like an occupation ill-suited to the craft characterisation. We should bear in mind, however, that not all crafts are or were associated with manufacture. Socrates' comparison of the teacher with a midwife in *Meno* is a highly influential account of the teacher as a craftworker and, furthermore, one whose work is freighted with spiritual and religious significance. *Meno* stands near the beginning of a dominant philosophical tradition that sees the teacher as a special kind of craftworker. The material that the

---

[4] The qualification is necessary due to the possible indirect influence of science, mediated through commonsense (see Chapter 4). This is a significant issue for teaching. It is doubtful whether craftwork in a purely non-technical form can exist in a world where investigations into the properties of materials, which are the sphere of operation of the craftworker, are ubiquitous.

[5] See Cuomo (2007). See also Keller ([1854–1855] 1951) for an account of the close links between art and craft in the mid-nineteenth century in his autobiographical *Bildungsroman, Der Grüne Heinrich* (Green Henry).

[6] For more on this using the example of the monumental mason, see Lenz (1989). Adam Smith's famous passage on the self-love of the craftworker (*Wealth of Nations*, vol. 1) deliberately attempts to subvert this image by noting the self-love of the tradesman and conflating self-interest with self-love. See Lynch and Walsh (2003) for a much more nuanced treatment of the relationship between pride in work and commercial exigency.

teacher works on is the mind and soul of the pupil. His instrument is dialectic. Of course, the Socratic example is associated with the metaphysical doctrine of *metempsychosis* or the transmigration of souls. The model cannot work in quite the same way for the *didactic* rather than the *dialectical* teacher, that is, one who conveys subject knowledge or some specialised form of know-how.

However, with modification it can be made to work in a way that emphasises the aesthetic and spiritual nature of the occupation. In what follows, an attempt will be made to do so. It will be necessary to look more closely at the know-how involved in craft practice and in teaching conceived as a craft practice in particular. It is clear that craftworkers need a medium on which to work. We noted that paradigmatically this would be a material medium such as clay, wood or stone, but it could also include human material as people to be served or as, in the case of teaching, people to whom something (allegedly) beneficial was to be done. Work on the medium requires various kinds of know-how, which will almost certainly but not exclusively include skills of some kind. These are usually thought to be the skills of pedagogy, primarily those involved in interaction with the pupil (and in classical discussions, it does tend to be the pupil – including discussions such as those of Rousseau).[7] Secondarily, however, they involve the relationship with a class of pupils as well as with individuals within that class, and this is often seen as a form of management relationship, hence the popularity of 'classroom management' and of 'how to' books such as Michael Marland's *The Craft of the Classroom* (Marland 1975). As we shall see, however, to describe the pedagogical know-how (either of the tutor like Socrates or Rousseau or of the classroom teacher) only in terms of 'skills' is to seriously mistake what is involved. However, although there is agreement that 'skills' are not enough, there is little agreement on what else is needed.

As well as know-how, it is assumed that teachers have at their disposal another sort of material, that which they teach the pupil.[8] This is the subject matter and can be an academic subject or some form of know-how, perhaps also informed by academic knowledge. Once again, this is not particularly controversial. As we have noted, however, the two dimensions of subject knowledge that we noted in Chapter 4 are not so frequently noticed, and it is often assumed by

---

[7] See Rousseau (1762a) for a somewhat different variant of the Socratic approach. See Pestalozzi for an adaptation of Rousseuvian pedagogy for mass education (Pestalozzi [1801] (1915).

[8] See the discussion of 'to teach' as a triadic relationship in Chapter 1.

the proponents of teaching as a craft that the aspect of subject knowledge considered from the point of view of presenting the subject to the pupils is something that can be acquired 'on the job' through experience and the drawing on of one's expert grasp of the subject as a whole. Given, though, that such insight often arises from epistemological reflection on the nature of one's subject, it would be surprising if this would be so without some ability to make sense of the subject matter from the point of view of the pupil and we can be reasonably sure that experience alone would not allow for this, without the ability to reflect and act on the problems with learning the subject that pupils may experience.

Know-How, Skill and Phronesis in Teaching
It will be helpful to look more closely at the know-how involved, first in the classroom and second in more institutionally and temporally extended dimensions. Like nearly all crafts, teaching involves the use of *techniques*, usually as a component of skills. A way of doing something, such as getting a class to sit in an orderly manner, is conducted in the 'operational conditions' pertaining to classroom teaching (e.g. there are 35 pupils, and they have just come in from a wet and windy playground at 3 p.m. on Friday afternoon). The skill consists in applying the relevant technique in the range of conditions that obtain in that school.[9] These skills and their proper exercise are enormously important elements in the repertoire of successful teachers, and it is no exaggeration to say that without their mastery, the lives of many teachers would be intolerable and their attempts at teaching ineffectual.

However, as has been observed many times before, successful teaching does not consist in the deployment of batteries of skills. Why? Because, as already argued, the aim of teaching is to enable pupils to learn what the teacher intends that they should learn, and the success criterion has to consist (except in unusual circumstances) in ensuring that at least a good proportion do actually learn what it is intended that they should learn. The problem here is that a teacher could successfully practice the battery of skills required for successful teaching and still fail to meet this condition. Possessing the requisite skills in keeping order, presenting material, sequencing a lesson and wrapping things up in time are all necessary but taken together are not sufficient for successful teaching.

---

[9] For more on the technique–skill distinction, see Winch (2013c).

One solution to this puzzle is to maintain that no teacher is successfully teaching unless all the pupils learn what they are supposed to learn.[10] But this seems implausible, precisely because of the operational conditions in which most teachers have to work. It is impossible to guarantee complete success in teaching, even for the most expert and conscientious teachers. Too many unexpected events may take place; the waywardness of pupils cannot be adequately controlled for. We can expect, however, that teachers approach their work with seriousness and attention and make use of all the skills that are relevant to teach successfully. How should we understand this? Key to doing so are some concepts that are closely related to the concept of education but intimately related to schooling. These include: *lessons, terms, the school year, the syllabus* and *assessment.* Teachers work within a conceptual framework that requires that they have to *plan* lessons and extended sequences of work; they have to constantly *communicate, co-ordinate, control* and *evaluate*, not only within individual lessons and in relation to pupils, but also in the longer sequences in which the lessons make sense, with colleagues and parents as well. Their work depends not only on successfully negotiating the classroom second by second and minute by minute, but also in controlling extended syllabi and schemes of work within a school year and possibly beyond.

These activities – *planning, communicating, co-ordinating, controlling, evaluating* and others – are not to be identified with skills, although they need to be realised through the exercise of some skills, not necessarily the same ones in each instance. As already noted, one can exercise skills of planning, evaluating and so on, going through the motions of planning and evaluating but not actually doing so. If one does not approach the work of teaching with the necessary attention and seriousness, then one will not successfully teach but will only 'go through the motions' of doing so. One can plan a lesson in a book, even specifying what is going to happen minute by minute. But if the lesson itself follows no plan, then one cannot meaningfully be said to be capable of planning a lesson, as that will require that one is able to see the plan successfully through in the great majority of cases. The same point goes for the other 'adverbial verbs' of communicating, co-ordinating, controlling and evaluating.[11] Someone who

---

[10] See Kleinig (1982) for an approach along these lines.

[11] It is important to realise that the need to plan and so on is not peculiar to teaching or even just to other professions, but is an essential attribute of autonomous working (for the case of bricklaying, see Brockmann *et al.* 2010).

can successfully teach can demonstrably do all of these things over extended sequences such as the extent of a syllabus or a school year in the kinds of operational conditions that teachers face. It will be part of our criteria for success that most pupils learn much of what they are supposed to learn most of the time.[12] What we are looking for, however, is not a particular proportion, much less 100% of the material, 100% of the time with 100% of the pupils, but rather devotion, attention and seriousness in relation to the business in hand, realised in long-term success over the duration of a syllabus, a term or a school year. In this sense, teachers are managers of relatively long-term projects rather than executors of short-term tasks, even though successful tackling of the latter is important in the realisation of the former.

THEORY IN CRAFT INCLUDING EPISTEMIC ASCENT

As already noted, craftwork is not generally thought to involve the implementation of a theory in practice. The knowledge applied in a craft is generally non-systematic and local. It is transmitted in communities and workplaces, and acquired both informally and non-formally.[13] The craftworker is not expected to formally demonstrate that knowledge but to express it in action and explanation where necessary. Although this is an 'ideal type' of craft knowledge, it is important to remember that it exists and has existed for hundreds of years in an environment where systematic enquiry into the subjects relevant to the carrying out of the craft has been carried out. It is, therefore, not realistic to expect that some informal or unacknowledged influence of such enquiry has not seeped into the understanding of craftworkers and informed their practice, even though they may not be aware of the provenance of such knowledge.

Teaching raises these issues in a particular form. First is through the centrality of subject knowledge to the occupation and the need to organise it in an appropriate form for pupils. Second is in the views that teachers have on pedagogy and the capacity for learning of pupils. In both these areas, the results of plenty of systematic enquiry

---

[12] What that minimum proportion should be is something that should be (and often is) determined in relation to local circumstances.

[13] See, for example, the account in Sturt (1923). 'Non-formally' means that there may be instructional, training or demonstrative sequences in or near the workplace. 'Informally' means incidentally through observation and imitation and perhaps instruction during the course of work (see UNESCO 2012).

are available, whatever one may think of its value. This means that teachers need to adopt an attitude towards it. In the craft conception of teaching, it will be that such enquiries are largely irrelevant, since the relevant knowledge for teachers will be that of their subject. Their ability to devise appropriate teaching techniques and to judge the learning capacities of their pupils will be acquired through informal and non-formal learning. It is assumed, therefore, on the craft conception that such learning of non-systematic knowledge, perhaps directly embodied in the form of practical know-how, is superior to the results of whatever systematic enquiry might be available.

This does, however, raise a danger, because one is assuming that teaching can be practised as a craft while at the same time the elements of theory of teaching are widely available and indeed widely disseminated. What one learns informally has a provenance, and this may well be the result of the distillation into 'commonsense' in Gramsci's sense of various theoretical claims. Since the believer in such claims will quite likely be unaware of their provenance and how they may have been transformed in transmission, there is a strong danger that they will not be able to mount a critique of them, since they do not have available the systematic basis of what has been offered to them. It might be replied that this does not matter, since they will be able to test such propositions against the reality of the classroom. However, it is quite plausible to suggest that such beliefs have a propensity to be self-fulfilling, particularly in the light of evidence that pupils often respond to the expectations of their teachers in a way that is congruent with those expectations (Mackay 2007; Hattie 2009). If this is the case, and there are grounds to suggest that this is often so, then we cannot rely on teachers to critically assess theory in an informal way. One could go further and suggest that relying on such critique risks damaging the education of pupils through the transmission of inappropriate and harmful prejudices. Even those responsible for constructing theories of teaching and learning may be in the thrall of such prejudices themselves.[14]

A similar point can be made about pedagogic content knowledge (PCK). Although, on the craft view, it is the teacher's responsibility to reconfigure their subject knowledge into a form suitable for teaching, there is theoretical work aplenty available as to how this should be done, which can become transmitted informally into PCK. It might be held by a history teacher, for example, on the basis of

---

[14] For a good example in relation to the concept of intelligence, see Gould (1984).

an understanding of Piagetian developmental theory, that children under 15 are not capable of understanding historical events beyond the near past. As argued in Chapter 5, a grasp of Epistemic Ascent (a major component of PCK) depends on a critical approach to epistemological considerations in one's subject, and it is inappropriate to informally adopt precepts on such matters without critical reflection.

PRACTICAL KNOWLEDGE IN TEACHING

Such considerations bring us directly back to a consideration of the nature and role of practical knowledge in teaching. We have already argued that we need to conceive teachers' practical knowledge within the craft conception of teaching in a generous way and include transversal and project management abilities in the overall conception. But how does the craft teacher deploy practical knowledge in a way different from that of the technician teacher?

A useful starting point for considering this issue is the work of Michael Oakeshott in his influential essay 'Rationalism in Politics'.[15] Oakeshott opens his discussion by considering a distinction between two kinds of know-how: technical knowledge and practical knowledge. Technical knowledge involves the mastery of rule-based procedures on the analogy of recipes, while practical knowledge involves the ability to implement procedures with sensitivity to the situational and practical constraints of the locus of operation. It is learned through practice, ideally in operational situations, rather than through formal instruction. Understood in this way, and as Oakeshott himself expresses the matter, technical and practical knowledge are complementary.[16]

Seen thus, Oakeshott's account looks like a sophisticated attempt to show how theory needs to be mediated by situational and practical considerations if it is to be successfully applied along the lines of a technical enterprise or occupation. However, Oakeshott develops his argument in a different direction with a detailed account of the nature of politics as a practice. It is evident from Oakeshott's discussion that politics is a practical occupation that has no need for technical knowledge, but is pre-eminently a sphere in which practical

---

[15] First published in 1946. Available in *Rationalism in Politics* (Oakeshott 1962).

[16] Oakeshott (1962, pp. 7–9). See also the detailed and extensive discussion of the relationship between *techne* and *phronesis* in Dunne (1993, ch. 8), which makes a similar point to Oakeshott's and argues that despite some variation, this was also the predominant view of Aristotle. As the reader probably realises, Oakeshott's distinction is partly a reworking of Aristotle's.

knowledge should hold sway. Indeed, Oakeshott asserts that it is mistaken to think that 'rationalism', the putting into effect of theories, has any place in political practice, and to think that it does is likely to lead to disastrous results. Whatever the truth or otherwise of this assertion, it is clear that Oakeshott's discussion has taken a significant turn at this point. At the outset of his article, technical and practical knowledge are seen to be complementary. Subsequently, and in relation to politics, they are seen to be incompatible (Oakeshott 1962, esp. pp. 22–23). The interesting point for this discussion is whether or not teaching should be seen as a practice similar to what Oakeshott claims politics to be.

In effect, the craft conception of teaching asserts that this is the case. Teaching is not a technical occupation, and practical knowledge is the core of a teacher's know-how. To assert otherwise and to see technical and practical knowledge as complementary is to admit that the teacher is a professional technician (see Chapter 8). As a corollary of this view, educational theory has no role to play in the work of teachers. This is a view widely held within the philosophy of education, but I will take the view of Wilfred Carr as perhaps the most fully articulated explanation.

Carr argues that education (and, by implication, teaching) is a practice whose development is largely autonomous in the sense that it generates and solves its own problems from within, rather than from outside practice, and therefore has no need of a theoretically inspired set of problems. Teachers have to attend to their own development and the problems that they encounter through reflection on their practice. Professional growth is thus described as *phronesis* or ethically informed situated judgement, for which experience and the capacities for observation, reflection and modelling are both necessary and sufficient. It follows that a theoretical basis for reflection such as philosophy does not have a role to play in the development of such reflective abilities. This is obviously true of the deliverances of analytical philosophy, whose results are simply irrelevant to educational practice as they are concerned with theory rather than practice (e.g. W. Carr 2005, p. 624). There is, however, an important qualification. Practical philosophy, however, as a tool of philosophical reflection on practical issues, has, Carr maintains, been largely discarded and its obvious relevance to teachers discounted. But:

> Teaching practitioners to confront the limits of their own self-understanding in this way is the central task of practical philosophy. (W. Carr 2004, p. 62)

It is not clear from Carr's writing what practical philosophy consists of. For example, he does not mean analytical reflection on practical problems. There is, however, potentially an important insight in Carr's argument, namely that conceptual abilities can be brought to bear on the resolution of normative and practical questions in education. But if this is the case, it is hard to see how this could be done without some knowledge of philosophy, which cannot itself be gained through practice. The ability to reflect philosophically on one's occupation necessitates as a minimum a grasp of the conceptual field of education and teaching and an understanding that there are different and often contested interpretations of that field. It is hard to see how teachers, on Carr's conception of the occupation, could get by without an understanding of what such terms as *values*, *aims*, *curriculum*, *pedagogy* and *assessment* broadly mean. Unless they have such an understanding, they cannot engage in debates or reflection about different possible interpretations of such terminology. It is hard to see therefore how teachers could meaningfully reflect on the problems of their practice without some form of philosophical education.

The second claim is that empirical educational research is unreliable and, by implication, irrelevant (e.g. Barrow 1984; Barrow in Barrow and Foreman-Peck 2005). This is a dominant theme in the arguments of proponents of the craft conception of teaching. The claim rests on two arguments. The first is that much educational research is of poor quality, unreliable and therefore false. The second is that, however good it is, the findings of educational research are always defeasible and therefore cannot give the certainty that teachers need.[17]

The first argument is plausible in the sense that much educational research is and has been of poor quality. The answer is not to abandon it but to improve its quality. We know that careful analyses of research of the kind conducted by Hattie (2009) can give us a good idea of what has and what has not been achieved. Such meta-analyses, properly conducted, can point teachers and teacher educators in the direction of what is worthwhile. The second argument is also based on a true premise. Of course, educational research is defeasible. We cannot hope to attain certainty in most empirical enquiries, nor should we aspire to do so in educational research. This

---

[17] 'One should never act on a generalisation' (see Barrow 1976). This is self-refuting as a strictly universal proposition. It is anyway unwise to treat empirical generalisations such as those found in empirical educational research as if they were strict universal generalisations.

does not, however, make it irrelevant or useless. It reminds us that there can only be probability, not certainty, in this area.[18]

One might, however, press the issue further. If the opponent of any educational research is saying that its findings can all be shown to be false, then that is an important result since it follows that its contradictory is true (see discussion in Chapter 5). When an empirical claim or theory is shown to be false, then that is a significant advance in our understanding. The claim that they *could* be false is, however, not particularly useful without the presentation of substantive reasons, such as for example, falling below threshold standards of research quality. It gains conviction by an illegitimate conflation of empirical universal statements with their logical equivalents in formal logical doctrine. When the claim:

1. All As are Bs

is made as a result of an empirical investigation, it is invariably made with a rider concerning the degree of certainty with which it is to be taken, usually a certain level of probability. Very often as well, it is understood implicitly that there are certain contexts where the generalisation might not apply. But this is not what is meant by (1) in a logic textbook. For (1) to be false in that reading is simply for there to be a single negative counter-instance of the consequent, such as an example of a A that is not B. This, of course, is the basis of Popperian falsificationism. But it is wrong to think of the generalisations of empirical educational theory in this way. They are nearly always defeasible, and the conditions of their possible defeat need to be understood before they can be properly interpreted.[19] But all that this means is that the scope and limits of empirical educational research need to be properly understood by teachers as well as by those who critique and comment on research.

If this is the case, then the kind of phronesis-based craft conception of teaching, advocated by W. Carr and with somewhat different emphases by D. Carr, is not adequate for dealing with the deliverances, however imperfect they are, of educational theory in general and educational research in particular. By setting the bar for probity of research too high, they unjustifiably dismiss all of it, rather than

---

[18] See Aristotle (1925, bk. 1, ch. 3) on degrees of precision.
[19] And it follows, of course, that authors of such research need to make these defeasibility conditions clear.

those findings about which it is entirely justified to exercise scepticism. Whether craft teachers like it or not, theory has a role to play in their working lives. It is better that this role receives due acknowledgement rather than that it slips unacknowledged through the back door of the teacher's awareness and affects their work and attitudes willy-nilly through commonsense assimilation within the staffroom, through other informal channels or through popularisations in the educational or general press. For this reason, an acquaintance with standards and justifiable warrant within educational research is a necessary part of the intellectual equipment of teachers.

D. Carr, W. Carr and others also quite rightly emphasise the importance of a conceptual sensibility if teachers are going to engage in productive reflection on their work. But, as in the case of empirical theory, the ability to undertake worthwhile conceptual reflection on teaching cannot be acquired informally. While it is not desirable to dogmatically transmit philosophical theses about education (see Chapter 1), the ability to engage with educational issues in a philosophical way demands a certain degree of formal philosophical engagement either in initial teacher education or at an early stage in teachers' careers. Without some philosophical education about the practice of education, they will not normally have the resources to do so on their own. Neither will they be in a strong position to react to the deliverances of educational research, whether speculative or empirical, without having the critical faculties to make sense of it, appraise it and understand its scope and limits. The idea of teaching without theory of any kind, except that which is generated directly out of reflection on action, which seems to be central to the full-blooded craft conception of teaching, is unlikely to be functional in the conditions in which contemporary teachers working in the state systems in developed countries operate.

PHRONESIS AND ETHICAL CONSIDERATIONS IN TEACHING: A THEORY OF ONESELF

The above arguments have rejected some of the claims of the craft conception. It is a very different matter to seek to dismiss any craft elements from teaching, and that is not the aim of this chapter (see Chapter 8 for a fuller account of the craft elements in a more professionally oriented conception of teaching). However supportive or sceptical one might be about the benefits of educational theory, it remains the case that teachers do, as W. Carr and many other commentators have noted, need to reflect on their own experiences as teachers and to seek to make sense of them. They need to do this in order to develop the self-knowledge, resilience and enhanced expertise that they will need in order to have successful careers as teachers. There are two issues to be considered here: one is the development of *phronesis*, and the other is the development of self-knowledge. The two are closely connected.

We should envisage the deployment of Oakeshottian practical knowledge to be informed with a moral sensibility. Teaching, in common with many other occupations, has a significant moral dimension. It is difficult to peel apart the 'technical' situational judgements that teachers have to make as an element of their practical knowledge from the moral environment in which they operate. In addition, teachers are called upon to deal with situations in which the moral element is not just latent but actually dominant. Given the complexity and variety of the situations that teachers have to confront, that moral dimension cannot usually be seen as a matter of applying universal principles to particular situations without at the same time taking into account the particularity of those situations.

This particularistic sensibility is also part of a larger moral order within which teachers operate, which is partly formed by the principles, formal or informal, of the professional ethics under which they operate and also of the values which they espouse and those of the education system for which they work. The fact that these personal values and those of their education system are not always in alignment presents a considerable complication of this story, which is ripe for further investigation but which cannot be pursued here.[20] It is important, however, that the values that are relevant to teaching are not just those of the teacher, but those that underpin the education system (see Chapter 1), and the possibilities of disharmony between the two needs to be seriously considered when we look at the ways in which teachers see their own role.

It is often said that teachers need to reflect on their own practice, and this is not usually denied to the craft teacher. What, however, does the teacher reflect on? I will leave for the moment the confusing notion of 'reflection in practice', which I will take to be a way of pointing to teachers' ability to make situational judgements within the constraints of classroom practice. 'Reflection' is probably the wrong word for this kind of ability, particularly when it is supposed to take place in the course of what Beckett and Hager call 'hot action'.[21]

---

[20] See Cribb (2011).
[21] Beckett and Hager (2002).

This is more like the ability to make good judgements in the course of fast-moving and complex situations, which is, in any case, the characteristic ability of the 'professional', albeit in the case of the professional, classically conceived, drawing on appropriate theory to assist in making such judgements. More important for our purposes is the ability to reflect in relative tranquillity on what has gone on and how and why one has acted, and the lessons that may be drawn for the future from such reflection.

This ability, which might be described as a central element of the search for professional and personal self-knowledge, is quite distinct conceptually from the ability to reflect on the relevance of theoretical considerations for one's practice, although in practice the two may not be so easily distinguishable. This kind of reflection is personal: it concerns how *you* as an individual human being, who is also a teacher, come to understand yourself as a teacher, what your strengths are, where you need to learn, how you see your career developing and what ultimately is the role that teaching is going to play in your life. It goes without saying that the ability to ask these questions of oneself is important for someone who intends to make teaching a career; it is much less important for someone who envisages nothing more than a fleeting engagement with teaching. However, it may be that a recently qualified teacher might, on reflection, conclude that teaching was not for him or her and decide to leave the profession. This is an important consideration, and its relevance to the profession is reflected in the very high rates of attrition that are found in some countries such as the UK.[22] It is also highly relevant both to the selection of teachers for teacher education programmes and to their progress through them, as it is obviously desirable that the discovery that they are not suitable should be made sooner rather than later in their careers. However, acquiring resources that allow them to engage in critical self-reflection on their professional life is also important in initial teacher education in order to develop resilience and the ability to learn productively from key experiences within one's professional life. There is a good case to be made out that although much of this needs to be done in the course of work, the realisation that it is something necessary that needs to be done and provision of some preparation for doing it ought to take place before full entry into the profession and ideally during the very earliest phases of working within classroom conditions.

---

[22] House of Commons (2010).

There is a deeply personal aspect to the process of developing and maturing as a teacher and to the accompanying growth of practical wisdom and moral sensibility. The craft conception of teaching is correct in emphasising the crucial importance of this. However, teaching is more complicated than the craft conception is prepared to allow, and for this reason a way must be found of incorporating its insights into a conception that takes better account of the objective conditions in which teachers operate.

These conditions consist first in the conceptual field. Although educational reality is 'concept-dependent',[23] it is, nevertheless, an objective reality shared by those within and affected by the practice. The fact that there are often differing interpretations of the nature of that reality is a complicating factor, but not one that gives any warrant for dismissing the objective nature of the world in which teachers operate.[24] It serves, however, to pose a further level of challenge to the understanding that teachers have of their job and, in particular, of the ways in which they interact with pupils, parents and the wider society.

HOW SUBJECT KNOWLEDGE MIGHT INFORM CRAFT EXPERTISE

Teaching conceived as a craft differs from other crafts because the teacher brings their subject knowledge to the situation as the material to be taught to the pupil, and which the pupil must learn. It is assumed that teachers have acquired subject knowledge through formal education, at school or at university. They have become subject experts who have a good overview of their subject in the panoramic sense. Typically, they will not be active researchers within the subject and will be generalists in the sense that they have covered a wide syllabus and have undertaken a limited number of specialisms. They will have the intellectual equipment to acquire further specialist knowledge within the subject.

They will not, however, unless they have picked it up informally, have acquired PCK. This, as we saw in Chapter 5, is subject

---

[23] Cf. McNaughton (1988) and Searle (1995) for examples of philosophers who discuss the conceptual dependence of our moral and social understanding, respectively.

[24] The different ways in which different individuals (often in different roles) interpret this reality is closely related to the kind of permanent aspect-seeing described, for example, in Mulhall (1990). It does not imply a 'phenomenological' approach to educational reality in which there co-exist multiple and incompatible educational realities differentiated according to the different role-position of the individual. See Pring 2015 for a good discussion of this issue.

knowledge reconfigured to take account of the learning needs of pupils, a very significant component of which will include an understanding of Epistemic Ascent within the subject. If PCK were to be acquired through formal means, then it would have to be done through a teacher education programme of some kind. From the point of view of purist advocates of the craft conception, this would involve an unacceptable intrusion of educational theory into the formation of the teacher as craftworker. If the argument of Chapter 5 is right, the panoramic and the learner-oriented conceptualisations of a subject are distinct. One can have the panoramic view without the learner-oriented view, although it is difficult to conceive the contrary case, where the learner-oriented view can be acquired without the panoramic perspective. The informal alternative, whereby PCK is acquired through practice, is taken to be unproblematic or perhaps even automatic by some craft advocates.[25] However, no arguments or evidence have ever been produced that such knowledge is automatically acquired by the holder of a panoramic perspective. We are left, therefore, with a type of knowledge acquired experientially.

Although PCK is described as a type of knowledge, and although some form of ordering of subject knowledge is clearly implied by both the idea of the subject seen from a learner's perspective and the idea of Epistemic Ascent, ultimately PCK is a practical ability, demonstrated in a teacher's ability to present the subject in a favourable way for the pupil to begin to acquire a panoramic perspective on it, or to acquire mastery of the know-how involved. Whether or not there is a propositional or conceptual background to PCK is incidental to its manifestation in practical pedagogic ability. To suppose the contrary is to fall back on a discredited theoretical view of teachers' abilities, which suggests that they consist in being able to give an account of what they would do, rather than actually doing it (see Bengson and Moffett 2011).

It is worth putting this contention to the test, taking the example of the teaching of reading, one of the fundamental practical subjects that all primary school teachers have to ensure that their pupils have mastered. Clearly, they will have mastered the 'subject knowledge' in this instance: they will be able to read fluently and carry out a number of 'higher order' reading tasks.[26] Such fluency means that whatever technique they used to learn to read will have become automatic, and its precise nature probably long forgotten. Teachers will have

[25] DfE (2011).
[26] Beard (1990, chs. 7, 8) and Fairbairn and Winch (1996, 1.2).

acquired these abilities in a variety of ways, but they will be charged with teaching reading to children with a wide variety of abilities and backgrounds. What, then, is the nature of the PCK that the teacher can develop through classroom experience?

It is difficult to see how teachers could choose the methods of teaching reading appropriate to each child through experiential considerations alone. To take an example of children experiencing difficulties in learning to read, who are probably the ones with whom teachers will be most concerned, there will be a need to diagnose the difficulties that they are facing before developing a teaching strategy that will enable them to overcome those difficulties. In order to do this, teachers need to take into account at least two sets of factors. The first is broadly *linguistic* and includes an appreciation of the differences between the oral and written media, together with the phonological and graphological particularities of the target language. The second set of factors concerns the ways in which children learn to read (which is, of course, intimately related to the first set). The academic literature in both these areas makes it clear that they are highly complex and that there have been lively debates, as well as a growing body of reliable knowledge, both about the nature of the oral–literary distinction and about methods of learning to read. A key element in a teacher's success in teaching a child to read will be the diagnosis of what the difficulties experienced by the child are, and how to frame and execute plans of action that will overcome those difficulties. It is difficult to see how a teacher could become effective solely through the experience of teaching reading, even if she were to reflect deeply on her experiences in doing so. There is a hard-won and organised body of knowledge in both the areas described that has taken thousands of researchers many decades to acquire. To suppose that a teacher could, on her own through a process of reflection, come to grasp the most important elements in such complex bodies of knowledge is simply not credible. It is undoubtedly true that the teacher's own experience of the teaching of reading will be most important in acquiring her own PCK, but no serious case can be made out for claiming that the experience will, by itself, be sufficient.

At the very least, this example shows the dangers of leaving the acquisition of PCK to chance. A craft advocate might reply that the teaching of reading is not a typical case and that there are far fewer problems with the teaching of mathematics, science or history, for example. But this will need to be demonstrated; it cannot simply be asserted. Naturally, the problems of acquiring a form of PCK that is suited to children and young people who generally do not experience great difficulties in learning is going to be less than it is for those who work in complex and challenging educational environments. But the lack of difficulties that the former face should not be used as a reason for neglecting the needs of the latter.

CONCLUSION: WHAT A CRAFT-BASED TEACHING FORCE MIGHT LOOK LIKE

There can be no doubt that one can construct a 'good enough' teaching force on the craft model if one is not aiming for uniformly high achievement across the full ability range of pupils. Those who become teachers on the craft conception will probably be recruited directly by the schools who employ them and will be trained according to the needs and the peculiarities of the school or group of schools.[27] Ideally, they will be mentored in a 'community of practitioners' with someone who will attend to their learning needs. Experience will be, however, the main teacher, and they will need well-developed powers of reflection in order to profit from that experience to become expert teachers themselves. But, they will become teachers for the school in which they have been recruited and trained. They will not necessarily be able to adapt to the very different environments that other schools may offer. The craft-based teaching force will have a strong tendency to be a school-based teaching force rather than a national one. That in itself would be a major cause for concern in a state-regulated national education system.

---

[27] In England, this scenario may well come to fruition if the recommendations of DfE (2016) are put into effect through legislation.

7

The Teacher as Executive Technician, or the Temptations of 'Teacher Proof' Teaching

INTRODUCTION: DISTINCTION BETWEEN TECHNICIAN AND EXECUTIVE TECHNICIAN CLARIFIED

We now turn to the next character in the three-part typology of teachers and teaching – the executive technician. In order to understand the executive technician, it is necessary to clarify the word 'technician'. In the English context, the term 'technician' is used disparagingly when applied to teachers, as in 'the National Curriculum reduced teachers from professionals to mere technicians', a complaint often heard around 1988, the year of the Education Reform Act. Such sayings contrast the professional with the technician. However, the sociological literature on the professions often describes those who work in the professions as 'technicians', by which is meant that they are a species of workers who apply theory (often abstract, complex and difficult to acquire) to practice in fields such as medicine and the law. If teachers are indeed technicians in this sense, then they would have at their disposal a body of theory (which could include normative theory, such as a curriculum) that is to be applied in practice.[1] But very often, teachers and commentators who complain that teachers have been reduced to technicians do not believe that there is or could be an underpinning theory that governs teaching; they are objecting to the loss of the craft status of teaching.

But this raises the intriguing question as to why this loss of craft status is bemoaned, when the status of professional in the

---

[1] See Shulman (1986) on curriculum theory.

Teachers' Know-How: A Philosophical Investigation, First Edition. Christopher Winch.
© 2017 Christopher Winch. Editorial Organisation © Philosophy of Education Society of Great Britain.
Published 2017 by John Wiley & Sons, Ltd.

sociologist's sense promises to raise teachers to the position of the more established professions. The reason is that many teachers (and, as we saw in the previous chapter, several prominent commentators) do not believe that teaching either can or should be underpinned by theory. But they are not complaining either that teaching is losing its craft status through being underpinned by theory, since they do not believe that reforms like the National Curriculum provide teaching with a theory. So what is the objection to reforms that, like the National Curriculum, circumscribe the actions of teachers with a normative theory?

In order to understand this properly, we need to consider how theory is used in professional contexts. A theory θ should be capable of generating prescriptions or rules ρ which, when followed, result in practice π. Such a sequence is often described (and decried) as 'technical rationality'. Why should it be decried? The answer is that the move from θ to π via ρ is assumed to be unmediated by any craft knowledge or ability or, indeed, any situational judgement whatsoever. θ generates ρ, whose application leads to π without any mediating influence. But why should anyone think this? After all, Oakeshott, the scourge of technical rationality, argued in 'Rationalism in Politics' that there was a distinction between technical and practical knowledge (Oakeshott 1962). Technical knowledge is the know-how that enables the transition from θ to π. By itself, it is limited in effect and is in danger of becoming recipe-following, in effect relying on the ρ-to-π transition alone. But practical knowledge is supposed to mediate this transition by subjecting the application of prescriptions to situational constraints in which craft-style judgement becomes operative.[2] So technical knowledge and practical knowledge in Oakeshott's sense need not be incompatible, but should be complementary.

> These two sorts of knowledge, then, distinguishable but inseparable, are the twin components of knowledge involved in every concrete human activity. In a practical art, such as cookery, nobody supposes that the knowledge that belongs to a good cook is confined to what is or may be written in a cookery book; technique and what I have called practical knowledge combine to make skill in cookery wherever it exists. (Oakeshott 1962, p. 8)

---

[2] In Chapter 8, we will consider the transition from θ to π, but this is not the appropriate place in the discussion.

So why has this erroneous conception come about? In part, Oakeshott and others are themselves responsible. Oakeshott is primarily concerned with the practice of politics, hence the title of his influential article, and apparently thinks that politics is a form of pure craft activity that might become recipe-following when pursued by the inexperienced, but which even then needs an experienced prince or his vizier to help the fledgling prince interpret whatever recipes, such as 'The Prince' by Machiavelli, are available.[3] Whether or not we agree with Oakeshott about the role of theory in politics, the shift in the discussion, from consideration of activities that may require a mix of technical and practical knowledge to one that Oakeshott holds to be best practiced without theory, has had the unfortunate effect of leading commentators to think that technical and practical knowledge are incompatible with each other within the same activity.[4, 5] But there is no good reason for supposing this, and hence the claim is somewhat puzzling.

THE ALLURE OF THE EXECUTIVE TECHNICIAN: 'TEACHER PROOFING' DEFECTIVE CRAFT PRACTICES

The teacher whose role is to put into effect rules for classroom practice, without consultation of the theory that generated the rules in the first place, I call an 'executive technician' (an ET). In effect, an ET takes rules ρ and puts them into practice π without any mediation of theory θ. The overall model is based on *subsumptive reasoning*.[6] The ET applies norms, broadly speaking, on a *subsumptive* model. That is, the general form of the relationship between the action of the ET

---

[3] Oakeshott takes Machiavelli's 'The Prince' as his example of such a political recipe book. Even in Machiavelli's case, however, the recipes of statecraft do not derive from an *a priori* theory but from generalisations from experience.

[4] See also the discussion in Lave and Wenger (1991) on learning through legitimate peripheral participation. Dunne's commentary on Aristotle's treatment of techne and phronesis moves along similar lines to the early part of Oakeshott's discussion, but the conclusions drawn by some commentators appear to be that the two are incompatible.

[5] As pointed out in the previous chapter, it is important to distinguish between practical knowledge in Oakeshott's sense, which refers to the ability to make discretionary judgements appropriate to singular situations, with *phronesis*, which refers to that ability in the context of the practice of the virtues. Not all exercises of practical knowledge involve the virtues, and the latter are themselves, when practised, aspects of actions rather than a distinct species of action (see Winch 2010a, ch. 4).

[6] See Westphal (2011) for this term.

and the underpinning theoretical model that validates that action is as follows:

In situations of Type A, actions of Type F are called for.
This is a situation of Type A.
Therefore: Action of Type F is called for.[7]

In other words, the practical syllogism through which one's professional action is channelled leaves no discretion at the margins for situational judgement. The ET has to judge that he or she is indeed in situation A,[8] but having done so, selection of the action is automatic. But it is obvious that the subsumptive model of technical rationality contradicts a 'pure' version of the craft conception, as it is a central characteristic of the former that the core of professional activity involves the agent making situational judgements suited to the particular circumstances in which the agent finds himself.

The ET is, of course, an ideal type, like the craftworker of the previous chapter. However, he is also considered to be a desirable type of teacher by many policymakers, both in developing and developed countries. Why is this? There are two main reasons. The first, from the point of view of the policymaker concerned with the inadequacies of a craft-based teaching force, is to remedy the effects of poor craftsmanship by binding teachers firmly into practices that have a clear theoretical warrant. One does not need to convert the craftworker into a professional technician, an expensive, lengthy and unreliable process, but one can capture the advantages of the professional technician by, in effect, outsourcing the derivation of rules for practice from theory (the θ–ρ transition) to researchers or technologists of pedagogy whose specialism is to interrogate pedagogic theory in order to derive appropriate practice. 'Pedagogic Taylorism' thus conceived allows the relatively inexpensive and rapid conversion of a defective

---

[7] Notice how the logic of the subsumptive model works. The major premise tells the ET when ρ applies (note how θ does not enter the picture as far as the ET is concerned). The minor premise presupposes a recognitional ability on the part of the ET (see note 8), and the conclusion is a practical one, namely a personal injunction to do π.

[8] I am assuming that this recognition is unproblematic, but this might be excessively generous to the ET conception of teaching. It is not difficult to recognise that one is due to take a lesson in PE, for example; this is part of the 'good sense' that an operative in any occupation is expected to exercise. However, if it is important to recognise more subtle elements in a situation, it may be that a craft element necessarily enters the deliberations and actions of the teacher. Whether this can be done without undermining the very conception of the ET will be discussed in this chapter.

craft teaching force into an effective technical one.[9] An alternative possibility might be to replace a force of professional technicians (PTs) with ETs on the grounds that (1) they were too expensive; (2) their theoretical basis was inadequate; and (3) their ability to translate theory into effective practice was unsatisfactory. (1) is, however, a powerful motivation, particularly if a properly managed force of ETs can do nearly as good or as good a job as a force of PTs.

HOW THE THEORY–PRACTICE AND THEORY–REFLECTION–PRACTICE MODELS APPLY TO TEACHING

How would a teaching force consisting of ETs actually work? An obvious and indispensable desideratum is the availability of an adequate theoretical basis for practice. The second desideratum is a specialist workforce who can develop rules for the implementation of theory in practice. The third is a systematic network of trainers and training institutions that can inculcate in the teaching force the appropriate rules for practice. Let us take each condition in turn. There must exist an adequate body of theory or theories that is capable of generating rules that are *sufficient* to mandate effective practice.[10] Although we have argued against an unjustified scepticism about the worthwhileness of any empirical educational theory in relation to classroom practice, it is nevertheless the case that this condition is very demanding. In effect, the ET is only to judge whether or not *this rule R is to apply in this situation S*, and then to apply it without any qualification or modification. This is a problem because a theory, to be capable of generating such rules, must be very powerful predictively and must encompass the needs of a wide variety of situations and individual pupils. It is far from clear that a set of theories sufficient for teachers in all circumstances is available.[11] As

---

[9] Why would a craft force be thought to be inadequate? The principal reason would be that craft practices were defective as they were based on pedagogic traditions that failed to take account, either of up-to-date empirical research or of revised normative theory (such as the introduction of a national curriculum). Alternatively, they might be based on a distorted 'commonsense' derived from an inadequate but widely accepted theoretical basis.

[10] They cannot be merely necessary; otherwise, some form of craft knowledge or an alternative theoretical base would need to be possessed by the teachers. But, of course, 'sufficient' is a very demanding condition.

[11] Hence the temptation to use ETs in certain circumstances only, possibly with 'low fee' or 'lower class' pupils (discussed further in this chapter).

we shall argue in more detail in Chapter 8, for the PT such demands on theory are not necessary. It is the role of the researcher, perhaps with expertise in metastudies, to identify the relevant theory from the mass of data available as the empirical basis most suitable for the pedagogic needs of the pupils or the education system.

But the researcher is most probably poorly placed to prescribe the rules that the ET should follow: first, because the theory may well underdetermine what these rules are, and second, because the rules have to be comprehensible and useable by the ET. It is, therefore, likely that working closely with the researcher, a technologist of education who can understand and mediate the theory and prescribe in general terms what its mandates are in a wide range of situations, will be required at this stage. We should add that it is unlikely that such a technologist will be effective without a good knowledge of both the circumstances in which teachers will have to work and the capabilities of the teachers themselves. In addition, resources will need to be developed in order that the rules for practice be made operational. These will include, as well as a curriculum, schemes of work and lesson plans, which will prescribe in detail, often minute by minute, what the teacher should be doing at any given time. Aids to teaching such as textbooks will also be indispensable, and these will need to be written in such a way that the teacher will be incapable of misusing them – they will need to be tightly integrated into lesson plans if they are to be effective. The technologist will also have to consider the availability of other resources for transmitting information and for the pupils to use, and to take account of constraints such as class and classroom size in devising rules for practice.

This raises the question as to what precisely is the kind of normative structure within which the ET operates? I have used the term 'rules' in a generic sense so far, but more precision is needed. Clearly, ETs do not work with high-level principles except perhaps in relation to the broader occupational ethics which frame their action. The point about the rules within which ETs work is that they are subject to the minimum of interpretation, or maybe no interpretation at all. There is, therefore, a sense in which ETs are like Adam Smith's pinmaker, confined to rigid protocols in their work. The only difference with the Smithian pinmaker is that he, unlike the ET, performs only one operation over and over again.[12]

---

[12] Smith, *The Wealth of Nations* ([1776] 1981, vol. 1, bk. 1, pp. 14–15).

TEACHING AND THE FRAGMENTATION OF THE LABOUR PROCESS – HIGHER ORDER ABILITIES ARE EXERCISED OUTSIDE RATHER THAN INSIDE THE CLASSROOM

All education involves some degree of division of labour between, for example, teachers, inspectors and administrators, even though one person can often fulfil multiple roles. In the case of the craft teacher, however, we had a situation in which the teacher is responsible for extended forms of agency such as having the responsibility for teaching a class over an extended period of time, not to mention the responsibility for arranging lessons and schemes of work. ETs are, however, subject to a different process of the *fragmentation of labour*.[13] The activities of teaching are decomposed into elements, and the teacher in the classroom is only given a part of them, namely the execution of tasks in the classroom that are prescribed by others.

It is worthwhile dwelling on the implications of this for the everyday work of teachers. As we noted earlier, teaching has been traditionally thought of as an occupation where considerable independence has been exercised. Teachers are responsible on this view for planning, controlling, co-ordinating and evaluating their own work as well as exercising particular skills such as keeping discipline and explaining clearly. They have also been expected to carry out polymorphous roles within the classroom such as monitoring, communicating, adapting, improvising and so on. On the ET conception of teaching, most of these roles will either disappear or become protocol-driven. Thus, for example, a teacher might be told to ask certain questions at certain times only in a lesson. The textbook will probably need to be followed rigidly, with little room for deviation, interpretation or additional explanation. The extra-classroom functions of planning, communication and evaluation may well be removed to the hands of other specialists, curriculum designers and middle managers, for example.

The widespread use of ETs thus presupposes a more complex occupational structure for teaching, which involves layers of

---

[13] A valuable distinction made in Williams (2000). The division of labour is reflected in the existence of many occupations, each devoted to different aspects of human need. The occupation of teaching results from the division of labour. When occupations are decomposed into discrete tasks and these tasks are assigned to different individuals, one has the fragmentation of the labour process. Smith describes the most extreme form of this, where the manufacture of a simple object, a pin, is broken down into 12 separate stages, each performed by a separate individual who carries out only one task. Such a process has to, however, be *managed*, a point to which we will return.

management at the school level in order to carry out necessary tasks of planning, control, co-ordination, communication and evaluation which are beyond the competence of the ET, but also specific functions outside the school, such as the design and testing of classroom procedures and the fine-tuning of lesson protocols. This increased proportion of management resources should be regarded as a cost imposed by the ET conception of teaching.

Illustrative Examples from Literacy and Numeracy Strategies in England and Parateachers in India

Just to describe the work of the ET might seem to disparage it. Why would anyone want teachers like this? In fact, the idea of the ET is a very popular one with some policymakers, and there are various reasons why this might be so. We will look at each of these in turn:

1. Optimal exploitation of useful research findings;
2. Compensating for limited competence of craft-based teachers;
3. Organising low-cost mass education for lower-income groups.

Each of these three reasons is more salient than the others in different circumstances. (3), for example, is particularly influential in developing countries such as India. But the ET proposition also has a strong purchase in developed countries where doubts about the competence and/or commitment of the teaching force can be pervasive.

Optimal Exploitation of Research Findings   We have already noted that a vast amount of empirical research on teaching and learning is available. No teacher could access it all, and Hattie-like syntheses, which aggregate hundreds if not thousands of studies into findings of summaries and an evaluation of their findings in terms of the effectiveness of certain practices, are not sufficiently fine-grained to be directly exploitable within the classroom. Furthermore, even when potentially useful research has been identified, it by no means follows that there are ready rules at hand to enable it to be exploited. It is extremely wasteful, the thinking goes, to 'reinvent the wheel', both in relation to identifying exploitable research and in developing rules for its use. Furthermore, the efforts of each individual teacher to do this will be highly variable and fallible. Far better to use specialist technologists to identify 'good practice' and to devise protocols to implement it.[14]

For example, the literature on learning to read and teaching methods that are most effective is vast and requires a considerable amount of specialist knowledge to understand and to interpret it. Furthermore, there is likely to be more than one approach that is efficacious, and devising the right combination of these is likely to involve a considerable amount of trial and error. Another factor that cannot be ignored by educational planners is the cost involved in different methods, including the cost of training ETs. The problem from their perspective may well be to devise the optimum mix of effectiveness and cost-effectiveness (efficiency). Given what we know about the very variable results obtained by the teaching of reading, with typical 'failure rates' of between 15% and 20% in some developed countries, this is no mean challenge.[15]

Not surprisingly, then, various highly codified approaches have been devised in order to bring the optimum effect of research identified as valuable to bear on classroom practice. Examples in the UK include the Miskin approach, the West Dunbartonshire Literacy Initiative[16] and, last but not least, the National Literacy Strategy in England.[17] Literacy teaching is an area in which much detailed work on teaching and learning has been carried out, and the results appear unambiguous.[18] One might reasonably suppose that, with progress in the review of the research literature in other areas of teaching and learning, much more will come to be known about the best ways of exploiting the best research, and thus the scope for the effective deployment of ETs will increase.

---

[14] See Alexander (1992, ch. 11) on the sense of 'good practice' that should be used here.

[15] Such 'failure' would be constituted by not reaching a level of 'functional literacy', for example level 4 in the English National Curriculum. Figures suggest that failure to reach this level by the age of 11 means that it is unlikely that progress to this level will be made in the future. (Save the Children Fund, *Read On, Get On* (report), 2014, pp. 4, 49.). See also https://www. gov.uk/government/speeches/david-laws-speaks-to-the-national-education-trust-on-raising-standards.

[16] Miskin and Archbold (2007) and Mackay (2006).

[17] There is evidence that in this latter case, the research base was presented *post hoc*, rather compromising one of the major stated advantages of the ET model.

[18] That is, the results of the research that invariably recommend a mixture of approaches in which synthetic phonics are part of the mix. Political interpretations of the research tend to present the use of synthetic phonics as the sole recommendation to be gleaned from the literature.

Compensating for Limited Competence of Craft Teachers   We noted in Chapter 6 that the craft conception of teaching does not allow research to play any significant role in teaching strategies or methods. The craft teacher relies on experience, subject knowledge and accumulated collective wisdom within the occupation, and these resources are sufficient. This is, however, a highly idealised picture of the craft teacher, and the reality is often very different. In the first place, it is unlikely that the accumulation of experience and reflection of individual teachers would ever bring them to the point where they reached the same conclusions about teaching as protocol-based systems based on systematic review of extant research. The accumulated experience of many different teachers might broaden the knowledge of individual teachers but would be unlikely, even if it could be collected, to match the thoroughness of a systematic review.

But in many ways, the situation is much worse than that. We have already noted the importance of 'commonsense' in framing the worldview of teachers. Like Keynes' businessmen who consider themselves practical men of affairs unencumbered by theory, they are often in the grip of discredited theory even when they do not know that they are.[19] Very often, 'theory' validates or reinforces commonly held prejudices, particularly those about the educability of certain categories of children. One does not need to look far to see the evidence for this. Psychometric theory not only underpinned British educational policy for a considerable part of the twentieth century but also was based on flimsy conceptual foundations and flawed evidence.[20] The same can be said for verbal deficit theory[21] and overambitious interpretations of developmental theory.[22] Coming a little more up to date, 'psycholinguistic' approaches to the teaching of reading and writing, based on a misunderstanding of Chomsky's work, dominated many English classrooms in the 1980s,[23] and the craze for the poorly conceptualised and thinly substantiated theory

---

[19] See Keynes's (1936, ch. 24) comments on faulty economic theory distilled into commonsense.

[20] For a good historical examination of British policy, see Gordon, *Verbal Deficit* (1981). For a good account of the rise and fall of the intelligence testing movement, see Gould, *The Mismeasure of Man* (1984).

[21] See Dittmar, *Sociolinguistics* (1976); and Winch, *Language, Ability and Educational Achievement* (1990).

[22] See Donaldson, *Children's Minds* (1978).

[23] See the near-messianic *Reading* by Smith (1985) for pedagogic advocacy based on the slimmest of evidence and a heady dose of Rousseau-esque progressivism.

of different 'learning styles'[24] in the late-twentieth and early-twenty-first centuries has had considerable and dubious effect on education, largely due to the enthusiasm of middle-level policymakers and teachers themselves.

This somewhat inglorious history of the use (or misuse) of educational research by teachers could serve as powerful evidence in favour of the institution of ETs in teaching. No longer would faulty or misinterpreted research be subject to mass implementation with potential (and sometimes actual) disastrous results, but the use of ETs would ensure the disciplined, effective and systematic introduction of the very best research findings according to the best designed and tested teaching protocols. Research, no longer a capricious mistress, would become a useful servant to education. Given the lack of expertise currently possessed by most teachers to critically appraise research and given the lack of expertise available in putting knowledge of that research into effective teaching strategies, the case for the wider use of ETs, even in developed countries like England, could begin to look unanswerable. A further advantage could well be the much-simplified training and professional development that could be offered to teachers in an ET-dominated educational environment.

Organising Low-Cost Mass Education for Lower-Income Groups   One motivation for the development of ETs in developing countries is the prospect of low-cost education. The thinking is that developing societies do not need to spend the same proportion of GDP on education as do developed societies. The World Bank, International Monetary Fund and other bodies have encouraged the development of alternative models of education. These include low-cost private education and the widespread use of parateachers in state schools. The general direction of thinking is that simplified forms of education, particularly those that provide a basic education for low-income groups, can be designed with the use of a semiskilled teaching force that operates according to tried and tested routines validated by educational research. The power of the advocates is often considerable, and their recommendations have often had significant weight with the governments of developing countries.[25]

---

[24] See Coffield (2004) for a comprehensive critique of the 'learning styles' literature.

[25] Unfortunately, research on parateachers focusses on the effect of contract status on effectiveness rather than training effects. The emphasis is therefore on the motivating effects of contractual insecurity rather than on the effectiveness of research on practice; see Kingdon *et al.* (2013).

Although by no means all parateachers have been trained as ETs, the model is a suitable one for low-cost mass education for the following reasons. First, training in classroom routines rather than extensive teacher education is all that is required. This is shorter than conventional teacher education, and for that reason alone of lower cost. Second, the content of training can be based on research and systematic review through which the most effective routines can be identified, evaluated and converted into viable classroom routines useable in a wide variety of contexts. Third, contractual insecurity and low pay will motivate the parateacher to be as effective as possible in the hope of future reward.[26] For these reasons, the ET model may prove attractive to developing countries. If, however, it is effective not just in providing a substandard education for pupils whose interests are not uppermost in the minds of policymakers but more generally, the model might be deemed to have wider applicability.

THE RELATIONSHIP BETWEEN CRAFT AND EXECUTIVE TECHNICIAN CONCEPTIONS OF TEACHING – TO WHAT EXTENT ARE THEY COMPATIBLE?

The craftworker and the ET are two models of the occupation of teaching that are favoured by policymakers. They sometimes appear simultaneously in policy discourse even if not necessarily within the same documents. We have already noted, for example, the fondness for the craft conception expressed in contemporary English policy papers. But the ET also appears on the stage. Proposed University Training Schools will, as part of their function, carry out research into effective teaching and learning. This research can then be disseminated across the education system. Such a proposal could be used to support the development of the 'professional technician' (see Chapter 8), but if the research is to be transmitted to the teaching force in England who are expected to put it into effect, then the ET rather than the professional technician model is being considered.[27]

Recall that the craftworker develops practice from experience and observation. That practice is sensitive to contextual features and thus may be expected to vary according to circumstance. The ET, on the other hand, makes use of routines that are insensitive to practice. The

---

[26] Kingdon *et al.* (2013). For a critique of this approach, see Nambissan (2015).

[27] There is some evidence that in England, the government wishes to move beyond this approach (DfE 2016), but does not indicate how teachers could be equipped to read original research papers on topics relevant to their teaching.

question quite naturally arises as to whether or not a hybrid 'craft–ET' model might not be developed, which would utilise the best features of each, the situational sensitivity of the craftworker with the research-based accuracy of the ET. The question needs to be resolved according to whether or not the two models are actually compatible, and if so, to what extent.

In the ET model theory, θ generates rules ρ, which must be applied in practice – what Oakeshott calls 'technical knowledge'. Why should not technical knowledge, embodied in ρ, be modified according to circumstances to yield a practice π, which is not just the blind application of ρ, but an appropriate adaptation of it, a form in other words of practical knowledge in Oakeshott's sense? In order to answer this, one has to ask oneself whether the rules ρ will retain their effectiveness when modified according to craft principles. It would be expected that an ET would modify or disapply instances of ρ when confronted with situations in which he judged that action straightforwardly based on a subsumptive inference was not justified.[28] Either the ET will be competent to do so, or he will not. If he is incompetent, then there is clearly no point in expecting him to do so. If, on the other hand, he does have a *prima facie* valid claim to competence, we need to ask on what basis this is mandated. The problem here is that the ET model has been introduced because the craft model, which it is intended to replace, is flawed – craftworkers' situational judgements based on 'commonsense' yield substandard practice. If this is so, then the ET's claim to situational competence is undermined. It cannot be the case that he both possesses an additional source of competence and that this source of competence is fundamentally flawed. The most that we might reasonably expect is that the ET relies on 'good sense' to carry out his work. He does not turn up drunk, is not systematically absent, does not teach when no children are present and so on. But following such precepts, which are marks of rational behaviour and occupational commitment as such, rather than teachers' craft knowledge, can be seen as a presupposition of being an ET rather than a complement to the repertoire of the ET. In other words,

---

[28] The ET applies norms, broadly speaking, on a *subsumptive* model (Westphal 2011). That is, the general form of the relationship between their action and the underpinning model is as follows:
In situations of Type A, actions of Type F are called for.
This is a situation of Type A
Therefore: Action of Type F is called for.
In other words, the practical syllogism through which one's professional action is channelled leaves no discretion at the margins for situational judgement.

the ET conception of teaching is based on the idea that the only kind of judgement that a teacher should make consists of exercising 'good sense'. Any attempt to exercise craft 'commonsense' will undermine the practice which rules generated by theory prescribe.

Of course, this is a general and abstract account of the incompatibility between the ET and craftworker. It implies that the same teacher cannot carry out the same activity as both ET and craftworker. But this is not to say, for example, that there are cases where a teacher is ET for some of the time and craftworker for the rest. The literacy and numeracy strategies in England were based on this supposition; outside the fields of literacy and numeracy, teachers were free to plan and practice their work within the constraints of the National Curriculum.[29] But what we cannot conclude is that a teacher could be a craftworker and an ET at the same time; the most we can conclude is that a hybrid model may exist in which the teacher is an ET part of the time and a craftworker the rest of the time.

But there remain policy issues. It is no good policymaker's thinking that the two models are completely compatible. If the craft model is not completely adequate (for the reasons that we have put forward), then careful thought must be given concerning the ways in which it needs to be modified and for which areas of the curriculum. There is, of course, an attitudinal issue that is significant. To be a craftworker is to adopt a certain attitude towards one's work, as someone in possession of expertise and a master of professional judgement. To become an ET, even for a section of one's work, is to relinquish one's professional attitude. It may be doubted whether this is a realistic position in which to put teachers who are fundamentally craftworkers in their general stance towards teaching. And, indeed, the same point works for executive technicians who are expected to be craftworkers for some elements of their work.

Executive Technicians and the Problem of Theory
As we saw above in the subsumptive model of rationality (a simplified form of what is sometimes called 'technical rationality'), the ET needs no theory, either explicit or implicit. It is a presupposition of the model that there is a strict division of labour between those who generate theory, those who devise procedures enjoined by the theory and those who put those procedures into effect. The ET belongs

---

[29] And, as we shall see in Chapter 8, it is possible to combine the professional technician model with the ET model in a similar fashion.

to this third group and is intellectually only equipped for this work. Attempts to take on the first and second roles will take him beyond his competence.[30] It is in fact quite important that the first two roles are not just functionally, but also in terms of personnel, separated from the third. If the ET takes an interest in the theory underpinning his practice, then he or she will do so as an amateur rather than an expert (remember that experts have been assigned the role of generating and utilising theory). Not only will the ET's engagement with educational theory necessarily be non-expert, but such an engagement will also threaten the effectiveness of the ET model. If the ET's 'understanding' of theory suggests that the theory θ, which generates practice, is not valid, then the rationale, such as it is, which mandates a specific action for an ET evaporates. The teacher can only proceed on the basis of blind obedience and must ignore the suggestions of his own understanding. In fact, teachers are quite likely to operate according to some informal understanding of theory through their acquaintance with popularised and simplified forms of theory that mandate certain kinds of action in the form of 'commonsense' encountered through professional conversations in the place of work (usually, one supposes, the staffroom). These two must be suppressed if they contradict θ, which is the mainspring of his professional action. But this may be difficult if the ET is unacquainted with θ in any case. If the ET is acquainted with θ and comes to reject it, his actions in the classroom will tend in many instances to be matters of bad faith.

WHAT AN EXECUTIVE TECHNICIAN TEACHING FORCE WOULD LOOK LIKE

Choosing a particular conception of teaching, and then sticking to it, has implications for the nature of the teaching force. In Chapter 10, we will consider models of teacher education. Before we do so however, it is worth considering what the attributes of an ET teaching force would be.

The ET model depends both on the division of labour and on the fragmentation of the labour process. It is evident that the role of the ET is primarily in the classroom, executing lesson plans according to prescriptions. Other roles such as governance, management, curriculum development, research and the development of pedagogic

---

[30] Which is not to say that he cannot tell the technologist (he who writes the procedures) that they are, in fact, unworkable and thus oblige him to revisit his work. But he cannot intervene either in the generation of the theory or in the primary derivation of procedures from that theory.

routines will be the proper province of other occupations (as, to some extent, they already are). But we should not lose sight of the fact that curriculum development is a highly demanding and specialised activity (see Chapters 8 and 9) and probably not the proper province of the teacher alone. However, teachers are normally expected, in countries such as England and in Northern Europe more generally, to produce schemes of work and lesson plans. It is not at all clear that this should be the proper province of a genuine ET teacher. This brings us to the issue of the fragmentation of the labour process. If we take seriously the idea that teachers have responsibility for their classes over an extended period, like an academic year (as they generally do according to the craft and professional technician models), then there opens a divide between these conceptions of teaching and the ET. The ET in pure form is a carrier out of routines devised by other specialists. This is necessary because the model adopted is to choose the optimum method of translating the implications of the best educational research into protocols that will maximise the effects of that research. Deviation from these protocols will diminish the effectiveness of the model. It follows that a significant element in a craft or professional technician teacher's work will not be required of an ET. The key element of know-how for an ET is concerned with classroom and lesson management, not with planning or evaluation.

First of all, ETs must be capable of holding a class's attention and maintaining discipline. They will need to do this in order to execute the lesson plan. Lesson management will then be the main competence required. The kind of lesson that an ET will be required to teach will consist of relatively short sequences of activity, punctuated by rapid transitions to other forms of activity. For example, in teaching writing, the ET might be expected first of all to indicate the lesson objectives to the class. There might follow a short instructional sequence during which a task is given and necessary information pertinent to carrying out that task is given, together with an opportunity for questioning from the class. There might then follow a short recapitulation session (from material taught in a previous lesson) to reinforce knowledge and abilities needed for today's lesson's next task. A possible next step will be dispersal of the class to work as individuals, pairs or groups and supervision of this element of the sequence. Towards the end of the lesson period, the class will be reassembled, and the results of their work reviewed and salient lessons drawn from the exercise. Finally, the class as a whole will review whether and to what extent lesson objectives have been met. After the lesson is over, it is highly likely that the ET will need to engage in some structured record keeping and prescribe some activities for individuals in the next individualised phase of the next lesson. It is also possible that some lessons will include a test to assess pupil progress. The ET will also need to have reasonable mastery of the technology associated with such teaching, such as the use of textbooks, teaching materials and whiteboards, not to mention electronic recording procedures and data management.

It is important to note that at this stage, no judgement of the quality of such a lesson is being offered.[31] Such practices may even be highly effective, not only in relative terms (e.g. in relation to incompetent craft or professional technician-style teaching) but also in terms of the legitimate objectives of an education system. The key point that I wish to emphasise here is that the ET has to work in a highly focussed way, concentrating particularly on lesson management and to a lesser extent on recording. The use of technology may well allow the results of each lesson or at least of periodic testing to be made known to the school management so that adjustments may be made where necessary to the routines being followed. If we think of teaching as a matter of forming plans (to teach certain matters to certain pupils over a certain period), putting them into effect (act in a justified way according to one's aims and mandated actions) and evaluating the success of what one has done, then this cycle of activity is split amongst different people, and the ET is only concerned with putting it into effect.[32]

It follows that such teachers can probably be readied for action in the classroom in a relatively short period. For those who require specialised subject knowledge in order to carry out their roles, one will have also to build in the time necessary for them to, for example, acquire a bachelor degree, although the ET model, with its insistence on sticking rigidly to procedures and textbooks, will render this to a large extent unnecessary. It is also unlikely that teachers of this type would be able to gain promotion to some of the more second-order functions associated with teaching without further education. Such a system of teaching, like other examples of fragmentation of the labour process, requires adequate line-management structures that are capable of planning, controlling, co-ordinating and evaluating the

---

[31] See Winch (1996a) on the issue of quality in pedagogy and also Jain *et al.* (2017).

[32] Whether the evaluative part of the cycle can be undertaken by an ET is a moot point. Where it is a box-ticking exercise devised by others, then probably the answer is 'yes'. Where it is a more complex evaluation of activities in relation to pupil understanding, requiring insight into pupil learning and understanding, then it is much more doubtful that an ET could undertake such a role. This is an important point to which we will return in Chapter 8.

work of a number of teachers, and this is a significantly different job from following protocols in the classroom. The ET model is likely to produce a highly stratified and tightly managed school workforce with different routes into different parts of the structure.[33]

A FINAL THOUGHT ABOUT THE ET MODEL OF TEACHING

Whatever its virtues, policymakers attracted by the ET model will need to confront two questions. The first is whether the ET model is optimum given the resources available to the education system. It may be relatively easy to arrive at a decision about this. The second and much more difficult one, probably to be decided at government level, is whether the ET model is actually the best possible one for the society or is the best that can be hoped for given the level of resources that a government is prepared to put into education (or, more controversially, into the education of some sections of the society, usually the poorer and less privileged members of that society).[34] It may well be that the ET is the model of the 'good enough' or 'satisficing' teacher, maybe perfectly adequate for the lower strata of society, but not satisfactory at all for those destined to lead the society or even, perhaps, to play a role in its governance.[35]

---

[33] There is a very interesting issue about the motivation of the ET, which cannot be addressed here but which is highly relevant. If the ET is motivated not by intrinsic satisfaction in doing a job that requires discretion and independence but by extrinsic rewards and punishments, then a major role of school management will be to allocate such rewards and punishments in order to maximise performance. In line with the rational egoist model of management thus assumed, they will also have to guard against ET teachers gaming the system in order to maximise rewards and minimise punishments.

[34] For a discussion of the shifting definitions of a 'good' education for different sections of society, see Winch (2014).

[35] See Smith ([1776] 1981, vol. 1, bk. 5, pp. 785–786) on the type of schoolmaster suitable for the education of children of the common people, with a view to steering them away from revolutionary demagogues rather than for taking part in a democratic polity.

8

The Teacher as a Professional Technician

This chapter will outline a third conception of the role of the teacher, which I will call that of the *professional technician* or *professional* for short. The professional teacher is one who most corresponds to the description of professional occupations described in the literature already discussed. Again, the professional described in this chapter will be an ideal type, whose attributes will be found to a greater or lesser degree in actual teachers around the world. Should this be a *preferred* model of what a teacher should be? The answer depends on what kind of education system a society wants and the degree to which it is prepared to invest in such a kind of education system. The concluding chapter will set out the options more clearly. But for now, it is necessary to enquire why the need for a professional teacher should arise. We will start by considering the shortcomings of the two models already described, that of the craftworker and that of the executive technician.

RESUMÉ OF PROBLEMS WITH CRAFT AND ET CONCEPTIONS

The strength of the craftworker lies in the ability to draw on experience and situational judgement to produce the right outcome. Underlying these strengths is usually a sound grasp of subject knowledge, particularly in the panoramic sense (see Chapter 5), and it is assumed without argument that the transformation of subject knowledge in this sense into subject knowledge in pedagogic mode is largely unproblematic, something that can be done through

Teachers' Know-How: A Philosophical Investigation, First Edition. Christopher Winch.
© 2017 Christopher Winch. Editorial Organisation © Philosophy of Education Society of Great Britain.
Published 2017 by John Wiley & Sons, Ltd.

experience and collectively implanted craft wisdom.[1] Similarly, knowledge about effective means of teaching and learning has similar sources. For aims and values, it is often asserted that a craft teacher is one who defines his own aims and values and that these should not be imposed.[2] We saw, in our discussion of commonsense and the craft teacher in Chapter 6, the kinds of problems that could arise from this way of looking at things.

The other potentially large problem with the craft conception as we saw was that theory about teaching and learning is eschewed. The craft teacher does not require theory in order to be effective, and theory may even disrupt and destabilise the practical knowledge required to teach effectively. One of the problems with this approach is that it makes large assumptions about the irrelevance of theory when, as was argued in Chapter 5, dispensing with it altogether is different from thinking that you have dispensed with it altogether, when it may reappear in a less than benign form as 'commonsense' if one is not aware of the problem. More generally, a problem with dismissing theory as false does not actually lead to its complete dismissal, since the contradictory of false theory will be true and thus at least potentially relevant to the teacher.

The executive technician (ET) model of teaching is quite different from the craft conception, although the two are often not clearly distinguished in the minds of policymakers. The ET uses theory indirectly through following protocols worked from extant research on teaching and learning. The ET has little discretion, and the exercise of situational judgement on his part will tend to undermine the protocols that form the basis of his expertise. The ET should be able to make up for the shortcomings of the craftworker by utilising the research that has the most warrant for effective practice. It is assumed by proponents of the ET model that some research is better than most craft belief in guiding teachers to be effective in getting

---

[1]   This view does not, unfortunately, have much to say to those teachers whose crucial expertise lies in teaching an ability such as reading or arithmetic. It is not enough to be able to read or subtract in order to be an effective teacher of these subjects. On the other hand, one is not teaching pupils a body of knowledge in teaching them to read and subtract. So the question must arise: what exactly is the subject matter of the craft teacher of, say, literacy, if there is no subject matter as such to teach?

[2]   This is potentially a large problem for those who argue that the craft conception should be the official one in a state-controlled education system. The state should, through some due process, lay down what the underpinning aims and values of the system should be. But it cannot guarantee that teachers should conform to these without at the same time requiring that they do so, perhaps as a condition of employment.

their pupils to learn what they are supposed to be learning. There are many intervention programmes and, less dramatically, highly structured textbooks and teaching programmes that are capable of guiding the ET. The ET will not require a great deal of teacher education, but will need training in the effective use of the protocols prescribed by research.

The attraction of the ET model is that one can obtain a highly effective teaching force at low cost and, at the same time, avoid the problems associated with the craftworker.[3] There is some evidence that approaches of this type may be effective in certain circumstances.[4] It might therefore be asked: 'What are the problems with the ET conception of teaching?' Indeed, if we assume that empirical research can provide a sound warrant for effective teaching, then what is there not to like about a system that is designed to ensure maximum effectiveness of the research through the development of protocols for teaching? Unlike the proponents of the craftworker conception who dismiss the relevance of empirical research, those who accept that it can have value and *necessarily* cannot be ignored, are in a quandary if they have reservations about ETs.

THE GENERAL IDEA OF THE PROFESSIONAL TECHNICIAN

In this section, an attempt will be made to show how there could be a viable alternative to both the craftworker and ET conceptions of teaching. We have already discussed the potential shortcomings of the craftworker. What are those of the ET? The main problem with the ET conception is that teachers are deprived of the possibility of exercising discretion in teaching situations and, indeed, in most of their spheres of activity. And, as was argued in Chapter 7, this is not just a practical limitation but a logical one. One cannot have one's activities prescribed in detail and yet at the same time exercise discretion in relation to precisely those activities. So it is worth asking whether such professional discretion should matter. In order to

---

[3] Proponents of the craftworker conception will, of course, protest that there is no research that could mandate such protocols and that therefore the ET conception is chimerical. This, however, as we have seen is itself a confused claim. The best that can be said about it is that it has to be argued in detail over particular cases, in full knowledge of the technical challenges involved in firstly establishing the quality of the research and, secondly, establishing the extent of its warrant for practice.

[4] The parateacher research in India (Nambissan 2015); the Miskin (2007) and Mackay (2006) work on the teaching of reading are also examples. The evidence from the NLS and NNS is patchier, but it is arguable that these programmes were not given sufficient time to work properly.

understand this, one should ask whether it is actually relevant to the task of teaching whether one has knowledge of individuals and of the dynamics of the class one is teaching.[5] If the answer is 'yes', then there is a major flaw with the ET conception. It may work as a kind of pedagogic poultice to be applied to flawed craft teachers, but in the nature of such measures it is a makeshift and unfitted for the development of excellence in teaching. And, if it is excellence one is after, then the development of the ET is a false path to follow.[6]

So what is lacking from the armoury of the craft teacher and the ET that the professional should be able to supply? In brief, the answer is that the professional neither seeks to deprive teachers of their craft knowledge nor ETs of the basing of their practice on sound research. The professional teacher operates in a complex and often unpredictable environment which requires the bringing to bear of judgements and action which are not just based on the perceived exigencies of the moment but also can be justified by appeal to systematic knowledge of what is best done in situations of that type, in other words by research. Such a teacher will also of course be guided by aims and values together with a conceptual framework for thinking about education and teaching, and these will be properly integrated into their own sense of self as a practitioner of an esteemed occupation.

Let us be more specific still. Teachers, in order to teach effectively, have to inform their understanding of what they are doing with an understanding of what their pupils are trying to do. If, as we saw in Chapter 1, teaching is a triadic relationship between teacher, pupil and what it is that the pupil is supposed to learn, then understanding of that relationship by the teacher will necessitate an understanding of the pupils *vis-à-vis* the teacher. A central part of that understanding will be that of understanding the problem of learning from the point of view of the pupil.[7] This in turn has a consequence for the

---

[5] Such knowledge is difficult to pin down in terms of conventional epistemological classification. It involves *acquaintance* and some beliefs about the characteristics of individuals and of the class. But it also involves knowing how one stands with others, and having a secure purchase on their perspective, in other words, an understanding of the nature of the individuals that one is teaching, both as individuals and as part of a social group. In an important sense, it involves *knowing how to go on* with the class and the individuals who compose it (see Wittgenstein 1953, II, xi, p. 223, for the idea of 'finding one's feet' with people).

[6] This is not to deny that a good case can be made for 'good enough' given limitations of resources and restrictions of aims for some classes of pupils.

[7] This will, of course, be a vicarious understanding to a certain extent, but the argument will be that some understanding of this kind is essential for teaching to move beyond the 'good enough'.

teacher. If S is to be taught to pupils and a success criterion for the teacher is that as many pupils as possible learn S, then the teacher will, as Flew (1976) argued, be concerned about whether and to what degree S is learned if he is serious about what he is doing. This has one direct consequence, that he will be concerned to find out whether or not pupils have actually learned S. In this respect he will be interested in assessing their progress *formatively*, that is, in the question as to whether and to what degree they have learned S. But this will also be relevant to the next stage, when it is the teacher's job to get the pupils to learn T, a task whose success depends on the prior learning of S. The teacher is, *pace* White (2000), not merely *monitoring* what the pupils are doing; he is also trying to learn for himself what it is that they have learned and, crucially, what they do not yet understand.

And here we get to the heart of the issue. Teachers who are serious about the learning of their pupils need an insight into the kinds of difficulties that they are facing in their learning. This is not just a question of knowing *them* in the sense described above (see footnote 5), but also understanding the *kind of difficulty* that they may be experiencing in learning S.[8] The task involved is thus a complex one. It involves understanding the pupil and understanding the type of difficulty involved in learning, but it involves the difficulty embedded in understanding the latter, which is to do both with the element in S that is the source of the difficulty and with the nature of the difficulty of the task of learning S from the point of view of the pupil. It might seem that this second leg of understanding is nothing more than a restatement of the first, but this is not so. The nature of the learning difficulty is of a type, and the understanding of that type is what the teacher needs to get a grip of as well as the personal characteristics of the pupils who are experiencing that difficulty.[9]

If this analysis is right, then teachers need to have the kind of craft understanding that proponents of the craft model so esteem. But it will not be adequate since the type of element in S, which is difficult for some pupils to learn, will also need to be complemented by

In any case, we should not confuse 'understanding how someone perceives a certain situation' with 'experiencing the situation the same as they do'.

[8] It is equally important for teachers to recognise where able pupils need further challenges and where they find the going too easy. The ability to do this is the other side of the coin in terms of recognising where pupils experience difficulties.

[9] See Hattie (2009, pp. 173–178) on the empirical evidence that understanding and being able to act on pupil difficulties comprises one of the most effective pedagogical attributes that empirical research on effective teaching has identified.

an understanding of the type of difficulty that learning that element presents. Understanding the first type involves what we have called the *learning aspect* of subject knowledge; understanding the second involves drawing on what is collectively known, through systematic enquiry, of that kind of difficulty in learning S. Thus, pedagogic content knowledge and insight into questions of epistemic ascent are important in the first instance and understanding of the research into the learning question is required for the second instance. And such understanding has to be integrated with understanding of the personal characteristics of the pupil and how that can be managed within a particular classroom environment. Here, the protocol knowledge of the ET will not be adequate because (a) it will only at best include a generalised diagnostic element that does not take account of individual characteristics, and (b) the prescription of routines will not allow for much, if any, in the way of the kind of situational judgement involved in formative assessment and recalibrating a lesson to take account of emerging knowledge about learning. Finally, protocols for teaching a lesson are not adequate for a teacher who needs to be aware of individual characteristics as a necessary part of conducting a lesson.[10]

HOW THE THEORY–REFLECTION–PRACTICE MODEL MIGHT APPLY TO TEACHING

It is often said that a teacher of this type will need to be 'reflective'. It is much less clear to what extent this claim has substance. In order to get clearer about this issue, we need to return to a distinction already made in Chapter 5 between the need for teachers to gain occupational self-knowledge and their need to be able to reflect, in a more impersonal way, on how systematic knowledge may or may not inform professional judgement. The two related but distinct needs are often confused within the literature.[11] A teacher, like other workers, needs to be able to gain a perspective on teaching that gives a good insight into his or her own strengths and weaknesses and avenues for future development. This involves the capacity to reflect on one's work and to use those reflections in future work.[12] They may include

[10] This is not a plea for extreme forms of differentiation or 'personalised learning' in which the integrity of class teaching is fundamentally disrupted, but a plea for the need to take account of the individual characteristics of members of the class being taught.

[11] See for example in the work of Donald Schön (1987), whose model of reflection appears to short-circuit the systematic knowledge that is said to underpin professions.

[12] A further problem with the Schön approach concerns the concept of 'reflection in action'. The term is confusing as it suggests that there is a space for such reflection in the context of classroom

reflection on interactions with pupils, colleagues, parents and administrators. Teachers need to be able to cope with setbacks as well as with triumphs, and they need a resilience that allows them to reflect on mistakes without being crushed by them. They need to be able to identify their strengths and to build on those in order to develop their own careers. They need to discover their limits as teachers and become comfortable with them without losing enthusiasm for teaching over the 'long haul'. If one is going to make a successful career of teaching, this capacity is essential and its beginnings should be developed from an early stage.[13]

This capacity should be distinguished from the ability to use theory or systematic knowledge to inform one's professional judgement in situations of teaching.[14] Chapters 3 and 5 have already pointed to the need for teachers to have a conceptual map of education to enable them to frame educational thinking and judgement. We will have more to say about the early development of this in Chapter 10. Suffice it here to say that the considerations about the nature of education outlined in Chapter 1 are an essential framework for the making of informed judgements. However, the theory that teachers need to operate with can by no means be confined to philosophical and conceptual considerations. If they are professionals rather than craftworkers or executive technicians in the senses outlined in the previous two chapters, then it is important that they engage with empirical theory[15] about teaching and learning so as to assess its relevance to their own practice.

Unlike the ET, the professional will not have a purely passive relationship to underlying theory. If there are any theory-based protocols to be followed, then they must be self-legislated by the teacher himself. But it is more likely that the professional will not wish to

work or operational conditions more generally. As Beckett and Hager (2002) point out, this is often simply not realistic. This is not to exclude the role of professional judgement in action, which on the argument of this chapter is an essential feature of the work of the professional teacher. But the terminology used should better reflect the nature of the activity, and 'reflection' is not an ideal term for this kind of *in situ* professional judgement. Schön's concept of 'reflection on action' better represents the focus of this discussion.

13 See remarks in previous chapters on the Germanic *Bildungsroman* and its preoccupation with personal development through sustained occupational engagement.

14 And, as we shall see in the next chapter, in situations that are not directly related to work in the classroom.

15 By 'empirical theory' is here meant a body of knowledge that is developed from a systematic investigation of educational reality. Of course this has to be framed conceptually, but empirical research is concerned with what actually takes place, either in natural situations or as the result of a controlled intervention.

govern himself solely through protocols but use deliverances of theory which he deems useful to inform professional judgement and to plan and assess his work. The ability to do this requires a reflective capacity of a different kind from the one described above. Teachers need to be able to interrogate theory in order to inform their own practice and, subsequently, to reflect on the relevance of that theory for their practice. The kind of reflective cycle that is involved here is likely to go from consideration of the relevant empirical theory θ and its implications for practice π, back to a consideration of the theory and its relevance to practice. The cycle thus looks like $\theta > \pi > \theta$, and, although it does not preclude the use of protocols, it is more likely that a teacher who actively engages with theory relevant to practice is less likely to feel the need to rely on protocols, either self- or other-developed, in order to guide practice.

WHY WE ARE 'DOOMED' TO TAKE ACCOUNT OF EDUCATIONAL RESEARCH: TEACHER AS TECHNICIAN, TEACHER AS TECHNOLOGIST

Why, though, would teachers wish to engage with theory when we have examined models that suggest that they do not need to do so? And, as we have seen, many commentators have argued that educational theory (including empirical theory) has little or nothing to offer to teachers. The answer in this chapter is that teachers have no choice but to engage with educational theory, and they can do so either actively or passively. Passive engagement can take two principal forms. The first we have seen in the case of the ET in Chapter 7. Teachers make use of protocols derived from theory to inform their practice without having to engage directly with the theory. The second is the model that we saw embodied in the craftworker teacher. Theory appears in the guise of commonsense, which is appropriated unconsciously as part of the experiential heritage and wisdom of the profession. This kind of engagement with theory is a form of professional self-deception. It has been argued that all that empirical research on education seems to be able to do is to tell us what we already knew about good teaching and education.[16]

This is indeed sometimes the case. But this should not lead us to dismiss educational research. There are all kinds of practices and propositions that teachers are certain about (in a subjective sense of

---

[16] See White (1997) on school effectiveness research for example.

'certainty', i.e. as an attitude or state of mind), which may unfortunately nevertheless not be true or which may even be conceptually muddled. That teachers feel certain about such things does not make them true.[17] Indeed, all too often it turns out that they are false or at least ill-founded in relation to evidential support. Those on the other hand who pour scorn on educational research on the grounds that it is usually false or at least overgeneralised deserve a different response. If a theory T is improperly supported by evidence, then one does not have sufficient grounds for believing that it is likely to be true. If T is not supported by any evidence or if the evidence suggests that T is false, then one has good grounds for believing in the truth of not-T. For example, if none of the claims made in favour of the creole interference hypothesis for explaining learning difficulties amongst creole speaking children turn out to be supported by a sound evidential base, then one has no good grounds for believing in the truth of the creole interference hypothesis. If, on the contrary, the evidence points to the falsity of the hypothesis, then one has good grounds for rejecting it and believing the proposition *The creole interference hypothesis is false* (i.e. believing *that* proposition to be true).[18] It is almost certainly the case that there are many educational theories based upon hypotheses that have been decisively refuted, and these provide us with a valuable resource that tells us what guidance we should not take in framing teaching strategies. These are not just trivial matters. We know that we have little or no reason to believe certain forms of psychometric theory about 'intelligence', that verbal deficit theories have largely been falsified and that there is a considerable amount of non-corroborating evidence for psycholinguistic theories about reading and writing.[19] These findings suggest that approaches underpinned by such theories should be avoided by teachers when they frame a rationale for their pedagogic practice. The fact that there are also many theories underpinned by uncorroborated hypotheses is also useful to know. Once again, such theories cannot provide a

---

[17] Which is not to say that there is much about which we are certain that it does not make sense to doubt (see Rhees 2002; Moyal-Sharrock 2007). But empirical generalisations about learning and educability are usually capable of being intelligibly doubted.

[18] Cf. Winch and Gingell (1994) for an account of the creole interference hypothesis. In brief, it claims that children's difficulties with reading and writing in creole speaking environments result from the facility with the creole mothertongue impeding articulation in the standard form used in reading and writing.

[19] There has recently been a revival of interest in genetics and educational achievement (see Shakeshaft *et al.* 2013), but there are problems about the methodology and assumptions of such research that entitle us to regard it with some scepticism (Rose 2014).

warrant for teaching practices, and teachers should take account of this. But we also know that there are theories for which a considerable amount of cumulative empirical evidence exists in study after study.[20] Many of these studies also look at the effectiveness of pedagogies based on them. Such studies provide *prima facie* reasons for teachers to take them seriously as possible bases for elements of their own practice. Of course, one may complain that the deliverances of such theories amount to no more than 'commonsense'. 'We knew that anyway – we didn't need a researcher to tell us' might be the retort. But if some version of a theory T is embodied in a teacher's outlook on education (their personal commonsense), then that is not a good reason to regard it with indifference. As we have already noted, many beliefs about which we feel certain turn out to be false. It is actually useful and informative to find that some of them may actually be true and that some theories and propositions that we firmly believed to be false are in fact actually quite likely to be true.[21] We can conclude from this that despite the proper caution with which teachers should approach the deliverances of empirical educational research, engagement with it is unavoidable and the craft idea that it can safely be ignored is, in fact, chimerical. Educational theory is part of the world of teachers whether they like it or not. It is far better to master it than be mastered by it.

HOW TEACHERS SHOULD ENGAGE WITH RESEARCH: DIFFERENT LEVELS OF ENGAGEMENT AND THE ONE APPROPRIATE FOR THE QUALIFIED TEACHER; POSSIBLE PROGRESSION IN RESEARCH EXPERTISE

Such reflections quite properly raise the question as to what exactly should be the relationship between teachers and educational research. One answer should be dismissed at the outset, namely that teachers should conduct their own academic educational research independently of any assistance. This is not a promising answer because the conduct of educational research is a highly demanding

---

[20]   See Hattie (2009).

[21]   Another version of the 'commonsense' objection to educational research is that the deliverances of research are, where true, largely tautological (see White 1997). Thus, to be told that good teaching requires a teacher with good subject knowledge, good discipline, a well-structured lesson, effective assessment procedures and so on is essentially to say something trivially true. However, good research, which delivers such conclusions, should inform its readers what good subject knowledge looks like or what a well-structured lesson consists of, and these are not by any means trivial truths.

and specialised occupation which requires different kinds of know-how from those required for teaching.[22] It is not fair to expect teachers to be able to take on such a role.

How, then, should they be expected to engage with educational research? One of the problems with the educational research literature is that it is often difficult to understand and interpret. This is not just because it is sometimes (often) badly or obscurely expressed, it is because the subject matter is by its nature difficult and demanding. To approach it profitably requires an understanding of the kinds of problems dealt with, the methods used and the strength of the conclusions given the evidence and arguments presented. This is why it will be argued in Chapter 10 that the initial teacher education required for a professional teacher should include a good grounding in methodological questions in education research so that the professional can make an informed judgement about the research. It is important to appreciate that this involves an understanding of not just Hattie-like metasurveys, but the work that underpins those surveys as well. If research is to guide practice, it is unlikely that it will do so just through generalisations, but rather through some detailed consideration of how theoretical considerations were put to work in practice and how such practices might bear on what a particular teacher is trying to do. Therefore, teachers need to be able to engage with the primary as well as with the secondary literature if they are to make productive use of educational research. One should not doubt that this is in itself a demanding requirement for an intending teacher and furthermore a necessary requirement for any further progression as a researcher. But it is essential if teachers are to be able to use educational research as independent agents, able to form their own judgements on the basis of their readings of such research. Nothing less will do if research is to form part of professional judgement.

THE SCOPE AND LIMITS OF TEACHER EXPERTISE – A DISCUSSION OF THE TEACHER'S ROLE IN DEVELOPING AIMS, CURRICULUM, PEDAGOGY AND ASSESSMENT

Up until this point, in this chapter and Chapters 6 and 7, discussion of teachers' work has been largely confined to their role in the classroom. This was, by and large, suitable for the ET. The craft teacher,

---

[22] See Foreman-Peck and Winch (2000) for more on the history of practitioner-based research in education. The view above does not of course suggest that teachers have no role to play in the conduct of educational research. There will be more detail on this in this chapter and the next.

however, is expected to be able to engage in curriculum innovation, planning and evaluation. The professional will be expected to do these things and more. A teacher who is unable to act independently in planning and evaluating their work is in the position where they are subordinate to someone else who takes on these roles. However, the carrying out of such second-order activities as managing a year's work for a class is not an ability that one can reliably expect to be picked up 'on the job'; it requires instruction, discussion and practice. For this reason, the craft model is poorly suited to the development of the capacity for independent action outside the classroom.

Central to the work of an independent teacher (independence being one of the primary characteristics of the professional teacher) is the capacity to plan not just individual lessons, but an integrated sequence designed to fulfil some intermediate aims. In this sense the professional teacher is a project manager, overseeing a sequence from inception to evaluation. What, then, is the degree of independence that can reasonably be expected? We can say with some confidence that teachers should not be given sole responsibility for determining the values and aims that underpin the education system, for reasons that will be discussed in more detail in Chapter 9.[23] Likewise, although this is more controversial, there are strong arguments for maintaining that individual teachers should not have sole discretion in curriculum design. Neither should they be able to determine all the instruments for assessment for all the purposes that their society has deemed necessary.[24] If teachers are to be more than ETs, it is also reasonable to expect them to exercise considerable discretion with respect to the array of pedagogical methods to be used.[25]

Within these constraints, however, the discretionary scope of the professional teacher is considerable. Planning a sequence of work has already been mentioned. This involves working within a curriculum structure to achieve aims that contribute to the overall aims of the system. Even if teachers are expected to work with structured materials such as textbooks, they will want to organise their work so as to make maximum use of their own expertise as well as of that

---

[23] For some discussion of the relationship between aims and values in education, see Winch in Gingell (2014). For a discussion of the accountability relationship within public education systems, see Winch (1996a).

[24] This issue is closely related to, although not identical with, the accountability issue.

[25] This range of discretion has, of course, to be exercised with colleagues in the context of the institutions in which they work. The roles of the second-order abilities of co-ordination and communication are, therefore, very important.

embodied in the textbook. The work planned may then use the text-book as a starting point within which the teacher has a good deal of scope for innovation.[26] It might be objected that the very idea of a textbook undermines teacher independence and reduces teachers to the status of ETs. For some textbooks, this may well be the case. Indeed, the operation of the ET model does heavily depend on struc-tured 'teacher-proof' materials. Properly designed and used, how-ever, textbooks have an important function in ensuring co-ordination of longer sequences of learning and in ensuring that important ele-ments in the curriculum are not left out. Their design should be suffi-ciently flexible to ensure that this need is fulfilled without sacrificing teacher discretion. Alternatively, they should be used by teachers in a discretionary way so as to ensure that teacher expertise is used to best effect.

At the core of teachers' work in the classroom is the way in which they actually teach. A professional teacher should have a large amount of discretion in such choice. They have the responsibility for choosing the best mix of methods to suit the aims of the lessons that they are teaching. Very often, however, they are not allowed to do this or are put under considerable pressure to adopt a preferred method of pedagogy, usually by an authority such as a headteacher or an inspec-tor.[27] How far is such prescription compatible with a teacher being a professional in the sense of this chapter?

The Shoals of Good Practice
Alexander (1992) distinguishes between four principal senses in which the term 'good practice' is used. First, practice that is in accor-dance with a teacher's values (or, more strongly, expressive of them); second, practice with which the teacher feels comfortable; third, practice prescribed by an authority figure; and fourth, practice that seems to be mandated by research evidence. Each of these concep-tions of good practice raises complex issues. A useful starting point is Alexander's discussion of the ambiguity of the term 'good practice' when used in relation to this issue.

As regards the first, it appears to be entirely reasonable to expect independent teachers to ensure that their practices do not

---

[26] See Mili's (2014) research on pedagogy and subject expertise in the contemporary Indian context.

[27] There are also political pressures to adopt 'child-centred' approaches or to engage in Continuous Comprehensive Assessment as in India as a result of recent reforms.

conflict with their values. However, a problem arises when not everyone shares the same values. An accountable education system will embody a scheme of implementation of values agreed on. These cannot involve compromise about the values as such, as we cannot reasonably expect individuals to negotiate away values that they take to be central to their conceptions of self-worth. The best we can do in such circumstances, it seems, is to negotiate practices that involve compromises concerning the *implementation* of values, which will not be too onerous for those who have to implement those practices. There is no denying that such a compromise may be potentially disturbing for teachers and other public servants who have to serve what is determined to be a common good. The potential and sometimes actual conflict between personal values and those of the institutions one serves may well be a constant or at least recurrent source of tension. This tension is one that teachers have to deal with in their reflections on themselves as teachers and the extent to which they feel comfortable with and able to develop in that role.[28]

In relation to Alexander's second sense of 'good practice', it is also a vital part of teachers' reflections on their own practice that they determine ways of working that they feel comfortable with and are 'authentic' in the sense that they are ones that they have freely chosen, albeit within the constraints described above. This does not mean, however, that such comfort with certain practices should be immutable. Teachers may have to test themselves if they think that the practices that they adopt are no longer as effective as they might be. Again, this kind of self-testing ought to be a proper part of teachers' personal reflective cycles. Taking Alexander's third conception of good practice, one would expect the ET (although not the craft teacher) to comply with authorities as to exactly what pedagogy they should use. This cannot be the case for professional teachers, who should be expected to use their own judgement to pursue their selected pedagogical course of action. If the idea of a professional teacher is to have any substance within a public education system, then a considerable amount of discretion about the choice of pedagogical methods is necessary. This does not mean that they are entitled simply to justify courses of action by saying 'This is in accord with my values' or 'This is what I feel comfortable with', for reasons that have already been noted. It is necessary, rather, to show that

---

[28] See discussion in Cribb (2011) and Weil (1955, 1958) *Oppression et Liberte*, translated as *Oppression and Liberty*, pp. 93–94 of the English edition.

a teacher's actions are in conformity with the values that underpin the education in which he or she has committed to working within[29] and that, rather than merely being comfortable with a certain way of working, it is one that allows her to work effectively within the envelope of her own abilities and character.

This does not mean therefore that professional teachers should be entitled to do just as they like. We have already noted constraints that arise under Alexander's first two conceptions of good practice. What about the fourth, that good practice is what is mandated by evidence, including empirical research evidence? It is central to the idea of a professional technician that teachers have the ability to make judgements based on an underpinning body of systematic knowledge. At the very least, such teachers should be able to understand and interpret the relevance of such research to their own personal circumstances. They will also need to interpret it in the light of their values and the kinds of ways of working with which they feel comfortable (see above). But, given these reservations, should research that apparently mandates certain courses of action have normative force for teachers?

If research (carefully investigated) suggests that a certain course of action is likely to be the most effective in achieving a goal that a teacher has set, then it looks as if the general default attitude of benevolence towards one's pupils suggests that the research should have normative force for the teacher. Professional teachers then have a *prima facie* duty to investigate and interpret such research and to incorporate it into their practice if they are satisfied that it is the best way of achieving their ends.[30]

The main issue concerning *assessment* that bears on teachers' professional discretion and judgement is that of the use of assessment in order to inform decisions about teaching or *formative* assessment. It has already been argued that the use of formative assessment in some form or other is a necessary condition for being

[29] Which is also to say that they should have a role in determining what those values are. See the discussion in Chapter 9 of this book.

[30] They should, of course, be able to and should be encouraged to discuss the issues that the research raises with their colleagues, and they should also be able to revise their views in the light of evidence from their teaching. This is not to sanction mindless experimentation with methods at the expense of pupil well-being. If benevolence suggests the adoption of a practice, then there should be a default inclination to adopt it. But such decisions also have to be revisable, for the same reasons. The key issue is the need for a responsible and informed adoption of a particular practice.

serious about teaching. But an attitude towards it is not enough. For-mative assessment involves judging whether or not objectives have been met and, if they have been exceeded or not fulfilled, why that is likely to be so. Such an ability involves know-how underpinned by an understanding not only of the subject matter being taught but also of the pupil and how they are responding. Insight gained from teach-ing experience and personal knowledge of the pupil is also likely to be critical to the development of such an ability.[31] There is good rea-son to think that this complex form of know-how, which is generally agreed to be often in short supply, is a critical part of the pedagogical armoury of professional teachers.

The foregoing discussion suggests that although the professional teacher is quite distinct from the craftworker teacher, there is an irre-ducible element of craft practice within the make-up of the success-ful professional. Norms of action that may be mandated by research have to be adopted in ways that correspond to the situations in which teachers find themselves. Even if they develop a *techne* out of that research, it has to be applied in ways appropriate to their situations.[32] The professional is quite distinct from the craftworker, but craft elements consisting of personal discretion and situational awareness based on experience are essential elements in his or her make-up.

THE CIVIC ROLE OF THE PROFESSIONAL TEACHER

Central to the work of teachers is the need for effective communica-tion and co-ordination, not just with pupils but also with colleagues. Teachers with a wide range of personal discretion and well-founded experience and judgement should be capable, to a large extent, of running their own affairs. This implies that there should be a con-siderable degree of internal democracy within the schools and col-leges within which they work. We have already seen that teachers of this kind need to be independent within the classroom. We have also noted that they need to co-ordinate and communicate with their colleagues to a high degree if they are to plan, control and evaluate effectively. If they are not to fall back into the position of accepting positional authority figures, then they will need to have an impor-tant say in decision making. It may be doubted that the governing

---

[31] Including the ability to challenge one's own perceptions of what a pupil is capable of, which may in turn involve assessing the impression that pupils might wish to give of their abilities.

[32] See the discussion in Oakeshott (1962, ch. 1).

structures in British schools as they currently exist are suited to this role.[33]

WHICH CONCEPTION OF TEACHING?

This chapter and Chapters 6 and 7 have looked at three possible, and indeed plausible, conceptions of teaching and their relationships. All are viable within their own limitations. Which one should a society choose for its education system? A lot depends on whether one is prepared to settle for a system that is 'good enough', and the absence of resources may dictate that this is just what one should do. However, we have produced good reasons to suppose that, in a society where resources are available and where there is a clear commitment to educate all future citizens to exercise the full range of their abilities, the type of teacher required will be the type who can bring that about. Doing so requires having sufficient insight into a pupil's potential and difficulties in learning (as well as being aware where there is insufficient challenge) to make this possible. This suggests a teacher who has the best intellectual resources available at their disposal and the capacity to make the best use of those resources. The craftworker and the executive technician will not have such resources and capacities available to them. The conclusion seems to follow that the professional technician is the preferred model for a society with those kinds of aspirations. In Chapter 9, we will look further at the ramifications of the adoption of this model.

---

[33] This is not to say that teachers are not under an obligation to abide by decisions collectively made, even if they disagree with them. This aspect of the 'General Will' is one of the preconditions of democratic action; see Rousseau ch. 7, [1762b], (1913), p. 15.

9

Teaching as an Occupation

Up until now, this book has tended to focus on the 'core activities' of teaching, associated with working with pupils in the classroom. The argument of the past three chapters has focussed on the strengths and weaknesses of three distinct but related conceptions of teaching: craftworker, executive technician and professional. The professional conception, it was argued, is the most suitable one for education systems in developed countries, not least because it is capable of combining the strengths of the other two and avoiding their weaknesses, while having distinctive strengths of its own.[1] So far, the argument has focussed on teachers' ability to act effectively in the classroom, promoting learning. But a professional teacher has a much broader potential occupational capacity which is, in turn, bound up with the idea of a *career* in teaching. We need to examine in detail what this involves.

TEACHING IS MORE THAN JUST A SUCCESSION OF LESSONS

We have introduced and defended the claim that teaching involves more than possessing and utilising *skills* within the classroom. Teachers have to *plan, communicate, co-ordinate, control* and *evaluate* what they are doing in the classroom and, as was argued in Chapter 3,

---

[1] It might be thought surprising, given the arguments of Chapter 7, that any aspect of the ET should receive endorsement. Yet the argument of that chapter does not preclude the possibility that there may be some, albeit temporary, assignments that teachers have to fulfil that may be best served by functioning as an ET even though one is, for the most part, a professional.

Teachers' Know-How: A Philosophical Investigation, First Edition. Christopher Winch.
© 2017 Christopher Winch. Editorial Organisation © Philosophy of Education Society of Great Britain.
Published 2017 by John Wiley & Sons, Ltd.

such activities cannot be reduced to skills but are essential charac-
terisations of what it is to teach.[2] The importance of these second-
order forms of know-how make clear why some authorities have
described teaching as 'polymorphous' or irreducible to the possession of a defined set of skills. But these second-order abilities are
just as important within the activities that take place outside the classroom, as essential preliminaries and consequences of the work that
goes on in the classroom. Chapter 3 drew attention to the *project
management* aspect of teaching, of the need to see it as an integrated
sequence of teaching a curriculum over an extended period such as
an academic year. The ability to work independently (but also in
co-ordination with colleagues) in order to make teaching a coherent
activity is essential for this extra-classroom element in a teacher's
work. If not in the very earliest stages of teaching, at any rate quite
soon after, teachers will need to show such ability to a high degree.

TEACHING AS A CAREER

Once we have acknowledged the temporally extended nature of
teaching, we can go on to consider the ramifications of thinking of it
like that. One important element of joining an occupation is to consider it as an autonomous decision to pursue a certain course of life
which will, in part, shape one's identity and make a contribution to
individual well-being by providing a continuing source of satisfaction and a sense of self-worth. Such is the German concept of a *Beruf*
(Greinert 2007; Hanf 2011). It is bound up with the idea of self-
consciously becoming and being a member of an occupation and with
an identification with the ideals, ethics and sources of self-knowledge
and satisfaction that such an identification can bring.[3] It goes without
saying that a necessary condition for an occupation to attain something like the status of a *Beruf* is that it is well-regarded: by its practitioners, by their employers and by the wider public who are affected
by the occupation. The more limited conceptions of teaching, particularly that of the ET, are less likely to attain such a status.

There are both intrinsic and instrumental reasons for wishing to
make teaching more like a *Beruf* and less like a job. Taking the intrinsic reasons first, having an occupation that gives one a sense of self-
worth and the opportunity for personal development is a necessary
component of *autonomy*, or the ability to choose a course of life that

---

[2] With the possible exception of the ET (see Chapter 8).
[3] See Higgins, *The Good Life of Teaching* (2011), for example, chapters 2 and 6.

we consider to be a necessary component of a worthwhile kind of life in the kind of society in which we exist.[4] We have already in Chapter 5 considered the importance of the ability to gain self-knowledge as a source of continuing personal satisfaction in a career in teaching. Bound up with this is the possibility of developing as an individual through taking on new roles and challenges, increasing understanding of what the occupation involves and assuming greater responsibility and leadership throughout a working life.

Instrumental reasons are also important. The existence of a committed and knowledgeable corps of teachers whose occupation is well-regarded within society is a very good way of attracting the potentially most able and dedicated young people to teaching. Such teachers, possessing the ability to teach well and effectively, are likely to be the most important elements in a successful education system.[5] Such a system in turn is likely to produce a well and appropriately educated population and to make the most of the potential of young people. To adopt such a view of teaching is to go beyond the 'good enough' or satisficing model and to think in terms of excellence, which is quite appropriate for wealthy developed societies who consider their own worth and prosperity to be bound up, at least partly, with the possession of good education systems.

To consider teaching as a career is, then, to consider oneself as the member of an occupation (or, if you like, a profession) with its own traditions and standards of excellence. This in turn involves seeing it as a means through which one can develop as a teacher and as a human being more generally. This further implies that one commit oneself to teaching for a working lifetime or a significant part thereof. Teaching becomes a form of self-expression, as service to others and to one's society. There is an obvious benefit to having a dedicated long-term corps of teachers. The experience gained by individual teachers is not lost; attrition and the wasteful deployment of resources are minimised. Last, but not least, teachers with a long-term commitment are able to assume roles of leadership, guidance and counselling and to represent teaching to the wider society.

So, what are the possible forms of a career in teaching? There are a number of areas in which teachers can develop, both in the technical aspect of their expertise and in their relationships with parents, pupils, colleagues and the public. This chapter will examine the

---

[4] See Raz (1986) for such an account of autonomy (ch. 14). See Winch (2005) for a consideration of the necessary conditions for achieving autonomy in this sense.

[5] See, for example, OECD (2014, p. 89),

different ways in which teaching as a career can develop. Some of these routes are well-established, but largely in an informal sense. The proposal for professional teachers is that these be recognised pathways, grounded in specific forms of expertise often acquired through routes that require both theoretical study and practice, often leading to further qualifications. This is not only to ensure that the teachers concerned have the necessary expertise, but also to provide a basis for further career development.

Growing Expertise in Work in the Classroom (Pedagogy)

Many teachers will see their careers primarily as developing expertise as classroom teachers. There are at least two elements to this. The first is concerned with developing a better understanding of what might be called the theoretical elements of teaching, such as what research may have to contribute to teachers' understanding of their work. This clearly involves strengthening the scholarly aspect of their work, but it also necessarily involves a second element, namely that of understanding the implications of such research and, where appropriate, applying knowledge gained from it. This itself involves the craft element of expertise in teaching, which can only really be gained through extensive work within the classroom. However, filling this role in a way that most benefits a school and its other teachers may well involve taking on a further role such as that of mentoring or educating new or intending teachers. The key point, however, is that teachers undertaking such roles should be aware of: the research into pedagogy, the bearing that it has on classroom practice in particular schools and, last but by no means least, the expertise needed to counsel colleagues in a productive way.

Ability to Configure the Curriculum

It is often said (and we have no cause to dissent) that the knowledge that teachers have of their subject matter is a key element of their ability to teach well. But this knowledge of their subject matter needs to be organised not just in terms of its logical structure, but also in what we have called a mode suitable for imparting to those who are learning the subject. It follows that teachers' subject knowledge must embrace this element. One important way in which to do so is through interpretation of the formal curriculum into a form suitable for the design of programmes and schemes of work, textbooks and teaching materials and lesson plans. Subject specialists who have the ability to do this are of great value within and beyond the school. However, the ability to do so depends on the development of an understanding of epistemic ascent and pedagogic content knowledge as these apply to their own subjects. Heightened study of the curriculum area, particularly as it relates to approaching the subject from the point of view of learning, is important, but it is most fruitfully acquired if done so by someone who has already effectively acquired a considerable degree of pedagogic content knowledge. As in the case with a pedagogic specialism, a good grasp of the research relating to curriculum studies and to curriculum studies in the relevant subject is an important prerequisite for carrying out this role effectively.

Co-ordination of Work within and between Cohorts
Very closely related to this role and one that is probably best fulfilled by someone who is a curriculum specialist is that of co-ordinator. In order for teaching to be effective, it is necessary not just that good work occurs in individual classrooms, but also that the work between classrooms is properly co-ordinated to maximise progression and to eliminate, as far as possible, duplication of content. To do this successfully requires a lot of ability, including the ability to interpret the curriculum (see above) but also to co-ordinate the work of different people and to persuade them of the correctness of a course of action, after discussing the options. This role of subject co-ordination is a very important one within a school.

Diagnosis and Assessment
Although the ability to diagnose difficulties, and also cases where the pupil finds learning insufficiently challenging, are critical to effective work in the classroom, they are very often areas of work that teachers find very difficult to deal with. Understanding what are realistic but demanding expectations is also difficult, not to mention the devising of strategies, techniques and materials for diagnosis and consequent planning of subsequent work. So important and difficult is this aspect of teachers' work that it is arguably an area in which individuals can develop their subject expertise in particular ways so that they are able not just to be extremely effective in this aspect of their work themselves, but also effective in helping other teachers to develop expertise. Assessment and diagnosis is often a complex and difficult area of scholarship to master. Once again, not only practical experience, but also the ability to use research to develop what is practically valuable and to separate out what is not, are important elements in the fulfilment of this role.

Pastoral Work

All manners of considerations affect the ability of pupils to benefit effectively from schooling. These include cultural, ethnic, domestic and friendship factors, not to mention family, health and emotional difficulties. Clearly there are limits to the extent to which teachers can and should involve themselves in these matters, but at the same time a failure to appreciate their importance can also be very damaging to the prospects of successful teaching. There is room for teachers who wish to gain a specific understanding of the way in which individual pupils are affected by these factors, to develop a specialism in the area and to work with classroom teachers in understanding and solving extra-educational problems that pupils may be having. It is helpful to have someone within a school who has both a theoretical understanding of the issues and good practical experience of dealing with them, to take on such a role as counsellor both to the leadership of the school and also to teachers who are having difficulty in understanding why some children are having particular difficulties at school. The role is not that of representing pupils who are in trouble at school but in helping schools and teachers to understand the nature of some of the difficulties and to help in devising solutions.

Mentoring and Teacher Education

Implicit in what has been argued so far about the importance of the professional model of teaching is, on the one hand, the importance of teacher education grounded in the reality of the school and, on the other hand, the continuing extension of the understanding and expertise of teachers who are already qualified. This very important role requires abilities that are not the same as those of the successful classroom teacher (although it presupposes those abilities) but involve an understanding of and empathy with adults who are developing within their profession. The acquisition of professional expertise and associated qualifications and licences is a 'high-stakes' activity for the person undertaking it. It is desirable that someone who takes on such a demanding role has a suitable preparation for doing so and also that suitable people take it on, as unsuitable or poor-quality mentoring and school-based teacher education can have disastrous consequences.

Leadership and Governance

A professional teaching force would be expected to work relatively independently, and this capability in turn implies flatter management structures than would otherwise be the case. But we have already seen that good co-ordination and communication are essential requirements in a successful school. However, schools also need to be given strategic direction and the capability of developing their own values and ethos.[6] This does not mean that schools need to be independent of the national school system, but that they do have a certain degree of freedom to implement national policies in a way suited to their own needs and preferences. Teachers should, therefore, be capable of acting effectively with other stakeholders such as parents and local authority representatives on the governing bodies of their schools. In addition, management know-how is needed in order to interpret national and school-specific policies and to ensure that they are implemented effectively. Given a body of teachers used to and capable of acting independently, such management has to be something more than 'command and control' but needs to depend to a high degree on consultation and co-operation. In Chapter 10, we shall see that these roles require preparation and that intending teachers should be aware of what they involve from the earliest stages of their careers.

As a more general point about the running of the school system, it is useful to distinguish between leadership, authority and counsel in the different roles that teachers have within and beyond schools. *Leadership*, the ability to persuade others of an opinion or the desirability of a course of action, is an attribute that can be acquired as a by-product of one's expertise, and one need not hold a formal position to exercise it, although it is to be hoped that those who are in positions of formal authority do also have the capacity for leadership. In this sense, the capacity for leadership is a form of authority if it rests on genuine expertise and on an ability to convey the outcome of that expertise to colleagues.[7] The primary attribute of leadership in teaching is, then, that of giving good counsel. Such an ability is at least to a large extent a function of professional experience together with an ability to reflect on and transmit what is valuable about that experience to colleagues and others concerned with the education system.[8]

---

[6] Values are the fundamental ethical commitments of the school, underpinned by both empirical and metaphysical beliefs. Ethos is the informal as well as formal normative framework, which embodies (or fails to embody) the school's values.

[7] It is more than power, because expertise lends a legitimacy to one's counsel which the exercise of rhetorical persuasion by itself could not.

[8] Peters' distinction between being *an authority* and being *in authority* is relevant here. The argument is that one should preferably be an authority in a relevant area prior to being put in authority in that area. See Peters (1967). See also de Jouvenel (1957, esp. ch. 5) for an insightful discussion of the concept of authority and how it relates to leadership.

Those who assume formal positions of responsibility should be capable of leading, but we need to be clear about what this involves in the context of a workforce of professional teachers. It has to involve consultation and persuasion if it is to be effective.[9] It is suggested then that all teachers, from their initial teacher education onwards, need to think of themselves as potential leaders. They may not assume formal positions of managerial responsibility, but in any event, their ability to give wise counsel is a valuable attribute for the profession.

A teacher in a position of authority is, ideally, a leader. If they are to be effective, they cannot just be managers who are charged with implementing decisions made at the governing body, local authority or national level. The operation of command and control can ensure obedience from the workforce and even a form of passive consent. But proposals implemented with less than full commitment are much less likely to be effective than those implemented with the active consent of the teachers involved.[10]

Inspection

Inspection involves judging on whether and to what extent what goes on in schools and classrooms is worthwhile, and giving an authoritative pronouncement on those questions. There are different models for doing this. Inspection in the UK is something that is done to teachers and schools, rather than an activity in which they themselves have a responsible role to play. A good case can be made out for a revised form of peer inspection in which relatively senior serving teachers themselves make up inspection teams (albeit moderated by a more permanent corps of inspection specialists, who could well include those from outside the education system). The advantages of such an approach are that it allows for the sharing of experiences through the system, allows the development and consolidation of a common

---

[9] This does not mean that decisions should not be taken and that, when appropriate, people be expected to implement them. This is true of the most democratic kinds of system (Rousseau [1762a] (1913), p. 15).

[10] Hume's discussion of the sources of obedience tends to emphasise the passive side of consent and does not take account of involvement; see Hume (1978, pt. 2, bk. 3, sec. X). By contrast, see Rousseau's discussion of this issue, which emphasises agreement and the consequences of being bound by freely chosen agreement. Organisations like schools need active consent from those working in them if they are to be effective. This is more likely to occur when those concerned have had a say in the decision making. They need to be persuaded, and it helps if a leader is capable of rationally persuading.

conceptual and terminological framework and allows teachers to take responsibility for making improvements to the system as a whole.[11]

Inspection involves the reporting on and assessment of activities within a school. The particular purposes of inspection can be varied and do, of course, include accountability for the effective deployment of public resources.[12] But there are other, inspection-related roles which are valuable to schools, and these include evaluation and advice. This is not the chapter in which to present a set of recommendations for a preferred system of inspection, but if such roles are desirable they should be available to schools, provided either locally or nationally.[13]

Such roles require lengthy preparation and people who have great experience of successful teaching. But it is not always realised that they need much more than that. There can be nothing worse than inspectors who make judgements according to their own prejudices and predilections unmediated by research and reflection. This includes those inspectors who make judgements on the basis of ill-considered fads with little evidence for their effectiveness. As well as being impartial and reflective, with good experience of teaching, inspectors need to be scholars who can thoroughly understand research evidence and integrate that understanding into their own work. 'Understanding' in this context means, among other things, an ability not only to see what the scope and limitations of research might be, but also to have a sound grasp of what its significance should be for those teachers who are subject to inspection. This requires an ability to make contextualised judgements about research findings and not to make blanket applications of conclusions that may be superficially drawn from research evidence. All professional teachers should be able to assess not only the probity of research but also its relevance to their own circumstances. But this ability needs to be extended, in the case of inspection, to the second-order judgement concerning how effectively teachers are doing so.

---

[11] This would involve, in the UK, a very different system of inspection than now exists. It would resemble the early stages of the kind of regime used in higher education at the turn of the twenty-first century in the UK. See Winch (2001) for a more detailed argument.

[12] The prime purpose of inspection in England and Wales.

[13] It is very important that those who take on such 'advisory' roles are genuinely knowledgeable and expert teachers. The purveyors of passing fads have no role to play in authoritative positions within the education system.

Post-Qualification Progression

In Chapter 10, it will be argued that the initial qualification for teachers should preferably be at masters level. However, it will also be argued that the attainment of this qualification should not occur until a certain amount of authentic teaching experience has been acquired. Pre-qualification entry should be at bachelors level with a proven capacity to be able to carry out further professionally oriented scholarship and, to a certain degree, research. This brings us to the issue of the extent to which teachers should also be researchers, something on which much has been written in the last 40 years or so. It is perhaps best to tackle this issue in relation to the kinds of careers that teachers may reasonably expect to pursue over a number of decades.

As a preliminary, we need to remind ourselves from the conclusion of Chapter 8 that the conception of the professional teacher includes the capacity for scholarship in relation to the bearing that conceptual understanding and understanding of research evidence has on professional judgement and action. It will be argued in Chapter 10 that the qualification leading to full licensure as a teacher should include the ability to evaluate some aspect of the work of the teacher aiming for the qualification. Does this mean that this study is advocating the often-articulated idea that teachers should also be researchers?

If by this it is meant that teachers should be regarded as having as much right and expertise to conduct research relevant to their teaching as a professionally qualified researcher with, for example, a PhD in educational research, then the answer is 'no'. On the other hand, the masters-level qualification that a fully licensed teacher ought to possess should provide the expertise to undertake further study leading to such a qualification. Neither does it preclude teachers who wish to develop a career in practically oriented research from working in teams of researchers on questions of practical importance, perhaps doing so as part of undertaking study for an advanced qualification in educational research.

It is worth reminding ourselves of just what a fully qualified researcher should be capable of. This includes being able to formulate a relevant and useful research question, to develop a strategy to address it, to choose and use appropriate methods, to assess the significance of findings and to evaluate whether and to what extent research questions posed have been answered. We should add that a qualified researcher should also be capable of commissioning and evaluating research carried out by others. It is obviously impractical and probably undesirable to expect newly qualified teachers to be capable of undertaking such complex project management activities, but it is certainly not unreasonable to expect that their masters-level initial qualifications should render them capable of aspiring to and acquiring such abilities. Such opportunities need not and probably should not be confined to study for a traditional PhD qualification. A professional qualification at doctoral level, such as the EdD now offered by many universities, is, in some ways, a more suitable qualification for such a career, for the following reasons.

First, it can offer a rigorous education in the research cycle that gives due account both to conceptual questions of understanding the field of education and to the formulation of research questions. Second, it is suited to the kinds of opportunities in which teachers have to formulate questions relevant to professional practice. Third, it provides schools with the resources to gain an enhanced understanding, both of what research has to say that might be relevant to them and also to provide an enhanced capacity for innovation and evaluation within the school setting.

Qualifications such as these may allow teachers to go on to pursue an academic career but should also open up other roles within teaching that are valuable to education and that require a high degree of research expertise to be done well. As already mentioned, inspection and advice is one such role, but curriculum design and evaluation is another that will require such abilities. Not least among the advantages that schools or groups of schools who have staff qualified at this level will possess is that they will be able to engage with universities and research institutes as partners in planning, carrying out and evaluating research relevant to their concerns, thus enhancing the research, development and evaluation capacity not only of the school system but also of practically oriented educational research as a whole.

Curriculum Evaluation and Design
Curriculum design and evaluation raise important questions about the scope and limits of teachers' own expertise and activities. Public education is the responsibility of the society as a whole, not of individual teachers. But it is absurd to imagine that the understanding and expertise possessed by teachers are irrelevant to curriculum design and evaluation. What the scope and limits of teacher action are within the context of a publicly funded and accountable education system raises some difficult questions. The curriculum is the prescribed content of education (Barrow 1984). It should bear a meaningful relationship to educational aims (White 2007), and these should reflect an

agreement about the values to be implemented within education (Winch 1996a, 2014). It is difficult to maintain that teachers and schools can be the sole custodians of the curriculum and thus indirectly of the society's values. On the other hand, to exclude them completely from consideration of what should be in the curriculum is to run the danger not only of losing the benefit of their expertise in rendering knowledge into a form suitable for pupil learning, but also of demoralising and deskilling the profession.

By itself, a national curriculum need not prescribe in detail what should go on in each lesson or even what should go on during the course of a school term. Much of the detail of the implementation of the curriculum needs to be left to schools and teachers to deal with, once we accept the professional conception of the teacher, someone who is capable of long-term planning, of configuring subject knowledge into a form suitable for pupil learning and of exercising discretion according to local circumstances.

If this is right, it will fall to the teaching profession to play a major role in the implementation of a national curriculum. We will come back to this shortly. But we can go further than this. A national curriculum is not merely an account of what should be learned, but it should present content in such a way that it is capable of being turned into effective programmes of study. Curriculum design in this macro sense is going to require expertise from teachers concerning selection of content and Epistemic Ascent.[14] It goes without saying that teachers engaged in this kind of activity should have not only very good experience of teaching their subjects but also a profound understanding of the epistemological issues concerning curriculum design in general and of those pertaining to their subject in particular. They should be able to understand and to assess the merits of developmental claims arising from psychology and to debate these with other specialists. It is unlikely that they will be able to do this without further study of curriculum design questions relating to their subject at a high (possibly doctoral) level.

When we move from the macro level to the meso level of syllabi and detailed programmes of study, the role of teachers will inevitably become more preponderant. Teachers or curriculum designers with a very strong teaching background will be needed to specify content and sequence of content, and to advise or to produce teaching materials including textbooks. As it is so important that this work is done

---

[14] For an account of Epistemic Ascent, see Chapter 5.

to the highest possible standard, this will need to be done collectively by subject experts, moderated by other stakeholders. Such work will be ongoing as there will be various reasons why syllabi and schemes of work will need to be modified, not only when changes are made to the national curriculum. It should, therefore, be a major career milestone for a teacher to be appointed to such a role, whether at a national, regional or school level.[15]

The Extended Civic Role of Teaching

Consideration of the role of teachers in the design and implementation of the curriculum draws attention to the scope and limits of teacher competence in the public sphere. Public education is ultimately the concern of the public, its political representatives and major stakeholders within the society. But teachers are part of this public as well, and their contribution to national discussions will be distinctive because it will be informed by detailed understanding of the problems associated with implementing an agreed curriculum. This is a good reason why they should be expected to contribute a particularly authoritative voice to discussions of curriculum, pedagogy, assessment and resources. This civic role of the profession is very important, but perhaps not always accorded the importance that it deserves. This is particularly the case where the society in which they practice their occupation has weak or non-existent social partnership arrangements. By 'social partnership' is meant the practice of co-operating and resolving conflicts through regular contact between the major interest groups within a sector, usually including trades unions, employers, government and possibly others, including local authorities and voluntary organisations.

Social partnership may occur at different levels in a society: national, regional, local or workplace-based. It is particularly beneficial if teachers can exercise at least a part of their civic role through such arrangements. By their very nature they bring teachers into

---

[15] We need to envisage the role of curriculum implementation taking place at various levels. Some material will be produced at the national level, for example, textbooks and some teachers' resource materials. Some may be designed for particular regions to take advantage of local or regional resources. But the role of a school curriculum organiser will be important, not only in interpreting this material for colleagues but for advising teachers on the detailed planning of schemes of work for a class for a term or year and even in terms of offering advice on the structure and content of particular lessons. See the section above on the role of the school curriculum specialist. Progression to work at a regional or national level should be a possible career path, undertaken through a combination of experience and further study.

contact with other stakeholders with potentially very different points of view which they will then have to understand and take account of. The ability to listen sympathetically, understand other points of view divergent from one's own, negotiate and compromise are essential attributes for working effectively within social partnership arrangements. Once again, such roles require not only appropriate personal qualities but also systematic preparation, which is arguably a responsibility of all professional teachers, particularly if social partnership arrangements exist at the school level.[16]

Management and Governance

If the arguments of this chapter are correct, teachers acquire the ability to act as leaders and counsellors of other teachers through being prepared for such roles from the outset of their teacher education and then through fulfilment of one of the kinds of responsibilities within a career path that has already been outlined in this chapter. But there is a separate function involved in the day-to-day co-ordination of the activities of the school, the devising of school policies, parent–stakeholder–school relationships and the operation of governance structures. According to the arguments of this book, teachers should be able to operate under conditions of trust and with relatively high levels of autonomy in their day-to-day working lives.

This means that they will not need to be excessively 'micro-managed' or subject to intrusive accountability procedures but will by and large be trusted not only to get on with the job, but also to undertake collectively those co-ordinative functions of education that constitute a large part of 'management'. But they should also be able to assist, through electing representatives, in the governance function and in the formulation of school policies. This still leaves a substantial role to 'senior management', but to the extent that teachers are able to be self-governing the role of senior management will be more consultative and concerned with command and control largely in the sense of ensuring that collectively agreed decisions are, in fact, implemented.[17] Preparation for this role should involve giving

---

[16] This could include representation on school governing bodies, but may also encompass a 'works council' for the school in which day-to-day or week-to-week matters are discussed and decided upon.

[17] A very big if here concerns the preparedness of governments and, to a lesser extent, local authorities to grant schools *de facto* autonomy and not to seek to interfere with the operation of the education system in the short to medium term by government directives. The abilities for schools to self-govern exist in inverse proportion to the tendency of governments to run the education

prospective school leaders a profound understanding of the system in which they operate, which should involve some academic preparation. Just as important, however, will also be the experience that they will have gained in earning the trust and co-operation of colleagues through the communicative and co-ordinative activities outlined earlier in this chapter as elements in career progression for professional teachers.

THE LONG HAUL AND ATTRITION

What advantages are there to considering teaching as a professional type of occupation[18] with a long-term career structure? The model suggested in this chapter is one where teachers gain in expertise, initially within the classroom and then increasingly in a number of roles that require both extensive experience of teaching and further academic study, some of which may take place within a 'workplace' setting. Alongside this, teachers should have the opportunities, both personal and institutional, to develop a civic role, not only in the management and governance of their own institutions, but also in interaction with civil society and the state. Such a model conserves expertise, gives stability to the teaching workforce and maintains its morale – all desirable attributes of a national teaching force. Not least, it enhances the prestige and reputation of teaching as an occupation and thus attracts high-quality applicants, initiating a virtuous circle of educational improvement.

The selection and education of intending teachers are hugely important and will be discussed in detail in Chapter 10. However, it is important that excessive attrition does not occur post qualification. If the route to full qualification and teacher is to be lengthy and demanding, the opportunities that arise at the end of that period should be good enough to retain teachers for a lifelong career. So, what can be done to minimise attrition?

There are a number of quite simple measures and then some which require more thought and institutional change. The first of these is

system through directives from the centre. When an education system is run in this way, particularly according to the standards of 'new public management', the kind of manipulative qualification such as the NPQH (National Professional Qualification for Headteachers) devised by a previous British government will be appropriate. This approach was roundly criticised by Smith (2002).

[18] By this I mean an occupation with most if not all of the characteristics of the classic profession, such as medicine or law. The argument for the professional technician type of teacher (Chapter 8) has been an argument for an occupation of just that kind (see Freidson 1986).

perhaps obvious but often neglected. Teachers are probably at their most vulnerable at the early stage of their careers post initial qualification. Inevitably, they have a lot to learn through experience. They need to be given the opportunities to learn without being given demanding roles that should best be carried out by more experienced teachers. It is the responsibility of those who exercise leadership within schools to ensure that this happens. There is a particular danger that, in a 'high-stakes' environment, where for example, inspection reports and examination results have important consequences for schools and individual careers, younger and less experienced teachers are exposed to great pressures and then discarded when it turns out that they are not quite ready to cope with them. Second, it is important that teachers, particularly junior teachers, are not treated as 'dogsbodies' and given tasks to do which, though pressing for the school, are not within the sphere of expertise of the teacher. This includes being asked to teach subjects that they are not qualified to teach,[19] having to teach classes that they are not yet ready to teach and not being supported by senior staff when they find themselves in confrontational situations with pupils, parents or other staff. Regrettably all too often these are common factors within school life, and their prevalence is to a large degree due to poor leadership, governance and management qualities within the more senior reaches of the teaching force.[20]

The fact that this is so is in part a reflection on the qualities of those recruited into the profession, but also on the quality of the initial and continuing education that they obtain. As intimated earlier, the idea that leadership is an important future role for teachers is one that should be developed as part of initial teacher education. Continuing professional development, particularly for those aspiring to management positions, should pay particular attention to the issue of treating staff fairly and properly. Management is not just about implementing decisions; it is about doing so in a way that respects the individuals who have to implement those decisions and thus involves understanding how they might feel about the way that decisions taken will affect them. Current education management doctrine seems far from doing so. In particular, outdated 'hydraulic' accounts of motivation, linked

---

[19] There is a large literature on this topic. See, for example, Ingersoll and Smith (2003), and MacDonald (1999).

[20] It would be wrong, of course, to attribute all of these failings to teachers. Other contributory factors include: inappropriate high-stakes accountability procedures, lack of resources, failure of governments to support teachers and opportunistic media campaigns.

to primitive incentive schemes of reward and punishment, seem to be the dominant paradigm, imported, no doubt, from among the worst practices in the private sector.

Finally, provision needs to be made for the very large proportion of teachers who leave the profession temporarily to raise a family. They are too important a resource to lose altogether, and every effort should be made to retain them within the profession, whether it be through part-time working opportunities or opportunities to gain further qualification, not to mention opportunities to resume a senior role if they have already achieved one.

This chapter has provided an outline of how teaching may be seen as a professional career and the kinds of opportunities that should be available to those who choose to make it a career. It should be added that it is also highly desirable that those whose careers take the trajectories outlined here should also be able to retain opportunities for working with pupils in classrooms. Most of the roles described here should not preclude that, but careful thought will need to be given to the institutional framework in which schools are organised and the kinds of links that they can have with other educational bodies without compromising the education of their pupils.

10
Teacher Education

INTRODUCTION

We have argued for a particular professional conception of a teacher. The question then arises as to how such teachers should be prepared for their occupation and what opportunities they should have in the course of their careers in order to develop their expertise. We will need to consider some general questions pertaining to teacher education as well as to the specifics of preparation to be a professional in the sense developed so far in this book. We will consider: the selection of potential teachers, different models of initial teacher education, early career qualification and career professional development. In the course of doing so, we will look at some of the contemporary debates concerning teacher education that are relevant to this question.

SELECTION AND RECRUITMENT

Getting suitable people into teaching is a great challenge. It is so important because without the appropriate potential in candidates, it is going to be difficult to meet the high expectations that one would expect from a professional teacher. The requirement for an executive technician or a craft-based teacher is likely to be less onerous. An important factor in getting the right candidates is, of course, that they themselves regard teaching as a highly valued occupation that gives them pride as well as adequate remuneration. This may seem obvious, but it is a genuine problem where teaching is poorly regarded

Teachers' Know-How: A Philosophical Investigation, First Edition. Christopher Winch.
© 2017 Christopher Winch. Editorial Organisation © Philosophy of Education Society of Great Britain.
Published 2017 by John Wiley & Sons, Ltd.

by the public or where it is seen to pose intractable problems for those practising it. Teaching cannot just be 'spun' into being a highly regarded profession; it needs to be seen to be so. If teachers are mistrusted, punished ('held accountable' in the current jargon) or seen not to have the support of the political class and the public, this is unlikely to happen. So anyone who is serious about this issue needs to think of the long-term interests of education and to eschew the political expediency of attacking educational institutions and their personnel.[1] It is no exaggeration to say that if suitable recruits to the profession cannot be found, then any project of founding a professional teaching force is going to be unsuccessful and something less will need to be settled for, with all the consequences that that has for the education system.

Initial Teacher Education

The usual main purpose of initial teacher education is to provide a preparation for those who wish to become teachers sufficient for them to practise the occupation independently or, perhaps, under varying degrees of supervision. Those who are sceptical about the value of teacher education maintain instead that some form of supervised practice is sufficient to prepare the intending teacher for his role.[2]

We need to distinguish three elements of becoming a recognised teacher. The first is to be allowed to teach in a specific school. This can be done by the school itself after satisfying itself that an individual is competent to teach within that school. The second is the idea of *occupational licensure.* The teacher is licensed by the state (or some recognised authority) to practise if he or she can find employment in a particular school. The third is the idea of *occupational qualification.* One receives a qualification that is a guarantee that the individual holding it has the attributes necessary to practice the occupation well. One might think that it would be necessary to receive the qualification first, then the licence to practice and finally the offer of employment. However, this is not always the case. In England at the time of writing, it is possible in some categories of school to gain

---

[1] Hume's interesting idea that politicians should make the long-term interests of the public their own short-term interests runs into the problem in a democratic society that politicians need to be re-elected, usually within a short time horizon. See Hume (1978, bk. III, pt. 2, p. 537).

[2] The evidential base for the effectiveness of teacher education (let alone different types of teacher education) is not good, and more work needs to be done on this (see Hattie 2009, pp. 108–112; and, for a contrasting view, Darling-Hammond 2000).

employment without occupational licensure or qualification. It is also possible to gain licensure ('qualified teacher status') without an occupational qualification. The craft conception of teaching currently prevalent in England is comfortable with such ideas. For example, an individual who seems suitable to the school can be offered a contract of employment without teaching experience, provided he submits himself to whatever programme of preparation the school wishes to provide. The ability to practise successfully within that school can then appear on his CV as an indication that he has indeed acquired the ability to teach in a school.

It is the claim of this book that the conception of a professional teacher is incompatible with this kind of preparation. The sequence should instead be:

Achievement of the professional qualification which contains within it occupational licensure.[3]
Offer of employment.

It is also a central part of the preparation of a professional teacher that the candidate has considerable experience of teaching, a considerable proportion of that experience being no more than lightly supervised. The question then arises as to whether or not that experience should be as an employee of a school (as an apprentice), or as a supernumerary working in the school (as an intern). It is important to point out that there is nothing in the preparation of the professional teacher that should preclude becoming an apprentice – in fact, there may be good pedagogic reasons for going down this route.[4]

The latter idea suggests that some kind of apprenticeship is necessary before one can become an independently operating teacher. Few, if any, commentators maintain that becoming a full-fledged teacher needs no preparation whatsoever. At the core of the conception of a professional teacher is the idea that there are two necessary conditions for occupational competence, itself a necessary condition for the development of occupational expertise.[5] The first is the ability to practise the core activities of a teacher, namely teaching in classrooms, planning and assessing one's own programme of work and

---

[3] There are further complications to which we shall refer in due course.
[4] This entails, of course, that we are clearer about the meaning of the term 'apprentice', about which more shortly.
[5] Although the English term 'competence' is used here, by it is meant something more akin to the German 'occupational capacity', an all-round ability to practice the occupation (see Hanf 2011).

co-operating effectively with other colleagues. The second is the application to practice of the underlying systematic knowledge and understanding (theory) that enable the former activities to be undertaken with the greatest effect. As argued in Chapter 8, this underlying systematic knowledge and understanding include both conceptual and empirical elements, closely connected with each other.

The question then arises as to how such a synthesis can best be achieved. It is a corollary of the professional conception of a teacher that the occupation will be intellectually demanding, and the understanding needed to teach effectively will entail ability to interrogate and make use of a wide variety of theoretically based materials. If we take Northern European models as examples, typical preparation times for the achievement of full teacher status will be between five and seven years, in contrast to the three to four years expected in England.

If the aim is to acquire teachers who have a good understanding of the conceptual and empirical world of education in which they operate, together with a good understanding of how their work impacts on the wider society, then they will need a philosophical introduction to the conceptual field of education. They will also need to understand the ethical presuppositions of teaching, the preconditions for empirical warrant for practice (which will include some fluency with the philosophy of the social sciences) and a good understanding of the conceptual framework of their own subjects, together with an ability to understand debates about its nature.[6]

It is important to understand that teachers will need not just information about philosophical positions concerning education, but also the ability to understand and navigate philosophical debates about educational matters. The reason for this is that although it is possible to construct a broadly based categorial framework for understanding education in any society, its particular manifestations and the contested nature of those manifestations in particular societies and epochs entail that there can be no conceptually watertight clearcut conception of education that can be applied across history and geopolitical space.[7] However, there are certain important elements of the conceptual field of any form of education, which is itself a universal human practice based on the limiting concepts of the

---

[6] See Winch (2012) for an earlier version of this argument.

[7] A view which R.S. Peters came to adopt in his much-neglected but important late work 'Essays on Educators' (1981); see ch. 3 especially.

biological cycle of human life.[8] These include *values*, or a community's beliefs about what is worthwhile in human life (which includes
metaphysical, ethical and empirical elements); *aims* or the overarching purposes for which education is pursued in any given society; the
curriculum or the content that is prescribed as a means to fulfil these
aims; *pedagogy* or the forms of teaching and learning employed to
ensure that the elements of the curriculum are learned; *assessment*
or the idea that there are success criteria for pedagogic processes
and *resources*, the means required to fulfil an educational endeavour.[9] This framework and the conceptual relationships between these
overarching concepts need to be acquired[10] in order to understand
the possibilities of different manifestations in particular *conceptions*
of education in different societies and times. It is especially important for intending teachers to understand the particular conceptions
of education in play in the societies in which they intend to teach.
Not only will they have to work within such conceptions, but they
will need to deal with the possibility that their society will contain
multiple and contested conceptions.[11]

Such debates have clear ethical implications, since they are
founded on questions about value, which teachers cannot ignore.
In particular, they need to engage with the professional values that
should underpin teaching, the occupation which they aspire to join,
as well as to understand the kinds of character attributes required of
a teacher and the particular abilities to negotiate the complex world
of teaching and education. How these matters are conceptualised is
an important element in the earlier stages of teacher education[12] and
has to serve as a foundation for the more detailed and practically oriented reflection that a teacher needs to be able to engage in during
his or her career.

It has been argued in this book that engagement with empirical
thinking about education in general and teaching and learning in
particular is unavoidable, even if teachers are not always aware of

---

[8] See Vico (1968) and Winch (1964) on limiting concepts.

[9] See Winch (1996a), Naik (1975) and Sarangapani (2010).

[10] A conception being a particular interpretation of a categorial concept. There is no direct implication that a conception be *contested*, but given a plurality of possible conceptions of a categorial
concept like education, its *contestability* seems assured.

[11] They will also have to contend with the reconciliation of their own values with those that inform
the education system that they are entering, a neglected area of discussion of professional ethics
(see Cribb 2011).

[12] By which is meant here that component of a programme that is specifically concerned with
preparation for working in schools, as opposed to the subject study.

it. 'Commonsense', it was argued in Chapter 6, is often a disguised and corrupted version of often dubious educational research. Teachers need to understand the nature of empirical research into educational matters, the difference between good and bad research and the nature of research-based warrant for action. Understanding empirical educational research involves engagement with three elements: how research into a human institution like education differs from research in the physical and biological sciences, and what counts as sound research of this kind; the actual content of that research in areas relevant to teachers' concerns; and the practical ability to assess (1) such research for its relevance to teachers' own practices, and (2) the relevance of such research to the formation of professional judgements.

Finally, an intending teacher's own personal education into the subject which he or she will eventually wish to teach is of the highest importance and, as argued in Chapter 4, will need to include three elements: first, the subject under the aspect of its philosophical presuppositions (which are often contested in a way that is highly relevant to curriculum design); second, the logical structure of its central concepts, propositions and empirical findings;[13] and, third, under the aspect of *Epistemic Ascent* or the way in which the subject material should be organised in a way suitable for learning. It is debateable whether such a demanding curriculum can be completed at the bachelors level or whether a four-year programme is necessary.[14]

It is desirable not only that such understandings be developed at a relatively early stage in a teacher's preparation, but also that they be subjected to validation and deepening in the practical environment of teaching, ideally through engagement in teaching itself. As noted, there are two broad models of how this should take place, whether it be through *apprenticeship* whereby the intending teacher is an employee, or through *internship*, whereby the intending teacher is supernumerary but authorised to work under supervision within the workplace.

Before considering the relative merits of apprenticeship and internship, it is important to get clear about what an apprenticeship

[13] Often to be understood in terms of material rather than formal implication (see Brandom 2000).

[14] Confusion is possible here because the UK has already had four-year bachelor degrees. There are some grounds for thinking that the time allocated to these programmes was not used optimally. However, a demanding curriculum of the kind envisaged here may well need such an extended period. A master degree in Europe usually requires the equivalent of two years of full-time study, whereas the UK norm is one year. We need to bear this in mind when trying to establish equivalents with other European practices.

actually entails. Although an apprentice is technically a junior employee in an organisation, it is important to realise that he or she not only is a *worker* in that environment, but also is there to learn to become a competent practitioner of the occupation. There can be tensions between these two roles.[15] The economic model underlying apprenticeship is that it is over a period self-financing for the employer, while the apprentice makes a trade-off between the wage of the fully qualified and the opportunity to learn to become a fully competent practitioner.[16] The employer thus recoups expenditure on employing a not fully productive worker over an extended period during the latter part of which the apprentice is quite productive, although not yet as well remunerated as a fully qualified worker. It is therefore in the interests of the employer for the apprentice to become as productive as possible as quickly as possible, and this entails that the apprentice acquires the knowledge necessary to become a productive employee. In Northern Europe and especially in the German-speaking countries of Germany, Austria and Switzerland, this is taken to mean that the apprentice spends considerable amounts of time outside the workplace acquiring this technical knowledge, which he or she is then expected to put to work on return to the workplace. Such systems are therefore known as 'dual', signifying that learning takes place in two interconnected environments, the workplace and the vocational college.[17]

It may well also be the case, however, that the state intends that personal and civic education should continue during the period of apprenticeship, and to this end, provision will be made within the college-based element of the learning programme for such a curriculum to be taught. In this case, because the goods provided are not directly to the benefit of the employer, the financing of those elements is taken on by the state. We can see, therefore, that there is a great deal more to the modern idea of an apprenticeship than just 'learning on the job' under the supervision of an experienced craftworker, and when considering apprenticeship as a model of teacher education we will have this more complex version in mind at all times.

The great advantage of apprenticeship over internship is that the apprentice has, by the very nature of the role, an established place in the organisation and is expected to take on responsibility from an

---

[15] See Ryan (2012) for a thoughtful discussion.
[16] For details, see Foreman-Peck (2004).
[17] See Winch (2006) for more on the philosophical foundations of the dual system of apprenticeship.

early stage, albeit in a graded way and initially under close supervision. In particular, the dual system is thought to provide the most effective way of ensuring that the systematic knowledge that underpins the practice of the occupation is used to maximum effect within the practice.[18] In the light of the argument above, this would be a very important consideration when apprenticeship-based teacher education for the professional conception of teaching is considered.

Nevertheless, there are potentially significant drawbacks to a mass dual-apprenticeship system for intending teachers. These include: the need for selection not to be in the exclusive hands of the employing school; the need for higher education involvement in the selection of candidates; the need for the apprentice to gain experience of a range of different educational institutions; the need to satisfy the requirements not just of the school of which he or she is an employee, but also of the range of schools for which he is intending to teach; the need for the economic model to work satisfactorily and last, but not least, the need for capacity for many apprentices within the school system. The last requirement, in particular, may not be easy to fulfil in a mass system.

Assuming that apprenticeship were to become a dominant form of teacher education for intending professional teachers, what would it look like? Given the needs mentioned above, it would be very important for the selection of candidates to be done with not only their employability in a particular school in mind, but also their potential to work in schools within a particular age range throughout the system. This implies that schools, although they may have the final word on whom they employ, will also need to defer to the assessments of higher education institutions and other stakeholders about the academic suitability of candidates.

Given that candidates are preparing for a qualification that will enable them to teach in a wide variety of conditions across the education system of a country, it is important that their experience is not just of one school, but of a variety. It is difficult for a single school to organise this. These considerations suggest organisational complexity. Let us suppose that schools pay their apprentices a salary. Ultimately, this will need to be financed by the state. Furthermore, the state will have to calculate a *per capita* sum that takes into account not only an apprentice-style salary, but also the expenses of providing the other elements of the apprenticeship, which will include

---

[18] See Bosch (2014) for a detailed defence of this view.

experience of working in other schools and a higher education element that may well take place outside the school. Schools will need to administer a global sum, a portion of which will need to be given to other parties to finance their contribution to the overall scheme of teacher education. Given the high levels of academic attainment in their own subjects that will be expected, the apprenticeship model is unlikely to be suited to routes into teaching that combine subject knowledge with teaching proficiency in one overarching qualification, like the B.Ed. in England. The reason is that candidates will spend too much time away from their schools studying their subjects to be of much use to the school that is paying their salary. Apprenticeship is more likely to be a viable option for those forms of teacher education that occur after the academic subject knowledge element of a teacher's education is completed. Qualifications such as the PGCE in England would be more suited to this model.

Many European countries prefer a model in which subject knowledge and teacher certification are combined within one qualification, which locates the intending teacher in a university. A typical pattern is for students to follow a bachelor-level qualification, which is mainly concerned with subject matter, very much like a typical subject degree, but with some education content and some school experience, then transition to a masters qualification in which the education element and school experience play a more significant role. The teacher emerges with an initial qualification in education at masters level, which then qualifies him or her for the next stage in progress to full occupational licensure. In Germany, for example, completion of the masters qualification is a prerequisite for the taking on of an apprenticeship role within a school for a two-year period, teaching on a limited basis under supervision. Occupational licensure only occurs at the conclusion of this two-year apprenticeship. There is thus a transition, between initial qualification and occupational licensure, from being a student who carries out periodic internships within schools, to being an apprentice within a particular school for the final stretch of the route towards becoming a licensed teacher.

Licensure Follows Qualification

On the surface, this model has much to recommend it. There is both time for a suitable emphasis on the personal acquisition of subject expertise and ample room for the development of the pedagogically oriented reconfiguration of that knowledge, not to mention other elements of educational theory, both conceptual and empirical, that will be needed. There is also a controlled entry into the business of teaching, which avoids much of the complexity of doing this through a school-based apprenticeship alone. There is, however, one major flaw with the route just outlined. I will leave aside the question of length, although I do not think that a seven-year preparation period for a career in teaching is excessive if one wishes to develop truly professional teachers. Post-licence attrition is also minimal in countries such as Germany, suggesting that there are real advantages in gaining a committed and highly experienced teaching force through such a route. Undoubtedly, the three to four-year total preparation time for a career in teaching in England is too little. Whether it is politically realistic to move towards a seven-year preparation is debateable. However, it should not be less than five years.

The main problem with the schema outlined above is the institutional disconnection between the university, responsible up to the achievement of the master degree and the school, responsible for the two-year probationary practice. This means that the benefits of integrating the university with the school-based elements of the programme are largely lost, and there is a danger of wastefulness of time and resources if schools and universities do not adequately co-ordinate with each other. An alternative model, which built on the virtues of the German one, would work as follows. First, assuming a degree programme that combines a high level of subject knowledge with the development of competence as a teacher, students would enter university to study at the bachelors level a subject which they would intend to teach at school. Normally, this would be a three-year programme. If, however, as in Germany, secondary school teachers are expected to teach two subjects, there would be ample justification for making such a degree a four-year or even five-year combined subject degree, with a considerable but not predominant element of school experience. The advantage of a five-year programme would be the opportunity for students to spend a considerable amount of time in schools putting the theoretical elements of their course into practice and reflecting on that process. This would all be done in very close co-ordination with schools, who would be closely involved with the development and teaching of the non-subject elements of the programme together with those elements of subject education with a pedagogical orientation.

Such a programme should be capable of providing a 'provisional licence' to teach, as in the German system. Unlike the German approach, it would issue in a bachelors rather than a masters qualification, although full occupational licensure should involve qualification at masters level.

This means in practice that having completed a three- (or preferably four-)year programme that is a qualification in teaching as well as in the subject to be taught, the intending teacher will seek employment in a school. During the next two to three years after initial appointment, teachers will teach in the capacity of advanced apprentices, who will be expected to study towards a masters-level qualification that will involve a considerable amount of reflection on and research in the school environment, consolidating and deepening their engagement with the issues that they encountered in their bachelor studies. This qualification would be something similar to the MTL (Masters in Teaching and Learning) programme which briefly existed in England and which is currently operating in Wales.[19]

For those who do not wish to take an education degree, there needs to be an alternative route to a master degree in education. The current PGCE qualification in England, although it has the virtue of being very tightly tied to working in schools, is simply too short to provide the resources for a career in teaching, nor does it issue a qualification at masters level. One way of addressing this situation would be to institute an apprenticeship route for graduates with a three-year programme closely allied to higher education. If, however, as is likely, schools are simply not capable either financially or logistically of accepting so many apprentices, then an alternative is to lengthen the PGCE, with the first year leading to a provisional licence, which then allows the aspiring teacher to gain employment as a higher apprentice who then has to go on to study for a similar masters programme to those who follow an education bachelors route.

THE TRAJECTORIES OF TEACHER EDUCATION IN THE UK, GERMANY AND INDIA

The recommendations in the section above will have an odd ring to many in the UK and the US concerned with teaching. Despite the attention paid to the educational success of countries such as Finland with an initial masters qualification as in Germany and other European countries, policymakers in England and the US are reluctant to adopt such a model of teacher education. This also applies to some developing countries such as India.[20] Why is this?

---

[19] See Burstow and Winch (2013) for an account and analysis of this development in England.

[20] It should also be noted that the Finnish model is cost-effective: 30% less per student than the US with class sizes about 50% of those in the US (Economist Intelligence Unit 2014).

Much of the reason is that countries like Finland and Germany adopt what in this book is described as the professional model of the teacher, whereas the 'Anglo-Saxons' incline towards a version of the craftworker or of the executive technician. Neither do they typically recruit the most academically able candidates into their system. In fact, it is probably no exaggeration to say that there is considerable suspicion in England of highly successful graduates engaging in teaching, at least for the 'long haul'.

The craft model was described in detail in Chapter 6. Craft teachers learn how to teach in the classroom, and educational theory is largely irrelevant, if not actually harmful, to their practice. Consequently, the pressure is on to introduce a form of apprenticeship that is not much like that described earlier in this chapter – one that is much more like the traditional mediaeval time-serving apprenticeship, which involved almost solely 'learning on the job'. We have argued that the craft model can be relied on to produce a 'good enough' teacher who is competent within a narrow range of professional situations. In particular, it may well be the case that with pupils coming from highly educated backgrounds, with strong motivation, in small classes, and in a highly predictable and secure environment, the teacher with a strong academic subject background may well achieve good results (although not, perhaps, the best that could possibly be achieved with a more extended teacher education). But this is not the environment in which most teachers have to work, which is complex, unpredictable, full of heterogeneity and very often involves working with pupils whose aspirations and those of their parents may not be very high, or if they are, may be handicapped by a lack of cultural and social capital. For an education system with the ambition to raise expectations and to fully unlock the potential of all pupils, the 'good enough' teacher will not be good enough.

It might be thought that the craft teacher should be fully trusted to use his experience to the best effect. But curiously, the craft model, although accompanied by the rhetoric of 'the teacher knows best', operates in an environment where that precept is not followed in practice. Education systems like those of the US and England have designed accountability systems that are based on the assumption that teachers will not do their best if they are not directed by a system of accountability, which in practice involves the distribution of rewards and punishments. Paradoxically, the belief in craftworkers is contradicted by the accountability regime in which they have to operate. When we combine this paradox with the evidence of very high attrition rates from the profession in these countries, it is reasonable to conclude that the status of teachers is not high, that expectations of them are low and that they cannot be trusted to do what they are supposed to do. Such considerations do not suggest that basing teacher education on a craft model is likely to be a sound policy.

TOWARDS A TEACHER EDUCATION CURRICULUM

We have established that, apart from the subject studies element of an intending teacher's studies, which can be undertaken without reference to teaching, all the rest of the programme (which could be expected to constitute between a half and a third of a five to six-year programme) should be undertaken in close association with schools or whatever other educational institution is relevant to the intending teacher's future career. We also observed that an understanding of the conceptual geography of education should be introduced at an early stage of the professional part of the programme, and the more complex understanding that should be built on that should occur in close conjunction with work in schools. The same goes for the recent history, legal framework and administrative arrangements for education in their country. It is important that this is not introduced as a list of facts, but that it is introduced within the conceptual framework outlined, and that intending teachers develop an understanding of the relationship between this history and framework and the conceptions of education that have emerged in their society, and how resolution of the claims of competing conceptions have (or have not) taken place.

Of particular importance will be the development of subject knowledge in a form apt for teaching and learning (PCK). As argued in Chapter 5, this will include, as a central element, an understanding of the concept of Epistemic Ascent, which will then need to be applied to the subject that the intending teacher is preparing to teach.[21] As PCK is primarily a matter of know-how, albeit informed by a conceptual understanding of the subject under a certain aspect, it needs to be developed over the course of the bachelor-level element of the programme as a central element in practical experience in schools, but also through discussion and reflection with tutors, teachers and other students (interns or apprentices) working in different schools. Intending teachers will also need to engage closely with the research literature on this topic and assess its relevance to their own practice.

---

[21] And, as argued in Chapter 5, this includes practical subjects as well as academic ones.

A further, very important element in the conceptual side of initial teacher education rests in the relationship between ethics and professional work. It goes without saying that education needs an ethical code, preferably one founded on the idea of benevolence in relation to the long-term interests of pupils. It is preferable, in keeping with the approach that has been advocated all along in this book, that the ability to make independent professional judgements should be the core attribute of professional teachers. That being so, there is a good case for setting out the ethical requirements of teaching in terms of principles to be interpreted, rather than protocols to be obeyed.[22] As well as a grounding in ethical theory, which should cover virtue and deontological approaches, as well as utilitarian ones, teachers should consider a wide variety of cases in which ethical judgements are called for. These should be taken from known situations in teaching, personal experience and also literature.[23] They should also be encouraged to think about the personal characteristics required of teachers, both those that imply self-mastery and also those which involve co-operation with others. Part of the assessment of their abilities as teachers should include whether or not they have developed such attributes to a sufficient degree[24] and whether they are capable of developing this form of awareness through their careers.

Empirical Research

Much more difficult is the issue of how empirical research on teaching and learning is presented to students. The difficulty arises from a necessary tension in such understandings. On the one hand, it is desirable that teachers develop an independent and critical perspective on empirical research (just as they should on the conceptual elements of education), but at the same time it is important that they have some sense of which research results in knowledge and which does not. We must bear in mind at all times that educational research,

---

[22] Cf. Cribb (2011). This does not imply, of course, that there should be no external explicit normative requirements on teachers.

[23] Cf. Simpson (1989).

[24] This might sound like an unusual requirement in the Anglo-American context, but the development of such personal characteristics is a common feature of professional-vocational education in Europe (Brockmann *et al.* 2010), and is implicit in the idea that education is in part a preparation for citizenship (Géhin 2007). See the important work of D. Carr (1999, 2003) for more on the relationship between teaching and the exercise of the virtues.

like most research into social phenomena, cannot yield certainty, or even the kind of warrant that we expect from work in the physical and biological sciences, which allows us, with a considerable degree of confidence, to develop technologies based on their findings.

It is self-evidently of greater value to students to be introduced to research that has achieved good standards of probity in methodology, that has been repeatedly confirmed (preferably in a variety of educational contexts), that has survived refutatory attempts and that has had some demonstrably efficacious effect on teaching and learning.[25] It is the primary task of those involved in curriculum design and teaching in the higher education component of a teacher education programme to do this. Given the rather vexed history of the way in which such research has been introduced in the past, it is probably desirable that a central body concerned with teacher education produce guidelines (perhaps using the criteria above) as to which kinds of research should go into such programmes and which should not.

Is this an unreasonable interference in academic freedom? I would argue not. Teaching, like other recognised professions and other occupations, is a national interest. It is also funded nationally. Like the health and legal professions, it should, if it aspires to the status of a regulated occupation, accept that there are minimum standards of education that all members of the occupation must satisfy. Just as doctors and nurses are not expected to be introduced to ill-founded empirical research, so it is also reasonable to expect that teachers should not be either, unless it is for reasons that will be mentioned shortly. It is important to realise that there are well-established and widely accepted ways of evaluating the quality of research, in respect of both methodology and methods and trustworthiness of findings. The independent body that should be responsible for regulating teacher education should have, as a major element in its responsibility, the evaluation of such research, probably using secondary sources such as metasurveys, as a guide.[26]

---

[25] Metasurveys of research have greatly contributed to our understanding of the quality and reliability of empirical educational research. However, they also need to be used with caution as they often either restricted themselves to certain methodologies or group together studies based on different assumptions and methodologies. I owe this point to Paul Cobb.

[26] It is important to realise that this does not mean that only intervention studies should be considered. This would be unduly restrictive. There are canons of quality across the range of methodologies for educational research.

Given that this is so, research that is most relevant and most trustworthy should be presented. It should also be clearly explained why it is to be regarded as trustworthy, relying on the work that students should already have undertaken on the philosophy of social research. The scope and limitations of even the best research should be made clear. Above all, it should not be presented as a set of protocols for practice, but in such a way as to encourage intending teachers to consider its relevance for their own circumstances and how they can make use of it. It is utopian, however, to suppose that one can avoid giving attention to research which, although influential (perhaps in the form of pervasive commonsense), does not possess good justificatory warrant. Such research programmes as psychometric studies of intelligence, verbal deficit theory, Piagetian developmental theory, work on 'learning styles' and work on 'psycholinguistic' methods of acquiring literacy, to take a few examples, may all be so pervasive (despite being discredited in many cases) that it may be unavoidable to introduce intending teachers to them. In such cases, it is important that they are presented impartially, and their strengths and weaknesses clearly explained. It should be left to intending teachers to form their own conclusions about the relevance of such research in their own work in the classroom, with their expectation that if they do think that there are elements of value in it, those will need to be justified.

This in turn implies that an important element of their education will be their development as *scholars*. A great deal can be accomplished through their subject studies. Within these studies, they should acquire the ability to read and analyse articles in academic journals and to appraise the quality of argument, methodology and evidence (where relevant). They should acquire this ability in parallel with an ability to do the same with the academic literature on educational matters, which they will also be studying.

The outcome of a four or five-year bachelor programme should be that intending teachers will be personal masters of their subject(s), but also highly competent to teach it in a variety of circumstances. They will have a good, though critical and practical, perspective on the deliverances of educational research, which will be seen through the prism of a robust conceptual framework for thinking about educational issues, which at the same time pays due regard to the contested and often fluid nature of particular conceptions. This set of abilities requires intending teachers to have considerable intellectual independence and subtlety and to be able to combine these attributes with a strong sense of how to apply their intellectual abilities and moral sensibility to practical situations in teaching. Teachers at this stage of their education should not only be given a professional qualification in teaching but should also receive a limited licence to practice.

Post-bachelor Teacher Education

Having employment in a school with the ability to work with a high degree of independence should be the expected outcome of this stage of a teacher's professional education. Whether an intending teacher has been an apprentice or an intern up to this stage, the following stage, since it involves significant responsibilities as a teacher, should be as a junior employee.[27] The link with higher education should be retained, and universities (unlike in Germany) should continue to play a highly significant role in the latter part of the professional education of teachers. The first three years in a full-time teaching post should make provision for the teacher to progress to a masters qualification, whose achievement will signify the ability to assume full responsibility for all the functions of a teacher, including the ability to co-ordinate and to take on certain leadership roles. Such a qualification should also give the ability to be able, with supervision from a qualified researcher (who may be employed within the school or be located in a university), to conduct evaluation of aspects of their own practice or of the operation of the school. In order to achieve such a qualification, teachers will need to spend a proportion of their time (probably not more than 20%) in a higher education environment and will need some timetable remission within their school, although a favourable contract for teachers, such as is to be found in countries like Finland, may make this unnecessary.

The focus of such a qualification should be to develop the professional abilities of the teacher, though deepening their understanding of their work, gaining a better understanding of how their work is situated within the education system and gaining the ability to assume leadership roles within and beyond the school. A significant part of the assessment of these abilities should be through the carrying out of a practical project concerned with their own work or that of the school, whether it be curricular, pedagogic, assessment-related, resource-related or pastoral. Both senior schoolteachers and university staff should share the responsibility for assessment of the candidate. On successful conclusion of this programme, full occupational licensure should be granted, and it would be normal to expect

---

[27] Which is, in effect, tantamount to saying that such a teacher is an advanced apprentice.

that such a teacher should be ready to assume some co-ordinative or management responsibility.

Continuing Professional Development

Although the path to full occupational licensure will be long and quite arduous, there should continue to be opportunities for teachers to develop through the acquisition of further qualifications. By this stage, teachers should be quite accomplished scholars in the practical matter of education. This may take the form of extended subject study at masters or doctoral level, or it may take the form of qualification in research or management and governance, curriculum development or assessment. We should bear in mind the variety of roles that teachers should aspire to fulfil during the course of a career (see Chapter 9). In this respect, they would continue to have the kind of ability to progress and develop that is customary, for example, in medicine. Whatever funded professional development they undertake should, however, benefit the education system as much as it benefits the teacher aspiring to a qualification.

CONCLUSION

Teacher education appropriate to a professional teacher as described in Chapter 8 has been described. It should be academically rigorous, should be closely co-ordinated with developing abilities in practical educational contexts and should equip teachers for a lifelong career in which they can attain the highest levels of responsibility. It should also, however, give them ample opportunities to develop as individuals. All this may sound demanding and far removed from what is currently available in the UK and US contexts. Something like it is, however, available in some countries, and the indications are that such demanding programmes of teacher education pay ample dividends in the form of a very able teaching force and consequent highly effective education.

Dear Sally + Jeff. It
was good to see you
both on Sunday and
thank you for Lunch and
of course the 'Grand Tour'.
of the house — it's absolutely
lovely & I can certainly
understand why you
wanted it. I'm glad that
Vi + Adrian were able to
come. It was nice to catch
up with their news.
Thanks again for an
enjoyable day.
love Margaret.

Sally + Jeff Hinchcliff
9 Grange Road
Beccles. Suffolk

T N R 3.4 9 N R

11
A Good Teacher?

The aim of this chapter is to try to answer the question 'What makes a teacher a good teacher?' or at least to frame this question so that it encourages intelligible answers. Part of the problem, of course, is that there is a lack of consensus about questions of pedagogic methods and effectiveness, and this is an inevitable consequence of the contests that pervade different and competing conceptions of education. So perhaps a better description of this chapter would be that it is one that is intended to help to frame a discussion of this issue with a view to also promoting the idea of a professional teacher outlined and defended in Chapters 8 and 9.

CATEGORIAL AND NON-CATEGORIAL ANSWERS TO THE QUESTION

The term 'good' in relation to teaching is potentially problematic since there may well be different conceptions of what a good teacher consists of. At the same time, empirical evidence is to some extent relevant since, when we have arrived at a conception of what a good teacher is, it will be possible to establish whether and to what extent someone is in fact a good teacher. In order to approach this question philosophically, we need to return to considerations discussed in Chapters 1 and 2. We established that there is a categorial answer to the question of what a teacher is, but also that this only takes us so far when considering what, in the 'here and now', makes a good teacher. In particular, we noted in Chapter 2 two features of teaching that might be called 'categorial'.

Teachers' Know-How: A Philosophical Investigation, First Edition. Christopher Winch.
© 2017 Christopher Winch. Editorial Organisation © Philosophy of Education Society of Great Britain.
Published 2017 by John Wiley & Sons, Ltd.

The first was that teaching is a tripartite relationship, even if some elements are implicit.[1] This implies that both subject matter and pupil are important elements in the relationship. The second categorial point is that when a teacher teaches, other things being equal, the pupil learns what the teacher intends that he should learn. What is more, if it is the teacher's intention that the pupil should learn what the teacher wishes that the pupil learns, then we can only attribute this intention to the teacher if the teacher *takes appropriate measures* to check that the pupil has learned what it is intended that he should learn and, by implication, that he should take appropriate measures to ensure that the pupil does so subsequently. If we cannot guarantee this, then we are entitled to doubt the seriousness of the teacher in the activity of teaching and, hence, whether or not the teacher is really teaching, as opposed to going through the motions of doing so. It belongs to the concept of a teacher, just as it does to any other occupation, that one can distinguish between a genuine and a fake example. This does not imply that such a distinction is always easy to make, but it must be possible. Otherwise, one has no clear grasp as to what it is that one means by calling something an occupation of such and such a kind.[2]

Thus, there is in a sense a threshold concept of teaching, which includes the tripartite relationship and also an attribution of seriousness, revealed in the seriousness of the teacher's intentions. In a minimal sense, the teacher is an agent of some kind.[3] A good teacher is, then, someone who is not only serious enough about what he or she is doing, but also able to fulfil his intentions to a considerable degree, perhaps more than most of his contemporaries.[4] And, as we saw, this can be evidenced by, among other things, teachers' ability to understand the difficulties (or lack of them) that pupils may be experiencing and the associated ability to respond appropriately to that understanding. The attribution of seriousness to genuine, as opposed

[1] In Chapter 3 we noted that it was, in a sense, implicitly *quadripartite*. We will return to this point.

[2] This is not a plea for essentialism – there may be boundary cases for some occupations, and necessary and sufficient criteria may vary according to context. This does not seem to be the case for teaching, however.

[3] Not forgetting, as was argued in Chapter 2, that there has to be an element of agency on the part of the pupil as well if a teacher can be said to be teaching.

[4] It is assumed that certain side constraints are observed here, such as that teaching is done in an ethically acceptable manner and that the intentions are sufficiently long term to count as educationally valuable for the pupil. This second is an important qualification. Even if we accept that education is preparation for something worthwhile, the question 'Worthwhile for whom?' is not yet answered.

to fake, teaching is important as it allows us to say that what makes a teacher a teacher – and, *a fortiori*, a good teacher – is that the *manner* in which he or she acts in and beyond the classroom is as important as what he or she actually does.

One way of approaching the issue of seriousness is through looking at intentions and how they are fulfilled. Like other purposive activities, teaching requires intentions, or, in this particular case, intended outcomes.[5] To have an intention is to be prepared to see it fulfilled and to take the appropriate steps to do so, which will involve attempting to control the activities that lead to the intended outcome and, where necessary, co-ordinating and communicating with others in order to do so. Furthermore, it will involve some evaluation of success and reflection on what success or lack of it holds for future activities.

So we can make some quite substantive points, not only about what it is to teach, but also in general terms about what it is to be a good teacher.[6]

AN APPROPRIATE CONCEPTION OF TEACHING?

Does this mean that we need to have a normative theory of teaching appropriate to the ideals that we hold in our society? It has been argued that educational aims rest on a more or less stable orientation towards the values that it is determined should be implemented within a society. This is a categorial point. But what values and hence what aims should concern us in an inquiry into the nature of a good teacher? Undoubtedly, the common discourse in contemporary economically developed and developing societies is one deeply infused with liberal – or, more precisely, liberal democratic – values. But beyond this there is little agreement. A liberal society should, it is generally agreed, exist for the benefit of all its members, even if the material outcomes for those members may vary enormously. Such a society should allow for civic engagement and should, in principle,

---

[5] It might immediately be replied that there are easily envisageable circumstances in which a teacher had no definite curricular outcome in mind, but rather the objective of inspiring or disturbing his pupils, which he was able to do through a series of *ad hoc* activities such as dialogue within the classroom. This does not in fact contradict the point made, since these are precisely intended outcomes. What is not acceptable is having absolutely no idea what one intends to do.

[6] As noted in Chapter 1, it would be odd to have a serious intention to teach and not get any pupil to learn the intended material. It is another matter, however, to precisely specify what proportion of the class should learn what proportion of the intended material. This question cannot be answered philosophically.

recognise *equality of opportunity*, that, at the very least, in a competition for scarce jobs, positions and offices, everyone should start with the absence of formal constraints on their progress.[7]

Absence of formal constraints does not, of course, imply absence of *material* constraints. One could argue that the absence of formal constraints in the presence of significant material constraints is nothing more than a fig leaf for the absence of genuine equality of opportunity.[8] On the other hand, building material considerations into considerations of substantive equality of opportunity makes it difficult to see where one should stop short of full material equality in terms of removing substantively unequal material barriers to equality of opportunity. Furthermore, the formal principle of equality of opportunity does not preclude an education system where education is not necessarily aimed at the benefit of the pupil, provided that the formal principle is met.

These considerations give good grounds for thinking that the principle of benefit to the pupil ought to be built into the conception of an education system worthy of a society that does more than pay lip service to the principle of equality of opportunity, and this applies even more to a society that recognises *autonomy* as a significant educational aim. The ability to rationally, authentically and independently make choices about one's course in life is thought to be a requisite of societies such as ours.[9] The capacity for autonomy not only requires adequate resourcing in terms of education and material resources, but also, if one wishes to avoid differential access to the opportunity to become autonomous, then the elimination or at least the reduction of material inequalities is a prerequisite. We can conclude, then, that not only should teaching in such a society be directed to the benefit of the pupil,[10] but also that it should be resourced in a way consistent with providing equal opportunities for developing autonomy.[11]

---

[7] That is, the general 'neoliberal' default position. See Hayek (1959) and Nozick (1974) for representative accounts. A variation is to be found in, for example, Rawls (1999) and dissent in, for example, Raz (1986).

[8] Rawls' assignment of *lexical priority* to greatest equal liberty and then to full equality of opportunity before the difference principle seems to fall within this stricture, as, according to this schema, questions about equality of opportunity need to be settled prior to material distributive questions.

[9] See Raz (1986, ch. 15).

[10] Formally, A teaches B to C for the benefit of C (and only secondarily for the benefit of other interested parties). In other words, C's interests always defeat those of others whenever there is a conflict.

[11] Whether this entails substantial material equality across the individuals in a society is a question beyond the scope of this book. It is important to recognise, however, that substantial material equality does not entail sameness of educational outcomes nor even of educational processes.

It is reasonable to conclude that teachers should teach for the benefit of their pupils without making any discrimination between aims for different pupils. We need to be careful in our formulation of this point. Given that, for example, the aims for all pupils on reaching adulthood should include the ability to develop as an individual and to participate fully in economic and civic life, it does *not* follow that the school trajectory of each pupil should be the same. The possession by a society of such overarching aims does not imply that all pupils follow the same academic trajectory, but it does entail that, whatever trajectory they follow, it is in their long-term interests to follow that trajectory. It seems to follow from this point that it may fall to a teacher to be quite central to the pupil in giving guidance as to what trajectory, given their abilities, interests and self-knowledge, they should follow.[12]

LEGITIMATE PEDAGOGY AND LONG-TERM INTERESTS OF PUPILS

We now need to look at what forms of pedagogy are used by a 'good' teacher. This in turn brings us to some interesting questions about how teachers can go about implementing such ideals of benevolence effectively. The argument in the previous section concluded that teaching should be done for the benefit of the pupil. But what does 'for the benefit of the pupil' mean? It is possible to give an answer to this question. If education is (categorially) a preparation for life, then the interests concerned have to be long-term ones that extend beyond the immediate horizons of what pupils are currently interested in, or even what may be in their short-term interests.

In other words, if we are going to take the benevolence injunction seriously, namely that A teaches B to C for C's benefit (i.e. to give C a good education that fulfils such aims as developing the capacity for rational autonomy), then teachers need to attend to what they consider to be the long-term interests of their pupils,[13] regardless of what the pupils, their parents or commentators may think is in the pupils' interests.[14] The criteria for determining this are related to the

---

[12] And, of course, it is a central responsibility of those teachers who are explicitly advising pupils about entry into the labour market that the full range of possibilities is made clear, even if this means that different pupils will inevitably take different routes into the labour market.

[13] They are not expected to make a judgement of these long-term interests on their own, but by paying regard to the aims of the education system and the values that underpin it, as well as their own personal inclinations (which they may often need to resist).

[14] It is of course an elementary point, hardly worth mentioning, that what interests the pupil and what is in his interests do not necessarily coincide (see Barrow and Woods 1975, pp. 121–130).

aims of education and legitimate pedagogy and have to be interpreted *in situ* by individual teachers. We have seen that, in order to be teaching, as opposed to seeming to teach, teachers must be serious in their purpose. A necessary condition of such seriousness is attendance to the long-term interests of pupils and the impact that these have on the work of the teacher.

A COUNTER VIEW: ROUSSEAUVIAN PEDAGOGY AND MORAL PSYCHOLOGY

This view is not accepted by many. Those influenced by Rousseau and his followers in particular will resist this way of putting the matter. Why? Rousseau was not, of course, committed to the view that education should not be in the long-term interests of children; indeed, he took this very seriously. But he also thought that the children's possibilities for enjoyment during education were important (partly because of high child mortality rates at the time that he was writing), and was convinced that a child's perception that his will was deliberately being thwarted (e.g. by a teacher) would have a long-term damaging psychological effect, leading to the development of a kind of slave mentality or at the very least a permanent attitude of paranoid suspicion towards other human beings. But Rousseau arrived at this view through a speculative moral psychology that held that the conscious imposition of will by one person on another (who is also conscious that another's will is being imposed on him) will lead to psychological damage to both the imposer and the imposee.[15]

Rousseau's view rests on a mistake about social norms, concerning both their nature and their origin. His belief that authority arises through reciprocal agreement about the binding power of agreements (a large part of what he means by the 'General Will') reflects a view that normativity rests on mutual consent unconstrained by asymmetric power or use of force. Where unconstrained mutual consent is absent, then wills are determined through the constraints of power or force. But since this robs subsequent action of the consent of a free being, then the unfreedom thereby endured has a lasting deleterious psychological effect. Rousseau's views on the nature of contractually imposed authority rest on a view about the sources of normativity. It is a consequence of these views that the bending of a pupil's

---

[15] Dent (1988) and Winch (1996b).

will, since it must necessarily occur, should be done by covert means. The child must always think that it is Nature, not Man, that is teaching him. This means, in turn, that the teacher's work must proceed largely by subterfuge, a process which is described in detail in his great work on education, *Émile ou de l'Education*.

There are two points to be made about this. First, any understanding of the normative character of human life must pay regard to the origins of normative order in what Baker and Hacker (1985) have called 'normative activities' such as instructing, correcting, explaining, training and so on, which form the basis of rule following, itself the basis of human action. Second, Rousseau's resort to pedagogical subterfuge smacks of desperation. It implicitly acknowledges that successful pedagogy involves the will of the teacher being imposed on the pupil, if educational objectives are to be attained; and it has to suggest that this can only be done by deception, without at the same time considering the deleterious effects of such a strategy on both teacher and pupil. The deleterious effects on the moral and psychological health of teachers should be obvious both in Rousseau's terms and in terms of those who do not agree with Rousseau about normativity. Teachers who routinely carry out their work by deceiving their pupils will develop undesirable character traits of deviousness and deceit, which will damage them psychologically. In Rousseau's terms, they will cultivate a desire to dominate and subjugate their fellow human beings, which will degrade them morally. Pupils, on the other hand, unless they are very young or very stupid, will sooner or later realise that they are being manipulated for reasons that they do not clearly perceive. Rather than being told that they must do F, because F is in their best interests (even if they do not, at the time, recognise it to be), they are persuaded to do F because they are led to believe that they have no choice or because it will please them to do so. The perception that their entire education is being stage-managed and that they are being manipulated is likely to bring about an attitude of cynicism and suspicion about teachers that will be extremely destructive of their educational prospects. One does not require an elaborate psychological theory to understand this – anyone who has been manipulated and deceived will understand the reactions that normally follow such revelations.

It is reasonable to conclude that a pedagogical approach that overtly considers pupil long-term rather than short-term interests, to the extent of overriding what the pupil is currently interested in, is more morally and psychologically defensible than one which relies on manipulation and deceit as routine.

Where did Rousseau go wrong in his anti-normative pedagogic prescriptions? It is important to understand that *Émile* is, to a considerable extent, a prolegomenon to the normative political philosophy outlined in the *Discourse on the Origins and Basis of Inequality* (Rousseau 1755) and *The Social Contract* (Rousseau 1762b). In these works, a legitimate normative order can only come about by the mutual consent of those who are free and equal. This, in turn, can only come about by those possessed of a healthy *amour propre*.[16] But a healthy *amour propre* cannot be attained through an education that imposes either overt constraint of which the pupil is aware or so little constraint that the pupil cannot recognise any boundaries whatsoever. Therefore, legitimate normative order can only arise through free and equal consent. Any other kind of normative order is the overt imposition of one will on another and thus damaging to the development of a healthy *amour propre*.

It is important to recognise the dubious nature of the premise that 'a healthy *amour propre* cannot be attained through an education that imposes overt constraint of which the pupil is aware'. Not only does this look like an empirical statement, which is more akin to speculative moral psychology (with no empirical basis), but also it misunderstands the foundations of normative order, which lie at the basis of human life. The *normative activities*[17] that underlie, and are necessary to, the learning of our native language and induction into society are not illegitimate (what would it mean to say that they were?) but are an essential part of what it means to become educated, *provided that they meet the requirements of justice*. Those requirements do not exclude the overt imposition of one will on another, but they exclude the unfair, unnecessary and cruel imposition of such a will. They must include the imposition of such a will, both to protect young children from harming themselves and other people, and in order to attend to their long-term interests. Teachers must attend to these interests within the requirements of justice. This means being serious about what they are doing in attending to those long-term interests, using all the expertise at their disposal. Beyond these requirements, the theoretical range of teaching methods available to teachers is wide. Indeed, it does not exclude those prescribed by Rousseau and his successors provided that they meet the criteria for just pedagogy described above.[18]

---

[16] See the discussion in Dent (1988).

[17] Baker and Hacker (1985).

[18] See Pestalozzi ([1801] 1915) for a modification of the Rousseauvian programme for mass education. Rousseau's own prescriptions are based on a one-to-one tutor–pupil relationship.

BEING SERIOUS ABOUT TEACHING

It is vital, but not always easy, to distinguish between the appearance of teaching (and good teaching) and the reality of teaching (and good teaching). As was argued in Chapter 5, teaching is not just a matter of the exercise of teaching skills, such as writing lesson plans, maintaining an orderly classroom, instructing effectively, keeping to time and so on. These can be exercised without much pupil learning taking place. The important issue is the presence of marks of seriousness in the teacher's work. One mark of such seriousness is, obviously enough, that pupils learn what it is intended that they should learn.[19] And if, apart from exceptional circumstances and over an extended period, only a small proportion of pupils do that, then it is reasonable to conclude that, although maybe a semblance of teaching is taking place, it is more of a semblance than a reality.

Kleinig's (1982) view, that all the pupils must be learning what the teacher intends them to learn if he can be said to be teaching, is too strict. The claim seems to start from the justified view that a teacher cannot teach a pupil who does not want to learn. As Dewey points out, the desire and the energy of the pupil are critical for successful learning to take place.[20] If, furthermore, we take it to be the case that pupils will want to learn, then their failure to do so in a teaching situation must normally be due to the failure of the teacher to teach effectively. So it seems to follow that a teacher whose pupils do not learn as intended has failed to teach. While it is true that learning cannot take place without some desire and energy on the part of the pupil, it by no means follows that such desire and energy are strong enough to achieve the desired outcome without the assistance of the teacher; otherwise, there would be little need for teachers, except to guide the pupil in the right direction.[21] To assert that this is so is to make an unjustified empirical claim, probably on metaphysical grounds.

It is a central part of a teacher's job not just to harness the motivation of pupils (which is clearly very important), but also to ensure that the motivation that they do have is augmented sufficiently for them to learn, or, failing that, to supply in pedagogical ability the missing

---

[19] And, as Kleinig pointed out (1982), teachers have to take some responsibility for the unintended learning consequences of their teaching.

[20] Dewey (1933).

[21] As indeed recommended by Dewey as the teacher's role. Likewise, the pupil's *amour de soi* in the Rousseauvian scheme should guarantee sufficient intrinsic motivation from the pupil. For Rousseau, *amour de soi* is a person's impulse to preserve his own well-being, as opposed to *amour propre*, or the sense of how one stands with other people. See Dent (1988) for a good treatment.

knowledge, wherewithal and energy.[22] This is where seriousness of purpose is important. Being serious involves taking steps to ensure that intended outcomes are fulfilled. If a teacher takes all such steps and learning still fails to take place, then that failure cannot be laid at the foot of the teacher.[23]

If one undertakes a task or a project and one is serious about ensuring success, then one should be capable of evaluating whether the project is successful or not. This is why, as was argued in Chapter 8, the ability to use formative assessment is important. This is not just about an attitude, although that is important, but it is also necessary that a teacher have a mastery of the techniques necessary to carry out formative assessment and to actually use them effectively. The use of such an approach will not guarantee success in teaching, but it will go a long way to ensure that a teacher has taken all the steps that he or she possibly can to ensure that all pupils learn all that it is intended that they should learn. Thus, a teacher who has mastered the abilities necessary to teach effectively and is serious about using them and does in fact exercise those abilities seriously can be said to be teaching.[24]

One might think that this mark of a teacher actually teaching is a categorial statement about what it is to be a teacher, as opposed to seeming to be a teacher, and it would be tempting to take this view. However tempting, it is however problematic. The argument in Chapter 8 was that a mark of professional teachers' seriousness is the ability to take steps to assess the success of their teaching. Although it is a necessary condition of such seriousness that teachers take such steps, it cannot be the case that the necessary condition includes the deployment of certain techniques that make it possible to conduct such an appraisal successfully. It is quite possible, for example, that craft teachers would take steps to ensure that they were successful without using effective techniques, using the best approach that was

---

[22] We must be very careful here. It is a logical impossibility for a teacher to do the pupil's learning for him. Some accountability systems seem to suggest that the failure to learn is the sole responsibility of the teacher. This in turn leads to the kind of perverse educational practice described in Birbalsingh (2011).

[23] Doing all that is necessary will also include avoiding unintended outcomes that will stand in the way of achieving the intended ones. It is not enough, in all conscience, to wish for the outcomes that one desires and to pursue those without regard to unintended ones that may be harmful to one's purpose.

[24] We should recall that this is not just a question of exercising a bundle of skills, but of seeing a project through to completion as fully as possible (see the discussion of project management in Chapter 4).

available to them. This might include marking work, questioning, and monitoring the demeanour and behaviour of the class.[25] Assuming that, given the limits of their expertise, this is the best that craft teachers could do, one would have to say that they were serious about what they were doing and hence teaching, even if they habitually achieved much less than total success.

It is also possible to see that teachers of the executive technician (ET) model could be serious and could also apply formative assessment techniques to their class. However, it is also possible that, unable to effectively diagnose the learning status of individual pupils (because the techniques that they had available were not adequate to do this), their efforts meet with limited success. In this case also, they show seriousness and do all that they can in order to achieve their objectives. They too can be said to be teaching.

The difference that exists between teachers who have expertise in the professional technician mode expounded in Chapter 8 and these others is that, in this case, there is an ability that goes beyond that of monitoring or of applying procedures without differentiation to a class, to an ability to understand the situation of individual pupils, not only through insight borne of acquaintance but also through the use of approaches that allow an accurate assessment of strengths and weaknesses, together with the ability to use such assessments to devise procedures, either for overcoming pupils' difficulties or for extending their work further.[26]

THE ROLE OF EMPIRICAL EVIDENCE IN DETERMINING WHO IS A GOOD TEACHER

So far, the argument concerning the quality of teachers and their teaching has been largely philosophical. A good teacher is someone who satisfies criteria for what it is to be a good teacher. It is an empirical matter to then determine whether or not an individual teacher is in fact a good one. But there is also empirical research

---

[25] See White (2000) for a defence of this view.

[26] This should not be taken as an endorsement of what is sometimes called 'personalised learning' or, more generally, the practice of teaching individuals who happen to be in a class, on an individual basis, as opposed to teaching a class in which there are individuals, each with their own requirements. There is no contradiction between teaching a common curriculum or syllabus to a class and attending to the progress of individuals through that common curriculum. There is no evidence that 'individualised' forms of teaching have any advantage over class-based teaching and some evidence that the latter approach may have some advantages (Hattie 2009, pp. 204–207).

on what constitutes a good teacher and there are also prescriptions, seemingly based on extensive research, which are used to determine the quality of teaching. These must be based, at least implicitly, on criteria for what constitutes good teaching. For example, good teaching might involve effective learning (in the achievement sense). Here, for example, is a recent account by OFSTED, the English school and college inspection agency:

- The teaching in all key stages and subjects promotes pupils' learning and progress across the curriculum.
- Teachers have consistently high expectations of pupils.
- Teachers improve the quality of learning by systematically and effectively checking pupils' understanding in lessons, and making appropriate interventions.
- Reading, writing, communication and mathematics are well taught.
- Teachers and other adults create a positive climate for learning in which pupils are interested and engaged.[27]
- Marking and constructive feedback from teachers contribute to pupils' learning.
- Teaching strategies, including setting appropriate homework, together with support and intervention, match individual needs.[28]

The problem with such sets of criteria is not that they are necessarily seriously misleading, but that they apply at a level of generality that makes them highly susceptible to subjective interpretation.[29] This is a more general problem with highly distilled research findings – that at the level of generality at which they are stated, they are of little use to teachers, except in pointing them in the right general direction. While this may be of initial use, it is of little further use in allowing teachers to work effectively in the circumstances in which they actually find themselves. A good teacher needs to go beyond such generalities to utilise, adapt or devise approaches that suit their own circumstances. This will involve a combination of good initial teacher education (which enables them to access research of the requisite detail and relevance, and then to consider its relevance

---

[27] This might well be an example of an ideologically loaded prescription, derived from the Deweyan principles discussed above. See footnote 29.

[28] OFSTED (2004).

[29] It should be noted that lists of criteria like these, although they may have some basis in empirical findings, are also politico-ideological statements.

to their own circumstances), research undertaken within the school and personal research and trial and error by teachers in their own classrooms.

Hattie's (2009) meta-analysis of teachers and teaching methods also corroborates the positions set out in this chapter, although his findings on the efficacy of teacher education on student achievement are not very reassuring and should prompt a re-think of how teacher education is carried out, perhaps along the lines of Chapter 10 of this book. However, he and the studies that he looks at corroborate the view that teachers should be well-qualified and academically able and, as far as their teaching methods are concerned, should be capable of gaining an insight and responding to difficulties and opportunities that pupils are experiencing and of finding ways of addressing these to the benefit of the pupils. As already remarked, however, such findings, however suggestive, can only point teachers and teacher educators in the direction of the relevant primary research, which must be interrogated if it is to be of substantial use to teachers.

A DEFENCE OF THE PROFESSIONAL CONCEPTION IN RELATION TO STATED AIMS AND VALUES

It has been no part of the argument of this book that the professional technician conception of a teacher is the only one possible under a categorial understanding of teaching. Craft and ET conceptions are capable of fitting the categorial requirements as well. However, it is the argument of the book that the professional model is best suited to the education system of a society based on the idea that all young people are entitled to the best education that they can possibly get which will fit them for an authentically chosen and worthwhile course in life.[30]

At the very least, this means that teachers will always teach for the primary benefit of those whom they are teaching.[31] But, given the differences in potential that may arise from class and ethnic differences in social and cultural capital, it cannot be the case that 'good enough' teaching will suffice for all pupils. It may well be sufficient for those who have academic ability and high levels of social and cultural capital to achieve commanding positions in their society, and even some with less than high levels of social and cultural capital, but it will be

---

[30] For a defence of such a formulation as an educational aim, see Winch (2005).

[31] This is not to ignore the public goods aspect of education, since it can be assumed that such public goods will be enhanced by educational aims directed to the individual in the way described.

quite inadequate for the bulk of the school population.[32] If anything, the need for the very best teachers is more pressing for those who lack advantages in social and cultural capital.

Why should this be? After all, many independent schools are very successful with teachers who have a good first or second degree and no further professional education. Why should not such teachers flourish in less promising environments as well? It has to be said that the work of all teachers is likely to be made less onerous where pupils are endowed with high levels of social and cultural capital, not to mention high motivation and a ready facility with academic subjects. It goes without saying that providing such desiderata, together with the removal of obstacles such as high relative income inequality, will make the work of teachers easier and their effectiveness greater. However, it is not possible for reforms to the education system *per se* to address such matters.

Teaching in schools with a great deal of diversity in background and potential involves working in a highly complex and often unpredictable environment. The complexity arises from the greatly varied mix of needs, attitudes, endowments and motivation of pupils. The unpredictability arises from the situations that are entailed by working with classes of such complexity. The insights that teachers need in order to be successful will come from a number of sources: from conceptual clarity about the educational environment and what they are trying to do, from a deep understanding of their subjects, including from the perspective of learning, from what good research is able to tell them about teaching in complex conditions and, of course, from their experience and that of their colleagues, which helps them put all the other sources of knowledge and understanding about their work into situational perspective.

The craft conception is inadequate because of its excessive reliance on experience, both to transform subject knowledge from the expert perspective to that of the pupil and also in forming an accurate view of the possibilities and limitations of the classes taught. The ET also lacks the ability to understand the conceptual environment in which he or she is working and is not capable of thinking through the implications of research for particular teaching situations. The ET model may, in particular, act as a temporary poultice for the damage caused by inadequate craft-based teaching, but it is likely to be

---

[32] Good teaching can never be a substitute for other barriers to full educational achievement, such as high levels of relative income inequality (see e.g. Wilkinson and Pickett 2009), but it will be desirable in any relative income scenario.

incapable of sustained performance over a long period because although it is a model which, at its best, makes good use of the best research in designing protocols for classroom action, it cannot by its nature allow teachers to assess and respond to the requirements of particular classroom situations. It is thus capable of lifting a very bad set of educational practices to a more effective level, but fails to equip teachers to bring the very best of their potential out of individual pupils.

In conclusion, a good teacher will be well-equipped in the following areas, although these are not exhaustive of what one may expect a teacher to acquire during the course of a lengthy career:

Good subject knowledge, not only from the perspective of the logical structure of the subject, but also in respect to both its philosophical underpinnings and its configuration in terms of learning progression.

Good conceptual grasp of the conceptual field of education and the relationships between its major elements, including a good understanding of the possibilities and limitations of empirical research into education for professional understanding.

A *sound ethical grasp of the aims of teaching*, together with the ability to apply broad ethical principles to complex educational situations.

An *ability to understand educational research* and quality criteria for assessing it, together with an understanding of how relevant it is to the teacher's own professional situation.

12

Some Outstanding Issues

The concluding chapter of this book will address a number of related topics that have not yet received explicit attention, although the approach taken to them should be implicit in what has been said in the foregoing chapters. In doing so, I will attempt to show how the professional technician conception of the teacher is the most suited to educational needs in developed societies.

DISCIPLINE AND CLASSROOM MANAGEMENT

How to manage a class and establish good and purposive relationships with one's pupils is probably the issue that most concerns intending teachers. It is also a major concern of the press and politicians. This book does not take the view that discipline is a non-issue, as if one only needs to make one's lessons interesting and then problems of maintaining an orderly and purposeful environment will disappear. Those that maintain this usually subscribe to a speculative moral psychology that maintains that there is an intrinsic motivation to learn, which teachers can obstruct but not eliminate. But there is little evidence to support what is, if not a metaphysical, then an empirical claim of great generality and little supporting evidence. There is a paradox here: it is the teacher's responsibility to teach and the pupil's responsibility to learn, but a teacher cannot teach if the pupil is unwilling to learn. So, it seems, despite the original assertion, that it is the teacher's responsibility to enable the pupil to learn.

It is useful to distinguish between *obedience* and *co-operation* in order to get clearer about this issue. A class that is obedient may well

Teachers' Know-How: A Philosophical Investigation, First Edition. Christopher Winch.
© 2017 Christopher Winch. Editorial Organisation © Philosophy of Education Society of Great Britain.
Published 2017 by John Wiley & Sons, Ltd.

reluctantly go through the motions necessary for learning to happen, but nevertheless not be actually doing so.[1] The same point goes for individual pupils. Without obedience on the part of all the individuals in a class, it is going to be difficult to get any of them to learn what it is intended that they should learn. At times, a teacher may have to settle for obedience on the part of some pupils *faut de mieux*, but this is hardly satisfactory. *Co-operation*, in the sense of paying attention and making an effort, is a minimal requirement for successful teaching and learning. Only in these circumstances will learning (in the task sense) take place. *Enthusiasm* on the part of pupils is clearly a desideratum for the best teaching and learning. Where there is enthusiasm, learning is more likely to be an achievement rather than just a task undertaken. Other things being equal, this requires a degree of enthusiasm on the part of teachers in order for it to be reciprocated by a class.[2]

It follows that, at the minimum, a teacher must be able to ensure that pupils at least go through the motions of carrying out activities that teachers intend them to. No one is, however, likely to claim that without co-operation (where pupils actually want to learn some of the things that their teachers wish them to learn) anything of value is going to happen. The ability to gain co-operation, or indeed obedience, does not depend, it should be emphasised, on the individual teacher in the classroom alone. It is critically dependent on the *culture* of the school (sometimes described as the system of beliefs and values that inform its work – which can be informal as well as formal) and its *ethos* (sometimes described as the affective relationship that exists between the staff and pupils and the elements that constitute its culture). It is, of course, the responsibility of teachers in positions of responsibility and leadership to secure culture and ethos.

However, there is absolutely no doubt that the ability to elicit co-operation and, preferably, enthusiasm from pupils depends to a great degree on the character and the ability of individual teachers.[3] As Carr has pointed out, a sense of justice and fairness (which entail

---

[1] That is, they perform certain activities associated with learning but do not actually learn anything significant (in the achievement sense of 'learning'). In other words, although they appear to be learning (in the task sense), closer inspection shows that they are not, and thus their achievement is limited at best.

[2] In case this sounds like 'folk psychology', it should be pointed out that there is a loose conceptual connection between the interest that one takes in a task and the degree of success that one receives. We understand this connection conceptually as much as empirically.

[3] See the work of David Carr, especially Carr (1999, esp. ch. 11), for a detailed treatment of this important topic.

consistency) are essential elements of a teacher's character in ensuring this. In addition, the ability to temper general principles with the particular needs of particular pupils in particular situations is essential to achieve such justice and fairness in the classroom. It is far better to be acquainted with the general qualities and principles needed at the outset of a teaching career than to learn these laboriously and wastefully through the making of numerous mistakes in the early years of teaching. At the same time, experience of teaching will give teachers the growing ability to make sound situational judgements.

But, of course, co-operation with the teacher (especially reluctant co-operation, i.e. mere obedience) can be no substitute for enthusiasm.[4] So teachers need to be enthusiastic about getting their pupils to learn and about the subjects that they teach. This is why recruiting individuals who are motivated to promote enthusiasm for learning the subject that they are teaching is extremely important.[5] But such individuals need also to have the ability to render the subject matter in a form appropriate for the learning of their pupils. This is an ability that usually has to be learned, both through teaching of the principles of how a subject is best learned (which, as we saw in Chapter 4, is complex and needs careful handling) and experience in adapting those principles to the needs of the pupils that one is teaching, but also through trial and error informed by such principles. But unless this can be achieved, it will be difficult to generate pupil enthusiasm. We can see that the ability to successfully manage a classroom requires: pre-existing abilities and character traits, character traits and abilities that are further developed through teacher education and experience, and working in a school which is capable of maintaining a strong culture and ethos – itself, largely an accomplishment of able and committed teachers with much experience. But the ability should be developed from the earliest stages of teacher education, both within the university and within the schools in which intending teachers are working. Both the purely practice-driven craft conception and the protocol-driven executive technician approaches are ill-suited to doing this, unlike the very thoroughly prepared

---

[4] It should be stressed here, too, that the generation of enthusiasm for schooling is not the sole responsibility of individual classroom teachers.

[5] By 'enthusiasm' is meant here a dispositional quality, not recurrent episodes of *feeling* enthusiastic (although these are obviously appropriate to someone who has such a disposition). The disposition to be interested about something and to be able to communicate that interest (and why one has it) is the important element in enthusiasm. It is also true that it would be difficult to ascribe enthusiasm to someone as one of their dispositions if they did not on appropriate occasions manifest *episodes* of enthusiasm.

professional technician conception defended in Chapter 8. This is a point to which we will return shortly.

RETENTION AND ATTRITION

By 'attrition' is meant the loss of teachers from the profession before they reach the age of retirement. Attrition is not a neutral phenomenon; it reflects problems with the way in which the profession is organised in particular countries as well as a loss of talent and experience, not to mention a waste of resources spent on teacher education. Attrition varies greatly across different countries. For example, post-qualification attrition rates in England are about 43% after five years of service, while in Germany they are nearer to 2%.[6] Some attrition will be due to teachers leaving the workforce for family reasons, although in such cases it should be evident that many will return after a few years, particularly if arrangements are in place to enable them to continue with their careers. Some will have good reasons for making a career change that have nothing to do with dissatisfaction with teaching.

However, it is probably true to say that in general, attrition reflects discontents and dysfunctions within an education system. There is some evidence to support this, for example teachers who give as their reasons for leaving: being asked to teach material for which they do not feel qualified, lack of support for classroom management issues within the school, inadequate teacher education, low status of the profession within the society, low pay, lack of ancillary support and lack of opportunities for career development. Given that all these factors are 'bads' rather than goods of the education system and given that a high rate of attrition is, other things being equal, also a bad thing for an education system, it is certainly worth trying to reduce it, if one is concerned with sustaining a system of the highest quality. On the other hand, if what one wants is a system that is 'good enough', then high attrition may be something to live with, despite the waste of talent, experience and money that it seems to entail. Lack of support for classroom management and disciplinary questions is important because although, as argued above, maintaining an orderly teaching and learning environment is a central part of the work of individual teachers, it is also the case that it is very difficult to maintain such an environment if the school as a whole is not well-run. Since schools

[6] House of Commons (2010).

are primarily run by teachers in leadership and management positions, such a failure reflects adversely on the kind of preparation that those teachers themselves received for their future leadership roles.

If we go through these attrition factors in more detail, we will see much more clearly that they are bads and have an adverse effect on the education of pupils as well. It is clearly a major defect to give teachers work for which they are not qualified. Evidently, they will not have a sufficient grasp of the material that they are teaching and pupils will suffer as a result. Furthermore, they will be put under stress and are likely to leave the profession as a result. It is a situation that almost invariably arises from poor management, be it within the school, through a failure of an education system to recruit properly qualified staff or through a failure to develop staff expertise in an area where it has not yet been developed. Inadequate teacher education is clearly the responsibility of the government, and in the case of England, a House of Commons committee enquiry drew attention to the link between an excessively short teacher education and high attrition rates.[7] Lack of status within society is not a responsibility of governments alone. Different societies have different views on the importance and value of education. However, it is arguable that it is not the business of governments merely to reflect such views, but to change them if it is within their power. There is a great deal that governments can do to enhance the status of teaching if they are prepared to put political and financial capital into doing so, rather than blaming teachers and schools solely for the perceived failings of education within the society. It is also evident that excessively low pay will be either a consequence or a cause of such low status, although it is also true that there is not a direct correlation between pay and status. Self-evidently again, the remedy lies largely in the hands of governments.

This point also applies to ancillary support and, just as important, to the way in which such support is deployed. If it is used ineffectively, or even to the detriment of teaching (e.g. giving ancillary staff difficult tasks that it is the proper business of the teacher to carry out), it has a potentially harmful effect. In passing, it should also be noted that although, in general, equipment to assist teachers is desirable, expensive computer equipment whose pedagogical value has not been demonstrated, and for the use of which teachers have not properly been prepared, can also represent both financial waste and

---

[7] House of Commons (2010).

opportunity costs within schools. Governments need to evaluate the claims of equipment entrepreneurs with a highly sceptical attitude and need to ensure that good professional development is available to make proper use of the opportunities represented by the availability of both ancillary staff and pedagogical equipment. Finally, lack of career development represents a failure of governments to think through what a high-quality teaching profession would look like, including how it will sustain satisfying careers over a working lifetime. Chapter 9 devoted space to illustrating how teaching careers can develop so as to gain the most from the expertise of experienced teachers and to afford them maximum satisfaction in their careers.

This brief survey of issues to do with attrition and retention suggests that poor rates represent deep-seated problems with education systems and that a large part of them are due to the inability or unwillingness of governments to think through what a quality education system looks like and what it requires in order to become actual. Those countries that suffer from such high rates (like England and the United States) and, at the same time, express aspirations to offer 'world-class education' need to look very carefully at how they are organising initial and continuing teacher education in particular.[8]

LEADERSHIP, GOVERNANCE AND MANAGEMENT

In Chapters 10 and 11, it was suggested that teachers should be prepared to take on positions of responsibility and leadership in educational matters as part of their career progression. It was also suggested that although teachers have the primary responsibility for making their classrooms places where pupils learn effectively, their task is made immeasurably more difficult by the absence of leadership within the school. This leadership has to be provided by senior teachers, including the headteacher. But like providing an orderly environment in the classroom, providing one at the level of the school is something for which one has to be prepared. And we know enough about this, including that there are no panaceas or substitutes for hard work and dedication, to understand that there are well enough established ways of providing this. They do, however, require what I called in Chapter 11 'leadership', that is, the ability to get one's proposals

---

[8] This is not to suggest that all that is needed to ensure a quality education system is to attend to the teachers. As I have argued elsewhere, it is critical that values, aims, curriculum and assessment are given careful thought (Winch 1996a).

accepted and acted upon. Obedience cannot be enough; active consent is required.

The task is made more complex because it is not just the active consent of colleagues that is required, vitally important though that is. Active consent needs to come from pupils, parents, the governing body and any other institutions or agencies that have some responsibility for the affairs of the school. As in other areas of teaching, it is not enough (although it is very helpful) to know and understand research into how to make a school happy, productive and orderly. Such knowledge is only of any use if the agents responsible are able to apply and adapt it to the circumstances in which they operate. But the prerequisite for success is to enable even inexperienced teachers to understand the general principles through which schools are well-run, together with illustrative case studies from a wide variety of circumstances. Once again, the kind of preparation appropriate to a professional conception of the teacher, which sows the seeds of leadership potential at the outset, is most appropriate for this.

STYLES OF LEADERSHIP[9]

Much is written about this issue, resulting in a veritable zoology of leadership styles.[10] It is worth remembering, however, that leadership has to operate within a system of governance and management. If the governance structures are fundamentally authoritarian, there are limitations as to how democratic a school leader can be. He or she may like to consult and delegate, but ultimately is able to take decisions that are his responsibility even though they may go against staff consensus. Likewise, leadership that operates in a market environment, or one with 'low trust' accountability arrangements,

---

[9] To recapitulate, *leadership* concerns the ability of someone to get their proposals accepted and implemented. *Governance* concerns the formal structures within which decisions are made and implemented. *Management* concerns the implementation of the detail of decisions made at governance level. One can be a leader without being a governor or a manager. It is better that people who are able to lead occupy governing and management positions. This suggests that qualities of leadership need to be developed from an early stage in a teacher's career, so that they are able to understand the abilities and qualities needed to lead other professionals. It is important to stress here that leadership is usually at its most effective if it is based on the ability to engender active consent for one's proposals through the use of rational argument, and when it is based on a high level of trust for those who are to undertake the implementation of those proposals.

[10] Which include transformational, transactional, collaborative, democratic, charismatic, consultative, delegatory and so on. It is, however, rarely profitable to talk of leadership styles without putting them in the context of the governance and management structures in which leadership is exercised.

or with severe sanctions for infractions of targets or criteria, will be constrained by circumstances. Again, if the management structures imposed on the school allow little room for individual autonomy and decision making, that will necessarily have an impact on the style of leadership of the school.

To simplify the discussion and to concentrate on the preferred conception of teaching and teachers that has been developed, particularly in Chapters 8 to 11, I will assume that schools are staffed by 'professional technicians' of the type argued for in Chapter 8, who are capable of pursuing careers along the lines indicated in Chapter 9. It is unnecessary to develop teachers of this kind unless one is willing to repose a high level of trust in their capabilities and a strong sense of professional duty and calling. One can assume, however, that given a teaching force of this kind, methods of governance and management, relying on punitive accountability measures, will be inappropriate. Likewise, the assumption that one has teachers who are accustomed to being trusted and to working both independently and co-operatively with colleagues will neutralise the requirement for highly iterated levels of management control in order that they carry out their work effectively. At the very least in such schools, even if the headteacher is able to make decisions independently of the wishes of his or her staff, it is unlikely that they would wish to in most circumstances, particularly if their active consent is usually required for implementation.[11]

ACCOUNTABILITY: COMMAND AND CONTROL, CIVIC ACCOUNTABILITY

How do the foregoing considerations affect the role of teachers in relation to the society in which they live, and in particular to their obligation to provide the goods, both public and private, which education has to provide? These are issues that the profession needs to have answers to in facing the public. There are, however, some ready guidelines that can be adopted in dealing with them.

---

[11] This is not to aspire to some ideal world in which leaders and teachers in positions of authority do not have to take decisions that are going to be unpopular with those who have to implement them. But this is a feature of democratic decision making as well. A central part of Rousseau's idea of the 'General Will' is that there is a principle of reciprocity at work. If you agree to be bound by the decisions of a collective to which you belong, then you must be bound whether or not you necessarily agree with the decision that has been collectively agreed. Arguably, this in turn is part of a larger 'do unto others' or Golden Rule principle of equal regard and reciprocal obligation. See Dent (1988) and O'Hagan (1999).

The idea of command and control is associated with the imperative in large and complex organisations, as well as in organisations that need to take rapid and decisive action in order to survive, to issue directives and have them obeyed, with the use of sanctions for failure to obey. This looks like the antithesis of democratic governance, and clearly in many cases it is. However, the need for the use of command and control is not so easy to eliminate, even in democratic organisations. To see this, consider a situation where a school has a democratic decision-making procedure for policy decisions. The senior figures in the school, who represent its most significant leadership element, have persuaded the staff that a certain course of action is necessary. The *governance structure* of the school has determined that a decision made by majority agreement has to be implemented by the person charged responsible for doing so. The decision requires implementation in detail by various individuals on a day-to-day basis. This is the *management* element of the implementation of the decision. It should be evident that once the agreement has been made, procedures need to be deployed to ensure that it is carried out. These may well involve the following of protocols. Thus, an element of command and control is necessary in order for democratic decision making to be implemented. More generally, the participants in a democratic decision-making process may be morally held to the agreement to abide by the results of such decision making, including the detailed implementation of the decision.

It is probably more helpful to view the contrast between command and control and democratic decision making as in most cases a question of degree rather than an absolute. However, it does make a real difference whether or not the practical implementation of that decision is made under a heavy apparatus of supervision or whether it is carried out largely independently by the implementers. There are two reasons why the former may be necessary: (1) limited competence on the part of the implementers and (2) low trust of the implementers. Obviously, if (1) applies, then (2) will do so as well. If, however, the implementers are highly competent and are capable of working together on the management of a project such as implementing a school policy (see Chapter 3 on project management ability), then the issue of trust would bear on whether or not the implementers can be relied on to implement mutually agreed decisions. Where accountability is *civic*,[12] then professionals (that is, the professional

---

[12] See Bottery (2003) for an account of civic forms of accountability in education and O'Neill (2002) for a sustained defence of civic accountability in public services more generally.

technician in the sense of this book) are generally trusted, through the operation of their own principles of professional ethics, to carry out such decisions. In such cases, the rigidity of command and control structures, although never completely indispensable, can be simplified and relaxed to a significant degree.

INWARD AND OUTWARD LOOKING CIVIC ACCOUNTABILITY

The argument of the previous section was that although command and control, even within a broadly democratic framework, cannot be entirely dispensed with, it can be considerably ameliorated by a sense of civic responsibility on the part of decision implementers. But does the notion of civic accountability have a role to play outside a school or educational institution, in relation both to other stakeholders and to the wider public and the government? One of the main contentions of this book has been to argue that teachers should, from their initial professional education onwards, have a good understanding of the place of their work within the concerns of the wider society and should, in particular, have a good idea of the role that education plays in their society and also give some thought to the role that it *should* play. This perception does not, of course, give them any unique authority to determine matters of the public interest in education, but their insights into the detailed working of educational policy and practice do give them insights, as citizens, into what may or may not be possible.[13]

They have the delicate and at times difficult role of balancing the defence of their own interests as employees or civil servants, with the broader interests of the society that they are employed to serve. Oppositional trade unionism, of the kind that represents teachers as employees in Victorian sweatshops, and teachers as workers who cannot and should not have a role in the management of their own affairs, is not compatible with this role.[14] It does suggest, however, that they be more ready than they have been in some countries to adopt a social partnership approach to industrial relations, where they co-operate on matters of common interest and seek to reach accommodation to mutual benefit on issues where they differ, and above

---

[13] And of course, it would be wrong, and foolish, to assume that there would be a unanimity of views amongst teachers on these questions.

[14] This is not to deny that teaching trade unions should not be robust in defending their members' interests.

all, take a role in leadership and governance matters at different levels of the education system, including at the level of government policy.

This in turn entails an ability to think about education in terms of the *goods* that it is or may be capable of providing, and to think of the provision of these goods as their main professional commitment. Education is itself a complex good, which is partly private (of benefit to those who are successfully educated) and partly public (of benefit to the wider society).[15] Teachers have to balance their own interests with a responsibility to take part in the affairs of their society, exercising that responsibility on the basis of their knowledge and experience of the complex world of education. This is, if you like, part of the necessary civic education of teachers that should begin during the period of initial teacher education and continue subsequently.

They should, for example, have something to say about the accountability arrangements of the education system based on their knowledge of what are and are not effective means of securing accountability, not on the basis of considering their own interests solely.[16]

EPILOGUE: TEACHING IN A MARKET SOCIETY

In concluding this book, it is necessary to reflect on the kind of society that exists in developed countries and particularly in the Anglo-American-Australian world of the 'liberal market economy'. Obviously, such a socio-economic environment has a profound effect on the aims of education, and on the way in which it is conducted. When it is conducted in terms of market or quasi-market principles, and when parents and children are encouraged to think of themselves as consumers of a service, whose providers are to be punished if they fail to 'deliver', this has a significant effect on the *manner* in which education is conducted and compromises any attempt to develop

---

[15] See Varian (2006) for an economist's definition.

[16] This is not to say that there will not be difficult issues. One of these is the potential clash between personal and occupational principles (see Cribb 2011). There are no easy answers here, but there remains a general principle, that one is bound by democratic decision making to carry out tasks that one may not oneself necessarily approve of. It may also be that one cannot find it possible to jointly implement such decisions and adhere to one's own chosen values (if one finds no further scope, for example, for implementing them). Such cases may legitimately call one's own commitment to the occupation of teaching into question.

a professional teaching force along the lines argued for in this book.

Teaching as a Service Occupation

While it is true to say that education is not a product in the physical sense, is it therefore a service? We need to distinguish between two senses of 'education' here. Sometimes education is referred to as a process, such as schooling, training, tutoring or self-instruction.[17] Sometimes it is referred to as the outcome, namely the change that someone undergoes as a result of experiencing an educational process. Some market-oriented thinkers see the work of schools and teachers as to provide the opportunities for pupils to become educated. This is, if you like, the 'product' that education is offering. But it is clearly not a product in the physical sense, although it may rely on physical assets in order to be realised as a process. It can thus also plausibly be considered as a service, like advertising or financial advice. However, the provision of an opportunity to someone does not imply an obligation on the providee to take the opportunity up, especially if they have paid for it. Furthermore, when the service provider rather than the putative consumer receives overt punishment for the consumer's failure to make use of the opportunity provided, the unenthusiastic consumer may feel even less inclined to take up the opportunity offered.[18]

None of this might perhaps matter in an environment where all pupils were enthusiastic about becoming educated. But we do not live in such an environment, and many pupils (and their parents) have relatively little interest in taking advantage of what education has to offer. The reasons for this are complex and varied and include cultural factors, social inequalities, the nature of the labour market and the impact of consumerism on personal dispositions. However, the result can often be that schools do more than they should to promote the appearance of pupil learning (in the achievement sense) and consequently fail to ensure that learning (in the task sense) is actually taking place. The danger is that pupils with already low levels of

[17] See Tooley (1998).

[18] It is worth pointing out that advocates of the 'opportunity' conception of education-as-a-process now place great hopes on the ability of private providers to actually get pupils to learn, rather than just provide opportunities to do so. It is difficult to maintain that an institution that does not care whether or not the opportunities are being taken up is actually genuinely providing such opportunities (as opposed to appearing to do so).

motivation will become even more demotivated as they perceive that their teachers see it as their primary responsibility to demonstrate tangible results in the form of exam and assessment grades, and not primarily their own responsibility.[19, 20]

In part, no doubt such extreme measures result from deep-seated dissatisfaction about the quality of the teaching force amongst politicians. It is also easier to blame other people for one's own failings, for example, in ensuring that there is a body of excellent teachers working in the system. But the result of such measures is hardly going to improve the quality of teachers and teaching, if that is to be judged by genuine as opposed to bogus achievements on the part of pupils. Such accountability measures undermine professional morale and discourage able and committed people from entering education, or, if they nevertheless do, they encourage them to leave early. We need to ask whether the development of a professional teaching force is compatible with the operation of an educational quasi-market based on high-stakes and punitive measures for non-performance. This is a major challenge facing any politician or party that seriously wishes to raise the quality of teaching within our schools today.

---

[19] How this process actually works is vividly (if perhaps unintentionally) described by a participant-observer in Birbalsingh (2011).

[20] This is to say nothing either about gaming strategies that schools may resort to in order to make their performance look better than it is, such as entering pupils for undemanding courses (in order to boost outcome statistics) or lowering achievement at the beginning of a value-added assessment cycle (to boost value-added scores). Where assessment of schools and teachers is high-stakes, with punishment as the feared outcome, as le Grand (2003) has observed, knights may be turned into knaves.

Bibliography

Alexander, R. (1992) *Policy and Practice in the Primary School* (London, Routledge).

Arendt, H. (1958) *The Human Condition* (Chicago, University of Chicago Press).

Aristotle (1925) *The Nichomachean Ethics*, edited by Ross, D. (London, Dent).

Baker, G.P., Hacker, P.M.S. (1984) *Language, Sense and Nonsense* (Oxford, Oxford University Press).

Baker, G.P., Hacker, P.M.S. (1985) *Wittgenstein: Rules, Grammar and Necessity* (Oxford, Blackwell).

Bakhurst, D. (2011) *The Formation of Reason* (Oxford, Wiley-Blackwell).

Barrow, R. (1976) *Commonsense and the Curriculum* (London, Allen and Unwin).

Barrow, R. (1984) *Giving Teaching Back to Teachers* (Sussex, Wheatsheaf).

Barrow, R. (2014) Swansong: The Price of Everything, in Gingell, J. (ed.) *Education and the Common Good: Essays in Honour of Robin Barrow* (Abingdon, Routledge), pp. 128–150.

Barrow, R., Foreman-Peck, L. (2005) *What Use is Educational Research? A Debate* (London, Philosophy of Education Society of Great Britain).

Barrow, R., Woods, R. (1975) *An Introduction to Philosophy of Education* (London, Methuen).

Beard, R. (1990) *Developing Reading 3–13* (2nd ed.) (London, Hodder).

Beckett, D., Hager, P. (2002), *Life, Work and Learning* (London, Routledge).

Bengson, J., Moffett, M. (2007) Know-how and Concept Possession. *Philosophical Studies*, 136: 31–57.

Bengson, J., Moffett, M. (eds.) (2011) *Knowing How: Essays in Knowledge, Mind and Action* (Oxford, Oxford University Press).

Benner, D. (2003) *Wilhelm Humboldt's Bildungstheorie* (Munich, Juventa).

Bernstein, B. (1971) *Class, Code and Control: Volume 1 – Theoretical Studies Towards a Sociology of Language* (London, Routledge).

Bernstein, B. (1973) *Class, Code and Control: Volume 2 – Applied Studies Towards a Sociology of Language* (London, Routledge).

Bernstein, B. (1977) *Class, Code and Control: Volume 3 – Towards a Theory of Educational Transmissions* (2nd ed.) (London, Routledge).

Birbalsingh, K. (2011) *To Miss with Love* (London, Penguin).

Teachers' Know-How: A Philosophical Investigation, First Edition. Christopher Winch.
© 2017 Christopher Winch. Editorial Organisation © Philosophy of Education Society of Great Britain.
Published 2017 by John Wiley & Sons, Ltd.

Bosch, G. (2014) Facharbeit, Berufe und berufliche Arbeitsmärkte. *WSI Mitteilungen*, 67 (1): 5–13.

Bottery, M. (2003) The Uses and Abuses of Quality: the need for a civic version, in Preedy, M., Glatter, R., Wise, C. (eds) *Strategic Leadership and Educational Improvement*, (Buckingham, Open University Press in association with Paul Chapman Press).

Brandom, R. (2000) *Articulating Reasons: An Introduction to Inferentialism* (Cambridge, MA, Harvard University Press).

Brandt, S. (2014) How Not to Read *Philosophical Investigations*: McDowell and Goldfarb on Wittgenstein on Understanding. *Philosophical Investigations*, 37 (4): 289–311.

Brockmann, M., Clarke, L., Winch, C. (2010) *Bricklaying is more than Flemish Bond* (Brussels, CLR). http://www.clr-news.org/CLR-Studies/Bricklaying_qualifications_final%20report.pdf (accessed 23 December 2016).

Brockmann, M., Clarke, L., Winch, C. (2011) *Knowledge, Skill and Competence in the European Labour Market* (Abingdon, Routledge).

Brogaard, B. (2011) Knowledge-how: A Unified Account, in Bengson, J., and Moffett, M. (eds.) *Knowing How: Essays in Knowledge, Mind and Action* (Oxford, Oxford University Press), pp. 136–160.

Bryant, P., Bradley, L. (1985) *Children's Reading Problems* (Oxford, Blackwell).

Burke, E. (1790) *Reflections on the Revolution in France*. Published by (London Penguin 1986).

Burt, C. (1955) The Evidence for the Concept of Intelligence, in Wiseman, S. (ed.) (1973) *Intelligence and Ability* (London, Penguin).

Butler, T., Webber, R. (2007) Classifying Pupils by Where They Live: How Well Does This Predict Variations in their GCSE Results? *Urban Studies*, 44 (7): 1229–1253.

Carr, D. (1979) The Logic of Knowing How and Ability. *Mind*, 88 (1): 394–409.

Carr, D. (1981) Knowledge in Practice. *American Philosophical Quarterly*, 18: 53–61.

Carr, D. (1999) *Professionalism and Ethics in Teaching* (London, Routledge).

Carr, D. (2003) *Making Sense of Education* (London, Routledge).

Carr, W. (2004) Philosophy and Education. *Journal of Philosophy and Education*, 38 (1): 55–83.

Carr, W. (2006) Education without Theory? *British Journal of Educational Studies*, 54 (2): 136–159.

Carr, W., with Hirst, P. (2005) Philosophy and Education: A Symposium. *Journal of Philosophy of Education*, 39 (4): 615–632.

Chomsky, N. (1965) *Aspects of the Theory of Syntax* (Cambridge, Cambridge University Press).

Clarke, L., Winch, C. (eds.) (2007) *Vocational Education: International Systems and Perspectives* (Abingdon, Routledge).

Clarke, L., Winch, C., Brockmann, M. (2013) Trade-based Skills versus Occupational Capacity: The Example of Bricklaying in Europe. *Work, Employment and Society*, 26 (2): 932–951.

Clay, M. (1979) *The Early Detection of Reading Difficulties* (3rd ed.) (Newcastle-upon-Tyne, Athenaeum Press).

Coffield, F., Moseley, D., Hall, E., Ecclestone, K. (2004) *Learning Styles and Pedagogy in Post-16 Learning: A Systematic and Critical Review* (London, Learning and Skills Research Centre).

Coles, M. (2007) *Qualifications Frameworks in Europe: Platforms for Qualifications, Integration and Reform* (Brussels, EU, Education and Culture DG).

Cooper, D. (1980) *Illusions of Equality* (London, Routledge).

Crawford, M. (2009) *Shop Class as Soulcraft* (Harmondsworth, Penguin).

Cribb, A. (2011) Beyond the Classroom Wall: Theorist Practitioner Relationships and Extra-Mural Ethics. *Ethical Theory and Moral Practice*, 4 (14): 383–396.

Cuomo, S. (2007) *Technology and Culture in Greek and Roman Antiquity* (Cambridge, Cambridge University Press).

Darling-Hammond, L. (2000) How Teacher Education Matters. *Journal of Teacher Education*, 51 (3): 166–173.

Davis, A. (2004) The Credentials of Brain-based Learning. *Journal of the Philosophy of Education*, 38 (1): 21–36.

Davis, A. (ed.) (2016) *Dyslexia, Developing the Debate* (London, Bloomsbury).

de Jouvenel, B. (1957) *Sovereignty* (Cambridge, Cambridge University Press).

Dent, N. (1988) *Rousseau* (Oxford, Blackwell).

Desmond, A., Moore, J. (1991) *Darwin* (London, Penguin).

Dewey, J. (1933) *How We Think* (Boston, D.C. Heath).

Dewey, J. (1938) *Experience and Education* (Indianapolis, Kappa Delta Pi).

DfE (2010) *The Importance of Teaching: The Schools White Paper* (London, HMSO)

DfE (2011) *Proposed Master Teacher Standards* (London, HMSO).

DfE (2016) *Educational Excellence Everywhere* (London, HMSO).

Dittmar, N. (1976) *Sociolinguistics* (London, Arnold).

Dreyfus, H.L., Dreyfus S.E. (1996) The Relationship of Theory and Practice in the Acquisition of Skill, in Benner, P., Tanner, C.A., Chesla, C.A. (eds.) *Expertise in Nursing Practice* (New York, Springer).

Dunne, J. (1993) *Back to the Rough Ground* (Chicago, University of Notre Dame Press).

Economist Intelligence Unit (2014) Does Money Buy Good Teachers? http://thelearning curve.pearson.com/articles/article/does-money-buy-good-teachers (accessed 23 December 2016).

Ellenbogen, S. (2003) *Wittgenstein's Account of Truth* (New York, SUNY Press).

Elliott, J. (2016) Dyslexia: Beyond the Debate, in Davis, A. (ed.) *Dyslexia* (London, Bloomsbury).

Elliott, J., Gibbs, S. (2008) Does Dyslexia Exist? *Journal of Philosophy of Education*, 42 (3–4): 475–491.

Eraut M. (1994). *Developing Professional Knowledge and Competence* (Brighton, Falmer Press).

Etzioni, A. (ed.) (1969) *The Semi-Professions and their Organization: Teachers, Nurses and Social Workers* (London, Collier-Macmillan).

Fairbairn, G., Winch, C. (1996) *Reading, Writing and Reasoning* (2nd ed.) (Buckingham, Open University Press).

Flew, A. (1976) *Equality, Sociology and Education* (London, Macmillan).

Flew, A. (1986) *Sociology, Equality and Education* (London, Macmillan).

Foreman-Peck, J. (2004) Spontaneous Disorder? A Very Short History of British Vocational Education and Training, 1563–1973. *Policy Futures in Education*, 2 (1): 72–101.

Foreman-Peck, L., Winch, C. (2000) Teacher Professionalism, Educational Aims and Action Research: The Evolution of Policy in the UK. *Teacher Development*, 4 (2): 165–176.

Freidson, E. (1986) *Professional Powers: A Study of the Institutionalization of Formal Knowledge* (Chicago, University of Chicago Press).

Gallie, W.B. (1956) Essentially Contested Concepts. *Proceedings of the Aristotelian Society*, 56: 167–198.

Galton, M. (1892) The Classification of Men According to their Natural Gifts. Excerpts from *Hereditary Genius*, chap. 3, pp. 14–38, in Wiseman, S. (ed.) (1973) *Intelligence*, pp. 25–36 (London, Macmillan).

Gascoigne, N., Thornton, T. (2013) *Tacit Knowledge* (Durham, Acumen).

Geach, P. (1957) *Mental Acts* (London, Routledge).

Géhin, J.P. (2007) Vocational Education in France: a turbulent history and a peripheral role, in Clarke and Winch (2007), pp. 34–48.

Gingell, J. (ed.) (2014) *Education and the Common Good: Essays in Honour of Robin Barrow* (Abingdon, Routledge).

Glasman, M. (1996). *Unnecessary Suffering: Managing Market Utopia* (London, Verso).

Goethe J. [1796] (1980) *Wilhelm Meister's Lehrjahre* (Frankfurt am Main, Fischer Verlag).

Gorard, S. (2006) Value Added is of Little Value. *Journal of Education Policy*, 21 (2): 235–243.

Gorard, S. (2010) Serious Doubts about School Effectiveness. *British Educational Research Journal*, 36 (5): 745–766.

Gordon, J.C.B. (1981) *Verbal Deficit: A Critique* (Norwich, University of East Anglia).

Gould, S.J. (1984) *The Mismeasure of Man* (London, Penguin).

Gould, S.J. (1989) *Wonderful Life* (New York, Norton).

Gramsci, A. (1975) *The Prison Notebooks* (London, Lawrence and Wishart).

Grant, G. (2009) *Hope and Despair in the American City: Why There are No Bad Schools in Raleigh* (Cambridge, MA, Harvard University Press).

Grant, M. (2014) *The Effects of a Systematic Synthetic Phonics Programme on Reading, Writing and Spelling.* http://rrf.org.uk/pdf/Grant%20Follow-Up%20Studies%20-%20May%202014.pdf (accessed 23 December 2016).

Green, A. (1990) *Education and State Formation* (London, Macmillan).

Greinert, W-D. (2007) The German Philosophy of Vocational Education, in Clarke, L., Winch, C. (eds.) *Vocational Education: International Systems and Perspectives* (Abingdon, Routledge), pp. 49–61.

Hacker, P.M.S. (2011) Wittgenstein on Grammar, Theses and Dogmatism. *Philosophical Investigations*, 35 (1): 1–17.

Hager, P. (2011) Refurbishing MacIntyre's Account of Practice. *Journal of Philosophy of Education*, 45 (3): 545–562.

Hamlyn, D. (1978) *Experience and the Growth of Understanding* (London, Routledge).

Hanf, G. (2011) *The Changing Relevance of the Beruf*, in Brockmann, M., Clarke, L., Hanf, G., Méhaut, P., Westerhuis, A., Winch, C., *Knowledge, Skills and Competence in the European Labour Market* (Abingdon, Routledge), pp. 50–67.

Hanfling, O. (2000) *Ordinary Language and Philosophy* (London, Routledge).

Harbourne, D. (2013) Learning from Others, in Baker, K. (ed.) 14–18: *A New Vision for Secondary Education* (London, Bloomsbury), pp. 105–114.

Hargreaves, D. (1996) *Teaching as a Research-based Profession: Possibilities and Prospects*, Teacher Training Agency Annual Lecture. https://eppi.ioe.ac.uk/cms/Portals/0/PDF%20reviews%20and%20summaries/TTA%20Hargreaves%20lecture.pdf (accessed 23 December 2014).

Hasek, J. [1923] (1993) *The Good Soldier Schweik* (London, Everyman).

Hasselberger, W. (2014) Human Agency, Reasons and Inter-subjective Understanding. *Philosophy*, 89 (347): 135–160.

Hattie, J. (2009) *Visible Learning* (Abingdon, Routledge).

Hayek, F. (1959) *The Constitution of Liberty* (London, Routledge).

Heilbronn, R., Foreman-Peck, L. (2015) *Philosophical Perspectives on Teacher Education* (Abingdon, Wiley).

Higgins, C. (2011) *The Good Life of Teaching* (Oxford, Wiley-Blackwell).

Hinchliffe, G. (2011) *Teacher as Service-provider: An Alternative Approach*, unpublished MS.

Hintz, D., Pöppel, G., Rekus, J. (2001) *Neues Schulpädagogisches Wörterbuch* (Weinheim, Juventa).

Hirst, P.H. (1965) Liberal Education and the Nature of Knowledge, in Archambault, R. (ed.) *Philosophical Analysis and Education* (London, Routledge).

Hirst, P.H. (1974) *Knowledge and the Curriculum* (London, Routledge).

Hirst, P.H., Peters, R.S. (1970) *The Logic of Education* (London, Routledge).

Hobbes, T. [1651] (1904) *Leviathan* (ed. Waller, A.R.) (Cambridge, Cambridge University Press).

Hogan, P. (2011) The Ethical Orientations of Education as a Practice in its Own Right. *Ethics and Education*, 6: 27–40.

House of Commons Children, Schools and Families Committee (2010) *Training of Teachers Fourth Report of Session 2009–10* (London, HMSO).

Hoyle, E. (1974) Professionality, Professionalism and Control in Teaching. *London Education Review*, 3 (2): 15–17.

Hume, D. [1739–1740] (1978) *A Treatise of Human Nature* (2nd ed.) (Oxford, Oxford University Press).

Hutchinson, P., Read, R. (2011) De-mystifying Tacit Knowing and Clues: A Comment on Henry et al. *Journal of Evaluation in Clinical Practice*, 17 (5): 944–947.

Ingersoll, R.M., Smith, T.M. (2003) The Wrong Solution to the Teacher Shortage, *Educational Leadership*, 60 (8): 30–33.

Ingersoll, R. (2013) Why High-Poverty Schools Have Difficulty Staffing their Classrooms with Qualified Teachers. *Evidence to Pennsylvania State Legislature*, 10 September 2013. https://www.americanprogress.org/issues/education/news/2004/11/19/1205/why-do-high-poverty-schools-have-difficulty-staffing-their-classrooms-with-qualified-teachers/ (accessed 23 December 2016).

Jain, M., Mehendale, A., Mukhopadhyay, M., Sarangapani, P.M. and Winch, C. (Eds), (2017) *School Education in India: Market, State and Quality* (New Delhi: Taylor and Francis).

Keller, G. [1854–1855] (1951) *Der Grüne Heinrich* (Zurich, Atlantis Verlag).

Kerschensteiner, G. [1901] (1964, 1968) Staatsbürgerliche Erziehung für der deutschen Jugend, available in *Ausgewählte Pädagogische Texte, Band 1* (Paderborn, Ferdinand Schöningh) (1964), *Band 2* (Paderborn, Ferdinand Schöningh) (1968).

Kerschensteiner, G. [1906] (1968) Produktiver Arbeit und ihr Erziehungswert, available in *Ausgewählte Pädagogische Texte, Band 2* (Paderborn, Ferdinand Schöningh).

Keynes, J. M. [1936] (1973) *The General Theory of Employment, Money and Interest* (2nd ed.) (London, Macmillan).

Kingdon, G., Aslam M., Rawal S., Das S. (2013) *Are contract teachers and para-teachers a costeffective intervention to address teacher shortage and improve learning outcomes?* (London, EPPI Centre Social Science Research Unit, Institute of Education, University College London).

Kipling, R. [1899] (1999) *Stalky and Co.* (Oxford, Oxford University Press).

Kleinig, J. (1982) *Philosophical Issues in Education* (London, Croom Helm; New York, St Martin's Press).

Kuhn, T. (1962) *The Structure of Scientific Revolutions* (Chicago, University of Chicago Press).

Lave, J., Wenger, E. (1991) *Situated Learning: Legitimate Peripheral Participation* (Cambridge, Cambridge University Press).

le Grand, J. (2003) *Motivation, Agency and Public Policy* (Oxford, Oxford University Press).

Lenz, S. (1989) *Die Klangprobe* (Hamburg, Hoffman and Campe).

Letwin, O. (1986) *Aims of Schooling: The Importance of Grounding* (London, Centre for Policy Studies).

Luntley, M. (2012) What do Nurses Know? *Nursing Philosophy*, 12 (1): 22–33.

Lynch, T., Walsh, A. (2003) The Mandevillean Conceit and the Profit-Motive. *Philosophy* 78: 43–62.

MacDonald, D. (1999) Teacher Attrition: A Review of Literature. *Teaching and Teacher Education* 15: 835–848.

MacIntyre, A. (1981) *After Virtue* (London, Duckworth).

Mackay, J. (2007) *The West Dunbartonshire Literacy Initiative* (West Dunbartonshire, West Dunbartonshire County Council).

Mackenzie, J. (2016) *From 'Forms of Knowledge' to 'Social Practices'*, unpublished MS.

Marland, M. (1975) *The Craft of the Classroom* (London, Heinemann).

Marx, K. [1887] (1964) *Capital*, vol. 1 (London, Lawrence and Wishart).

McNaughton, D. (1988) *Moral Vision* (Oxford, Blackwell).

Mili (2014) *What Should Teachers Know?* PhD diss., King's College, London.

Miskin, R., Archbold, T. (2007) *Read Write Inc. Phonics: Parent Handbook – Help Your Child Read with Phonics* (Oxford, Oxford University Press).

Mortimore, P., Sammons, P., Stoll, L., Lewis, D., Ecob, R. (1988) *School Matters* (London, Sage).

Moyal-Sharrock, D. (2007) *Understanding Wittgenstein's 'On Certainty'* (Basingstoke, Palgrave).

Mulhall, S. (1990) *On Being in the World* (London, Routledge).

Naik, J.P. (1975) *Equality, Quality and Quantity: The Elusive Triangle of Indian Education* (Bombay, Allied).

Nambissan, G. (2015) Poverty, Markets and Elementary Education in India. http://www. perspectivia.net/publikationen/trg-working-papers/nambissan_markets (accessed 23 December 2016).

Nozick, R. (1974) *Anarchy, State and Utopia*, (Oxford, Blackwell).

Oakeshott, M. (1962) *Rationalism in Politics* (London, Methuen).

OECD (2013a) *PISA 2012 Results: Excellence through Equity: Giving Every Student the Chance to Succeed*, vol. 2 (Geneva, PISA, OECD). http://dx.doi.org/10.1787/9789264201132-en (accessed 13 May 2016).

OECD (2013b) *Education at a Glance 2013: OECD Indicators* (Geneva, OECD). http://dx. doi.org/10.1787/eag-2013-en (accessed 13 May 2016).

OECD (2014) *Education at a Glance 2014: OECD Indicators* (Geneva, OECD). http://www. oecd.org/edu/Education-at-a-Glance-2014.pdf (accessed 13 May 2016).

OFSTED (2004) *Handbook of Inspection* (London, HMSO).

O'Hagan, T. (1999) *Rousseau* (London, Routledge).

O'Neill, O. (2002) *A Question of Trust* (Cambridge, Cambridge University Press).

Passmore, J. (1989) *The Philosophy of Teaching* (London, Duckworth).

Pestalozzi, J. H. [1801] (1915) *How Gertrude Teaches Her Children* (London, Allen & Unwin).

Peters, R.S. (1967) Authority, in Quinton, A. (ed.) *Political Philosophy* (Oxford, Oxford University Press), pp. 83–96.

Peters, R.S. (1981) *Essays on Educators* (London, Routledge).

Plato (1970) *Meno*, in *The Dialogues of Plato* (ed. Jowett, B.) (London, Sphere).

Polanyi, M. (1958) *Personal Knowledge* (London, Routledge).

Popper, K. (1965) Towards a Rational Theory of Tradition, chap. 4 in *Conjectures and Refutations* (London, Routledge).

Pring, R. (1992) Standards and Quality in Education, *British Journal of Educational Studies*, 40 (1): 4–22.

Pring, R. (2012) *The Life and Death of Secondary Education for All* (Abingdon, Routledge).

Pring, R. (2015) *The Philosophy of Educational Research* (3rd ed.) (Abingdon, Routledge).

Raz, J. (1986) *The Morality of Freedom* (Oxford, Clarendon).

Rhees, R. (2002) *Wittgenstein's 'On Certainty' – There Like Our Life* (ed. Phillips, D.Z.) (Oxford, Blackwell).

Rose, S. (2014) Is Genius in the Genes? *Times Education Supplement*, 24 January, 26–30.

Rousseau, J.-J. [1755] (1941) *Discourse on the Origins and Basis of Inequality* (London, Dent).

Rousseau, J.-J. [1762a] (1968) *Émile ou de l'Education* (Paris, Flammarion).

Rousseau, J.-J. [1762b] (1913) *The Social Contract* (London, Dent).

Rumfitt, I. (2002) Savoir Faire. *Journal of Philosophy, C*, 3: 158–166.

Ryan, P. (2012) Apprenticeship: Between Theory and Practice, School and Workplace, in Pilz, M. (ed.) *The Future of Vocational Education and Training in a Changing World* (Berlin, VS Verlag, Springer), pp. 403–432.

Ryle, G. (1946) Knowing How and Knowing That. *Proceedings of the Aristotelian Society*, 56: 212–225.

Ryle, G. (1949) *The Concept of Mind* (London, Hutchinson).

Ryle, G. (1979) *On Thinking* (London, Blackwell).

Sarangapani, P. (2010) *Notes on Quality*, unpublished MS.

Sarangapani, P. (2013) Learning Culture: School as Cultural Learning and Person Formation, unpublished paper delivered at First Azim Premji University International Philosophy of Education Conference. http://www.youtube.com/watch?v=P5lRvaVvF7o (accessed 13 May 2016).

Save the Children Fund (2014) *Read On, Get On* (London, Save the Children Fund). http://www.savethechildren.org.uk/resources/online-library/read-get (accessed 10 November 2014).

Schön, D. (1987) *Educating the Reflective Practitioner: Toward a New Design for Teaching and Learning in the Professions* (San Francisco, Jossey-Bass).

Searle, J.R. (1995) *The Construction of Social Reality* (London, Penguin).

Sennett, R. (2008) *The Craftsman* (London, Penguin).

Shakeshaft, N.G., Trzaskowski, M., McMillan, A., Rimfeld, K., Krapohl, E., Haworth, C.M.A., Dale, P.S., Plomin, R. (2013), Strong Genetic Influence on a UK Nationwide Test of Educational Achievement at the End of Compulsory Education at Age 16. *PLoS One*, 8 (12): 1–10.

Shalem, Y. (2014) What Binds Professional Judgement: The Case of Teaching, in Young, M., Muller, J. (eds.), *Knowledge, Expertise and the Professions* (Abingdon, Routledge), pp. 93–105.

Shulman, L. (1986) Those Who Understand: Knowledge Growth in Teaching. *Educational Researcher*, 15 (4): 4–14.

Smith, A. [1776] (1981) *The Wealth of Nations* (Indianapolis, Liberty Fund).

Simpson, E. (1989) *Good Lives and Moral Education* (New York: Peter Lang).

Smith, M. (2002) The School Leadership Initiative: An Ethically Flawed Project? *Journal of Philosophy of Education*, 36 (1): 21–40.

Stanley, J. (2011) *Know How* (Oxford, Oxford University Press).

Stanley, J., Williamson, T. (2001) Knowing How. *Journal of Philosophy*, 98 (8): 411–444.

Streeck, W. (1992) *Social Institutions and Economic Performance* (London, Sage).

Stretton, H., Orchard, L. (1994) *Public Good, Public Enterprise and Public Choice* (London, Macmillan).

Sturt, G. (1923) *The Wheelwright's Shop* (Cambridge, Cambridge University Press).

Taylor, F. (1911) *The Principles of Scientific Management* (New York, Norton).

Tizard, B., Farquhar, C., Blatchford P., Burke, J., Plewis, I. (1988) *Young Children at School in the Inner City* (Hove, Lawrence Erlbaum).

Tizard, B., Hughes, M. (1984) *Young Children Learning* (London, Fontana).

Tolkien, J.R.R. (1936) *The Hobbit* (London, Allen and Unwin).

Tooley, J. (1998) The 'Neo-liberal' Critique of State Intervention in Education: A Reply to Winch. *Journal of Philosophy of Education*, 32 (2): 267–281.

UNESCO (2012) *UNESCO GUIDELINES for the Recognition, Validation and Accreditation of the Outcomes of Non-formal and Informal Learning* (Paris, UNESCO).

Varian, H.R. (2006) *Intermediate Microeconomics* (7th ed.) (New York, Norton).

Vico, G. [1725] (1968) *The New Science* (trans. Bergin, T.H., Fisch, M.H.) (Ithaca, NY, Cornell University Press).

Weil, S. (1955) *Oppression et Liberté* (Paris, Gallimard), translated as *Oppression and Liberty* (1958) (London, Routledge).

Westphal, K. (2011). Norm Acquisition, Rational Judgement and Moral Particularism. Paper given at Gregynog Conference on Philosophy of Education, Wales. http://www.philosophy-of-education.org/conferences/Conference_details.asp?id=18"\t"_blank (accessed 9 September 2014).

White, A.R. (1982) *The Nature of Knowledge* (Totowa, NJ, Rowman and Littlefield).

White, J.P. (1997) Philosophical Perspectives on School Effectiveness and School Improvement, in White, J.P., Barber, M. (eds.) *Perspectives on School Effectiveness and School Improvement* (London, Institute of Education), pp. 41–60.

White, J.P. (2000) Thinking about Assessment. *Journal of Philosophy of Education*, 33 (2): 201–212.

White, J.P. (2002) Thinking about Assessment. *Journal of Philosophy of Education*, 33 (2): 201–212.

White, J.P. (2007) *What Schools Are For and Why*, IMPACT Paper No 14 (London, Philosophy of Education Society of Great Britain).

Wilkinson, R. (2005) *The Impact of Inequality: How to Make Sick Societies Healthier* (Abingdon, Routledge).

Wilkinson, R., Pickett, K. (2010) *The Spirit Level: Why Equality is Better for Everyone* (London, Penguin).

Williams, M. (2000) *Wealth without Nations* (London, Athol).

Willis, P. (1977) *Learning to Labour* (New York, Columbia University Press).

Winch, C. (1989) Reading and the Process of Reading. *Journal of Philosophy of Education*, 23 (2): 303–316.

Winch, C. (1990) *Language, Ability and Educational Achievement* (London, Routledge).

Winch, C. (1996a) *Quality and Education* (Oxford, Blackwell).

Winch, C. (1996b) Rousseau's Account of Learning; a Re-evaluation. *Educational Theory*, 46 (4): 415–428.

Winch, C. (1998) *The Philosophy of Human Learning* (London, Routledge).

Winch, C. (2006) Georg Kerschensteiner: Founding the German Dual System. *Oxford Review of Education*, 32 (3): 381–396.

Winch, C. (2009) Gilbert Ryle on Knowing How and the Possibility of Vocational Education. *Journal of Applied Philosophy*, 26 (1): 88–101.

Winch, C. (2010a) *Dimensions of Expertise* (London, Continuum).

Winch, C. (2010b) Vocational Education, Knowing How and Intelligence Concepts. *Journal of Philosophy of Education*, 44 (4): 551–567.

Winch, C. (2013a) Curriculum Design and Epistemic Ascent. *Journal of Philosophy of Education*, 47 (1): 128–146.

Winch, C. (2013b) Learning at Work and in the Workplace: Reflections on Paul Hager's Advocacy of Work-Based Learning. *Educational Philosophy and Theory*, 45 (1): 1205–1218.

Winch, C. (2013c) Three Kinds of Practical Knowledge. *Journal of Philosophy of Education*, 47 (2): 281–298.

Winch, C. (2014) Barrow on Liberal Education and Schooling, in Gingell, J. (ed.) *Education and the Common Good: Essays in Honour of Robin Barrow* (Abingdon, Routledge), pp. 113–127.

Winch, C., Gingell, J. (2004) *Philosophy and Educational Policy: A Critical Introduction* (London, Routledge).

Winch, P. (1964) Understanding a Primitive Society. *American Philosophical Quarterly*, 1 (4): 307–324.

Winch, P. (1965) The Universalizability of Moral Judgements. *The Monist*, 49 (2): 196–214.

Wiseman, S. (ed.) (1973) *Intelligence* (London, Penguin).

Wittgenstein, L. (1953) *Philosophical Investigations* (Oxford, Blackwell).

Young, M., Muller, J. (2014) Towards the Sociology of Professional Knowledge, in Young, M., Muller, J. (eds.) *Knowledge, Expertise and the Professions* (Abingdon, Routledge).

Index

Teachers' Know-How: A Philosophical Investigation, First Edition. Christopher Winch.
© 2017 Christopher Winch. Editorial Organisation © Philosophy of Education Society of Great Britain.
Published 2017 by John Wiley & Sons, Ltd.